Crime Scene

Megan Gilbert, fifteen, stood before a mirror in her parents' second-story master bathroom, pulling a brush through her long brown hair. Shortly after 5:15 P.M., she heard a commotion coming from outside, on Hill Street. A male voice shouted, "Get out! Get out!"

Startled, she spun around and peered out a window. Across the street and a few yards down the block, she could see a red compact car parked about eight feet from the curb, and a black vehicle angled in front of it. A man stood at the passenger door of the red vehicle, pointing something at the person seated inside. Megan drew a sharp breath when she realized the object could be a handgun. A sudden muted pop, much like a distant firecracker, followed by more identical bursts, verified Megan's fears. She rushed into the adjoining master bedroom, where the view was better.

The agitated gunman had circled to the other side of the red car. He stopped just outside the driver's open window.

The crack of yet another gunshot, perhaps two, reached Megan's ears.

Megan grabbed a telephone and dialed 911.

A radio call was sent out by the 911 dispatcher at 5:23 P.M. "Possible shooting in the fourteen hundred block of Hill Street. Two reported victims down."

IF I CAN'T HAVE YOU, NO ONE CAN

DON LASSETER

PINNACLE BOOKS
Kensington Publishing Corp.
http://www.kensingtonbooks.com

Some names have been changed to protect the privacy of individuals connected to this story.

PINNACLE BOOKS are published by

Kensington Publishing Corp.
850 Third Avenue
New York, NY 10022

All Kensington Titles, Imprints, and Distributed Lines are available at special quantity discounts for bulk purchases for sales promotions, premiums, fund-raising, and educational or institutional use. Special book excerpts or customized printings can also be created to fit specific needs. For details, write or phone the office of the Kensington special sales manager: Kensington Publishing Corp., 850 Third Avenue, New York, NY 10022, attn: Special Sales Department, Phone: 1-800-221-2647.

Pinnacle and the P logo Reg. U.S. Pat. & TM Off.

First Printing: November 2006

10 9 8 7 6 5 4 3 2 1

Printed in the United States of America

FOREWORD

Love is the most dangerous game of all. The eternal quest for romance can be a treacherous path littered with frustration, muddied with tears, and leading to disaster. It's a rare person who hasn't made that journey and endured the agony of a shattered love.

An attorney described it from the viewpoint of a cuckold: "For people who have been in love, you realize the pain and sleepless nights, the aches . . . day in, day out . . . I cannot take it anymore . . . the woman that I want to have kids with . . . she had a boyfriend."

Nearly everyone knows the lyrics of a song, from Elvis to Usher, that fits their own personal heartbreak. Certainly, some seekers of a blissful union may find roses and rapture along the way, but too many others discover nothing but painful misery.

And for some, the tragic trail ends in bloody, violent death.

Homicide detectives know that the usual suspects in murders of women are husbands or boyfriends. FBI statistics show why. They counted 14,408 murders committed in the United States in 2003, and stated that 3,215 of the victims were females. Of these slain women, 573 were killed by their husbands and 464 were murdered by boyfriends. This means an alarming 32 percent of female victims were killed by their mates or lovers.

As the author of several true crime books, I have frequently been asked if I have discovered any identifiable behavior patterns or social influences common in murderers. I cannot give a definitive answer. Psychologists and criminologists have examined this conundrum in countless probes but found few factors to reliably predict violent homicide. I think they should focus their microscopes on this matter of love.

I have seen defense attorneys seize the issue of love, or the absence of it, and weave it into the "abuse excuse." The client's criminal conduct, they claim, was caused by a traumatic childhood devoid of love. Mental health "experts" are called in to testify that physical and emotional mistreatment combined with an unfulfilled desire for affection led to the defendant's sociopathic behavior.

In some cases, it might be true. One serial killer described to me how his beautiful but amoral mother, from the backwoods of Kentucky, deserted him. He spoke of his desperate need for any sign of maternal love. When they were reunited, he received it in the most bizarre form. Soon after his thirteenth birthday, she injected him with heroin and sexually seduced him! Another man convicted of murder, who kept his female victim's body in a freezer three years, was allegedly scarred by his mother's coldness and obsessive protection from anything involving romance or sex during his formative years.

On the other hand, most of us know someone who endured painful formative years, yet managed to avoid a life of crime.

I believe the major difference in people who overcome traumatic beginnings and wind up leading lawful lives, and those who eventually turn to murder, does often relate to love. In numerous cases, I have observed that most men who kill *never felt they were truly loved* by anyone, while individuals who overcame fractious relations with their families still knew deep down that their parents or other close relatives actually did love them.

The other side of the love factor leading to murder stems from jealousy and rage at the discovery of betrayal, or even suspicion that the beloved mate may be straying. When a love triangle is exposed, the betrayed individual, in some cases, cannot stifle blind fury and the need for revenge. Since emotional frenzy is not grounded in logic, cuckolded mates often decide that the only solution is to kill the unfaithful partner's new lover. And all too often, a burst of deadly wrath results in slaughtering both the loved one and the unfortunate suitor. It's the old story: "If I can't have you, no one can."

For some time, I've wanted to explore the complexity of misbegotten love leading to murder. The case in this story contains all the elements and more. This book departs somewhat from the usual formula of true crime accounts by not only chronicling the perpetrator and the two victims' histories, but by detailing the adventures of a fourth key character's poignant, humorous, tragic, and incredible metamorphosis.

If I Can't Have You . . . traces the lives of four people along their paths of love, romance, betrayal, adventure, and heartbreak. At the point where the travels of these four—one woman, two men, and later a third man—reached a confluence, the outcome produced a tidal wave of tragic suffering. The survivors' roles in the matrix of life and death were changed forever.

—Don Lasseter, 2006

CHAPTER 1

"He's Going to Kill Me"

Turning to the first page of a blank spiral notebook, Sarah, age twenty-one, took a deep breath to control her trembling hands. She entered "3/27/03" in the upper right corner, then began pouring her emotional anguish into the new journal. On blue-lined sheets, Sarah neatly printed words revealing her torment over a convoluted love affair. In sentence after sentence, she spoke of fear that clouded every waking moment, gripping her because of the man's repeated threats:

"He told me that he had a gun in his car under his seat. He also told me that I'd better not tell anyone what's going on because if I do and if he goes to jail that he was going to find me and kill me."

During the next few days, Sarah filled eleven pages with dread that she was going to be murdered by a man who had already taken everything she had to give.

On March 28, she noted, "He told me that I better not get a restraining order on him because then I will be making a big mistake. He also told me nothing had better happen to him otherwise he was going to kill me when he gets out of jail."

Describing a recent confrontation at a community college, where Sarah took night classes, she told of being accosted by the man she had entrusted with deep affection. He had grabbed her with enough force to bruise her arm: "I opened the door to my class and he just pushed it shut. He then put his hands around my neck, choking me." She had managed to escape into the classroom, where a fellow student summoned a security guard.

Just a few months earlier, Sarah's meticulous printing had reflected something far different. Her words, in notes and letters, expressed passion and excitement rather than terror-filled predictions of doom. To the person who would eventually threaten her life, she wrote: "I love you so much . . . I love it when we are together." She decorated the paper's borders with cartoons of flowers and punctuated her sentences with happy faces.

While children under her care at a preschool took afternoon naps, she penned romantic letters to the man who was already a father: "I have 8 kids here. Hey baby, how many more kids do you want? I want 2 or 3! Gosh baby doll. I love you so much. I wish I were laying down with you right now. . . ."

Sarah didn't know how many women he had dated or bedded before they met, but she did know that one of them had given birth to this man's baby.

In sharp contrast, Sarah had previously experienced only one serious romance. A few weeks before the start of her senior year in high school, August 1999, she had fallen in love with a young man named Matt Corbett. In the previous semester, more than a few randy classmates had made passes at her, attracted by her budding five-foot figure, waist-length dark hair, luminous brown eyes, and ever-present smile. According to Sarah's mother, "she could light up a room with her smile."

Instead of all the potential suitors in her own school, Sarah chose Matt, who attended a separate school across town. He stood a sturdy five-ten, and was masculine, athletic, and powerful, which appealed to Sarah. Yet, he was gentle and considerate. It all began when they met because she dialed a wrong number.

Puppy love drove them at first. Before long, it blossomed into what playwright-poet Ben Jonson called "spiritual coupling of two souls." Their attachment inspired endless telephone calls, visits to each other's families, movie dates, and their attendance at her senior prom. After graduation, in 2000, when Matt acquired a car, and traded it for a power pickup, the couple found the freedom to spend even more time together. Now it was unequivocal love.

Sarah and Matt shared future dreams and plans. Computers fascinated Sarah and she spoke of entering the field of graphic design, but decided to teach in the preschool alongside her mother while attending college classes part-time. Matt planned to work after graduation, then attend college later.

Friends of the handsome couple felt certain they would stay together into marriage. But midway through 2002, Sarah found herself wondering if it was a good idea to make a lifetime commitment without the experience of dating others. From somewhere deep inside, she felt a stirring need. It grew steadily and screamed for fulfillment. Then, as summer dwindled away, she met a man who seemed to hold the answers to her restlessness.

It started with physical attraction, as most hookups do. Flirtation, a faster heartbeat, arousal, and something else captivated her. This mysterious guy, several years older

than Sarah, didn't show the patient respect exhibited by
Matt Corbett. He seemed more raw-edged, unpre-
dictable, almost dangerous in some ways. She sensed se-
crets in his existence, and felt a challenge to unravel
them. And it surprised Sarah that these characteristics
excited her. His moodiness sometimes frustrated Sarah,
but it didn't prevent her from seeking to fathom the per-
plexity of him.

When she learned that he had fathered a child by a
previous girlfriend, Sarah at first felt the flush of jealousy.
The urge to lash out boiled inside her, and she struggled
to avoid making threats of breaking up. Before long,
though, a maternal urge edged out the resentment,
and she began wondering what it would be like to bear
her own child. It surprised her when she found the
thought arousing.

For Sarah, this new turn in her life may have been
kick-started by infatuation, but it grew to something
beyond that. It was a new kind of love: thrilling, sexy, and
fun. Like a ride on a high-tech roller coaster, it reached
thrilling heights, then plunged downward with speed
that sucked the air from her lungs. Those sudden drops
in the new relationship sprang from temperamental
outbursts by both of them, something new to Sarah. It
hadn't been that way with Matt. Of course, it bothered
her when she and her paramour argued, and especially
when he appeared to be on the verge of slapping her.
She hated the altercations, but making up was filled with
warmth, desire, and intimacy.

Shadows of confusion sometimes pestered Sarah.
Gradually she realized that this brooding fellow seemed
capable of physical violence. Yet, for the first time in her
life, she understood something she had heard about
other women—that some were actually attracted to
danger.

How could this happen? Why would she stray from a solid, happy relationship with her longtime boyfriend? What would drive a young woman to risk losing something wonderful to pursue a dangerous course?

A prominent Los Angeles marriage counselor, Cosette D. Case, suggested certain possibilities:

> *Women who stray often rationalize their behavior. "I'm bored . . . If men can cheat or play the field, why can't I? . . . I'm not getting the attention I want from my current partner." It is also possible that Sarah was raised in a protective family with no conflicts or temperamental outbursts. If so, this might have made her so naive that she simply wasn't aware of the danger in this man. Even if she was, she may have just wanted to act out her sexual curiosity.*

Trying to analyze a woman and understand the motivations for her behavior—for most men—is like gazing at the calm Pacific Ocean during sunset on a summer evening. It is beautiful, inviting, mysterious. But hiding under that resplendent surface are sanguinary creatures and hazards beyond all imagination.

Perhaps Sarah was driven by an unfulfilled need, desire, or the lure of adventure. Maybe not. In all probability, not even she understood exactly what sent her spinning into something poet Robert Browning described as "interests on the dangerous edge of things."

Evidence exists to reveal that she had intimate relations with her lover. The first time she saw him nude, Sarah was probably amazed by the bold, giant tattoos that wrapped across his legs, a few inches above the knees. She had already seen the blue-ink inscription on his right inner arm. It spelled out the name of his five-year-old offspring. On the other arm was the child's birth date.

But enlarged cryptic block lettering on his thighs, filled in with geometric designs, likely mystified her. Her attempts to ask about them were met with sullen silence. She didn't want to believe they were gang-related, but couldn't think of any other explanation.

Other parts of his body presumably sent Sarah's temperature and libido soaring to different heights. If so, their lovemaking taught her new meanings of sexuality and released an inner self she had never known. All inhibitions vanished. When he wanted to photograph her in the nude, she acquiesced.

Sex games frequently produce consequences. By early September, Sarah found herself pregnant, and she expressed certainty that her new lover was the father. Not ready yet to bring a baby into the world, Sarah opted for an abortion.

All love affairs move through phases, and this one was no exception. In the fourth month, latent alarm signals that Sarah had perceived earlier, but ignored, grew in her mind.

His possessiveness seemed romantic at first. Little by little, though, his controlling demands began to annoy her. She tried to rationalize that his adoration drove him to insist on her complete devotion, yet she found herself flushed with anger.

Sarah sometimes tended to blame herself for misunderstandings between them. In a note to him, she said, "I really do love you so much. You really do make me happy. Honest. It's just me when I get mad. It has nothing to do with you. It's just me. . . . I get mad at myself and then I just end up taking it out on you and I'm sorry for doing that."

It became increasingly difficult for Sarah to pretend that certain aspects of his behavior didn't bother her. She tried to rationalize that the only thing of real importance was the future. Grasping for a way to change his attitude, Sarah considered moving away with him. She fantasized about places she'd like to live someday. In one love letter, she wrote, "Baby, are you really going to move with me when I go to Texas or Washington? I hope so. . . ."

As autumn weather embraced Southern California, and the sun dimmed in hazy, late afternoons, she discovered something else about him, something even more disturbing. He had been arrested and placed on probation for assaulting another woman. And his need for drugs, which she perceived as recreational, was habitual. It hadn't surprised Sarah when she first learned of his drug usage, and she had even consented to experiment with them herself. The thrill of forbidden pleasure faded, though, when it struck her like a slap on the face that his need for drugs was hard-core addiction. The realization left her disillusioned.

A notion seeded in Sarah's mind, took root, and grew. The whole thing had been a gigantic mistake. She should never have let herself get involved with this guy. After months of hiding the affair from her real love, Matt Corbett, she wondered if he could ever forgive her and start over.

It is not uncommon for a man to place the woman he loves on a pedestal so high that she inevitably must fall. Such men often have difficulty in accepting that the angel they love is subject to human foibles. She might harbor veiled sexual cravings or perhaps feel a need to escape outdated images of purity and innocence. The urge to explore carnal interests was once a privilege allowed only for men, but in modern times, women, too, have seized the freedom to sample forbidden pleasures.

Matt Corbett's gradual discovery that Sarah might be spending time with another man at first confused him, then hammered at his emotions. His beloved Sarah

couldn't do such a thing. In view of the fact that he spent
at least five evenings a week with her, he didn't see how
she could find the time for secret meetings with someone else. He asked her what was going on, but she
danced around his questions with vague answers. Several arguments between them just fanned the flames of
hurt. Rather than lash out emotionally, Matt tried to analyze the predicament. Maybe Sarah needed some space
for a little while. It was probably just infatuation. That's
the term Matt chose for her involvement with this new
guy. It had to be nothing more than infatuation. He rationalized that Sarah was just acting on curiosity that
most young women experience. It must be a phase she
would go through, and then realize what a mistake she
was making. Maybe it would be best to keep quiet while
she got it out of her system. Still, it was difficult to conceal the pain engulfing him.

As Sarah grew increasingly dissatisfied with the thorny
treatment from her second beau, she developed a new
understanding of how much she adored Matt Corbett.
She realized that she wanted to resume their idyllic romance. But a major problem stood in the way. Every fiber
of her being was paralyzed with terror that leaving the
second lover she had ever taken would result in him
killing her.

CHAPTER 2

"You Can't Hit Girls"

Most young men who find themselves adrift are spawned from indigent, dysfunctional families and miserable poverty, or abusive treatment by families and peers. A few, though, may grow up in lives filled with wealth and privilege, while others might simply rebel at nothing more than parental authority. Parents know that it is not an easy task to administer life's lessons along with appropriate punishment for misdeeds. The term "tough love" has been popularized to represent certain levels of discipline in child rearing. Such treatment may be misinterpreted by children and adolescents as an absence of love or unfair cruelty. Responsible parents can only hope that their treatment of offspring eventually molds the youngster into a responsible citizen who is grateful for the lessons, rather than a sociopath who turns to crime.

In the small western Massachusetts town of Agawam, nestled near the state's southern border, across the Connecticut River from Springfield, a baby arrived into

a large Irish family on February 9, 1959. Dennis John
Conway was the sixth child born to Mary and Donald
Conway, who struggled financially to make ends meet.
Within eight years, five more brothers and sisters would
be added for a total of eleven offspring.

Early childhood memories, usually sparse for most
people, are like tiny, faded snapshots. Few can recall anything about their first three or four years of life. Dennis
Conway's earliest recollections relate to the dismal
events in November 1963 when President John F. Kennedy was assassinated. Even though Conway was only
four, he remembered seeing everyone in tears. Irish
Catholics in Massachusetts, according to Conway, can-
onized the Kennedys, making JFK's death even more
profoundly tragic. In the Catholic school Dennis attended, the nuns held the president's family in particularly high esteem, so the grief made an indelible
imprint in the youngster's mind.

Of course, to a young child, the murder of a U.S. president was only a mysterious blur of events. For young
Dennis, death was an abstract concept with little emotional effect. He would later say that very few deaths im-
pacted him emotionally. Some would evoke a feeling of
melancholy, such as the slaying of John Lennon in December 1980. In his memory, the heaviest blow from the
Kennedy assassination fell on Mary Conway, Dennis's
mother. He recalled that she was "deeply upset" by it. His
mother's moods, personality, and her behavior would
turn out to have a major influence on Dennis's life.

In Dennis's retrospective view, Mary Conway seemed
to be from the same mold as President Kennedy's wife,
Jacqueline. Her carriage, dignity, intelligence, love of the
arts, and her interest in education all mirrored the
popular First Lady's characteristics. Perhaps these com-
parisons made it even more difficult for Dennis to

understand why the relationship with his mother turned abrasive and painful from the very beginning.

Education was a pillar of importance to Dennis's parents, and his began quite early. He was placed in school at the age of four, probably because Mrs. Conway was overwhelmed at having so many children around the house. He felt that his mother and father were polarized in their affection for him. "I was my dad's favorite son," he would recall, "but I sometimes felt I was my mom's least favorite kid."

The youngster found himself not only in the middle of the pack of eleven children, but also sandwiched between five sisters, two older, three younger. Dennis recalled, "Girls mature sooner, so when I was little, my sisters would kick my butt. Most of them were good athletes. Then, when I got a little older and big enough to give them a little payback, I learned you can't hit girls. My big brothers would kick my butt for hitting girls."

This uncomfortable position in the pecking order would be a continual source of agitation for Dennis during his hectic, mischievous childhood. Gradually he began to feel that he was the target of his mother's frustration. Fractious relations with her would lead him into rebellion and a vow to leave home as soon as possible.

Work was a top priority in the value system of Mary Conway, so all of the children were required to help in the house and yard from a very early age. Wasting time simply was not allowed. Chores were assigned, and she would "white glove" everything to make sure it was completed satisfactorily. Sometimes, when Dennis failed to meet her standards, he would try to figure out a way to avoid the consequences. On occasion, when he hedged a little on his duties, Dennis attempted to hide it from his parents, but with rare success. "I would over-estimate, in my mind, their reaction to whatever I did. Then, when I would realize that a few things had leaked out, they got madder at the lying and the covering up, more so than being angry about whatever the infraction I had committed."

Mary Conway expected her children to work, and would accept only two reasons for any absence from household chores. She regarded employment out-side the home as the best exemption, but would also reduce the domestic workload for participation in or-ganized sports. It didn't take long for Dennis to pursue both.

Athletics could not only satisfy his need for physical expression, but would also help gain the independ-ence he sought. Baseball and soccer both appealed to Dennis, but his favorite sport was hockey. Massachusetts winters create ice everywhere, and Dennis strapped on skates soon after learning to walk. At ten years of age, he earned a position as goalkeeper, or goalie, on an ice hockey team of eighteen boys. The red-clad skaters won a division championship in 1971 and posed for a team photograph.

Mark Faucette, a local hockey player and high-school classmate of Dennis's, continued to pursue the sport, and is still a National Hockey League referee today, identi-fied by the number 11 on his jersey.

Young athletes tend to form long-term friendships with team members, and Dennis kept in contact with sev-eral of his fellow hockey players. But two of the boys in the championship team photo were fated to die early. One member, as a young adult, would have his life cut short by alcoholism. Another teammate, Jimmy Sim-mons, a lanky kid with light brown hair, had a reputation of being one of the really nice guys. About a year after the photo was taken, Jimmy rode his bicycle to downtown Agawam. On Main Street, a car struck him. "That was the first time I ever knew someone who died," Conway recalled. It certainly wouldn't be his last confrontation with tragic death.

Dennis's interest in sports once received a boost from an unexpected source: his mother. It came as a surprise to him when she demonstrated an understanding of a personal dilemma he faced. In trying out for a baseball team, Dennis wanted to pitch. But the coach, Mr. Paisano, assigned him to third base. To Dennis's competitive mind, the setback was particularly hurtful. Sports was his own private and secret world, his refuge from frustrations at home. Once in a while, his father would attend a game in which Dennis played, but most of the time his athletic activities were completely separate from his family life. That's why it amazed him when his mother took an interest in his disappointment at losing the pitching job.

When Mary overheard Dennis grumbling about the coach's decision, she surprised him by going to the next game with him. Mary led him by the hand to the baseball diamond. Confronting the coach, she demanded, "Mr. Paisano, let the kid pitch! It means a lot to him. Why can't you let the kid pitch?"

Dennis later reported that he would never forget it. The coach capitulated and allowed Dennis to take the pitcher's mound at the next game. With a laugh, Dennis recalled, "Well, he let me pitch and I got completely shelled! That made me realize I still had some things to learn. I didn't want to pitch anymore. Back to third base, and that's fine. Mr Paisano said, 'Okay, but I don't want to tangle with his mother again.'"

Dennis's father took a completely different approach to parenthood. A native of Bayshore, on New York's

Long Island, Donald P. Conway, barrel-chested, stocky
with thin legs, sporting a thick mop of curly dark hair,
had joined the U.S. Navy at seventeen, and served
during WWII. Through a special educational program,
he gained postwar admittance to Harvard University.
Dennis recalled seeing a yearbook and learning that his
father had attended with actor Jack Lemmon and with
Robert F. Kennedy, who graduated in 1948.

Back in civilian life, Conway met and married Mary
E. Morgan, a bright young Bostonian. Some would call
it a match of "lace curtain Irish" and "shanty Irish."
She had earned a B.A. degree in English at the College
of Our Lady of the Elms for women, in Chicopee, Massachusetts.

Mary bore the first of their eleven babies, Morgan
Patrick, in 1951. To support the family, Conway made
a few stabs at entrepreneurial enterprises, but eventually decided to attend law school at night. After hanging up his shingle as a practicing attorney, he struggled
to make ends meet for a period of several years.

Energetic, always on the go, the senior Conway recognized the need to lift some of the burdens of child
rearing from his wife's shoulders. Nearly a dozen kids
represented a burden too heavy for any one person. To
help, he regularly gathered his brood on Sundays, and
took them to the rural woods in the Berkshires. Summers were for hiking in the forest or long bike rides. In
winter, he taught them to skate on a frozen pond, led
them in cross-country skiing, and showed them how to
trek with snowshoes. He was forty-five or fifty years old
when Dennis found an ad in the sports section about a
hockey rink that was going to start up an adult league.
He convinced his dad to start playing after a layoff of
more than two decades, and he continued until he was
seventy-seven.

In the first game Donald Conway played, he caught a slap shot to the head, close to his eye. It dislodged his glasses and gouged a deep cut in his face, requiring several stitches. Dennis recalled, "There I was, only thirteen years old, driving him to the hospital. My dad was all proud of the scar it left, regarding it as a badge of honor."

To Mary Conway, her husband had more important things to do than waste time on an ice rink. She pulled Dennis aside and complained, "Now he's gone a couple nights a week playing hockey." Later, though, she acknowledged that her husband's participation in sports was beneficial because "it kept his ticker going" and perhaps helped offset the fact that he smoked Pall Malls, with no filters, for forty-five years.

Donald Conway's love of hockey was so important to him, he traveled all the way to California to participate in a special event. Charles Schulz, the world-famous "Peanuts" cartoonist, and a renowned devotee of ice hockey, sponsored a senior tournament at his Santa Rosa rink every year. Conway played on a team called The Speed Limits with some of his childhood friends from Springfield. Once, Dennis made the trip to Santa Rosa to join his father and was privileged to referee the game.

The incessant smoking by Donald Conway bothered his friends and teammates. One year, his buddies said, "Conway, if we win this tournament, you gotta stop smoking." Dennis recalled it with a chuckle. "Here's this man with no vices. Didn't gamble, thought it was stupid. No drinking. Just smoking. They won. His pals crushed his cigarettes, sprinkled them over his head, and he never had another smoke. Very strong constitution. In fact, he became kind of an annoying born-again nonsmoker."

If the senior Conway was a laissez-faire, happy-go-lucky father, his wife, Mary, took the role of a rigid and strict disciplinarian. Standing slightly over five-six, she seemed much taller to her children. Like her husband, she had jet black hair, which caused Dennis later to quizzically muse, "Eleven kids, and not one with black hair." Even though she endured the rigors of eleven births, Mary miraculously maintained a trim figure. Irrespective of resentment about his mother's strict methods, Dennis would later speak of her as a "classy" woman. "I think part of her was a little annoyed by the uncouth of my dad. But neither of them ever swore. Never. Oh, every once in a while my dad would get around my uncle and copy him by saying 'hell,' but that's about it."

In Dennis's recollection, he said that his father had never struck him. "He hit my older brothers a few times until he realized it didn't work, then stopped." His mother, though, kept her own special weapon for administering punishment. When she decided that one of the children, usually Dennis, needed a smack on the posterior, she headed for a pink bread box in which she kept a green hairbrush. The bristles had long since fallen out, giving it the appearance of what Dennis described as a "toothless predator." It struck fear into the younger children. To make matters worse, Mary would sometimes order a sibling to help administer the punishment. Said Dennis, "I can still see it in my mind. She'd enlist our help to hold one of the little miscreant's legs for a spanking by the hairbrush. I can remember holding my little brother Andy's legs. Afterward, he gets down and does the run-crawl-cry up the stairs. I run after him to apologize. He is six; I'm twelve. He's at the top of the stairs; I'm at the bottom, and I say, 'Andy, I didn't mean to, she made me do it.' He turns, looks down at me, and says, 'Yeah, but you liked it.' I (shrugging shoulders) say, 'Well—yeah!'"

Of course, Dennis really didn't mean that he enjoyed participating in his brother's punishment. But it was a relief to see someone else other than himself getting the treatment. "Today," says Dennis, "I'm sure we would have referred to her green hairbrush as a 'weapon of ass destruction.'" Spankings hurt, but perhaps not as much as some of Mary Conway's words. Dennis knew that he was at the bottom of her affection list. He recalled, "It's funny, I used to wonder if I was adopted. I'd cry to myself and wonder how she could treat me like this because she was very clear about her favorites. This was mean of her, but she'd look me right in the eye and say, 'You know, I love all of you, but some of you I don't like very much.'"

As agitation grew between Dennis and his mother, he found additional reasons to escape the family environment. Since membership in organized social activities also ranked high in the Conway household, Dennis was both an altar boy and a Boy Scout. But his main escape took the form of part- time jobs.

From the age of thirteen, Dennis sought any type of employment available. He wanted to earn his own money, but most of all, he wanted time away from the chaos and pandemonium of home life with so many kids and the stringent rules of his mother.

"Saturday mornings 'Mummy'—we all called her 'Mummy'—would be in my room for a white-glove inspection." She'd open the drawers to see if the clothes were folded and stored just right. If they weren't, she'd pull them out of the drawers, throw them down, and demand they be refolded. Also, she'd announce, "I have chores for you to do." The shutters need to be pulled down and scraped. The yard needed weeding, raking, and hoeing. To Dennis, she morphed into a military drill instructor.

The labor became particularly burdensome to Dennis when his older brothers moved on. In Mary Conway's division of labor, her daughters performed indoor chores and the boys were assigned outdoor duties. Thus, Dennis inherited most of the yard work previously handled by brothers who left home. Weeds had to be pulled out by the roots, no churning them under with a hoe. If he tried that, and her inspection revealed a glimpse of green peeking between clods, there was "hell to pay." In the fall, leaves had to be raked every day. Dennis once proposed what he regarded as a logical alternative to daily raking, but his mother instantly rejected it. She snapped, "No, we can't wait until they have *all* fallen off the trees." When winter came, and rain turned to heavy snow, Dennis was sent outside to shovel it from the sidewalk and driveway. He began to think of himself as the family "chore boy."

To Dennis, the duties assigned to him bordered on slavery. It would take him a long time to realize that something else was taking place. In his youthful view, he couldn't yet grasp that his parents were trying to teach him the value of learning a powerful, enduring work ethic. His mother, perhaps unwittingly, but probably with full knowledge of what she was doing, inculcated in him a system of strong values and conditioning for facing life as an adult.

While still living at home, though, Dennis thought she seemed dictatorial. Mary held a particularly strong belief that wasting time was sinful, and television topped the list. On the few occasions she allowed her children to watch the tube, she kept a watchful eye on the programming, and insisted they could keep their hands busy simultaneously. In a disgusted voice, she would say,

"Well, if you are going to sit there and watch the idiot box, then do something useful." A hamper filled with freshly laundered socks would be placed in front of the kids. Their eyes would move busily between the screen and the duty of sorting and folding socks.

Another issue bothered Dennis about television. On the rare occasions the children were allowed to watch it, the older siblings imposed their preferences in program selection. They commandeered the rotary channel switch for the little black-and-white screen—long before anyone ever dreamed of a remote control. Joseph, for example, liked *Bonanza* and *Star Trek*. Dennis wasn't partial to either show, but could endure them. When his parents chose the channel, though, it was Lawrence Welk or the British program *Upstairs, Downstairs*. To Dennis, these were truly a waste of time. The only incidents of family unity regarding television entertainment came with an annual event, when *The Wizard of Oz* was aired. Everyone would gather in front of the twelve-inch screen and remained glued to it until Dorothy returned to Kansas with Toto.

Bored with most TV fare, Dennis and the younger children would leave the set to others and play board games instead, including Monopoly, Scrabble, Parcheesi, Battle Cry, or cards. Reading, though, consumed most of their leisure time.

Books became an important part of the Conway regimen. Said Dennis, "We were a family devoted to the printed word. Reading is the exercise that strengthens the muscle between the ears. And I was brought up with that, especially from my mother and her demand to stop watching the idiot box. Dad emphasized it. Reading takes you to all kinds of places, creates in the mind, expands vocabulary, and helps cr skill to string words together coherently." To

the reading habit, Dennis's father would drive his brood
to the library at least once a week. "We'd have to do
[book] reports and would get little gifts. He made it a
competition among my brothers and sisters. My dad was
always reading. Both mom and dad had big influence
on us liking books." The importance of the printed
word was furthered emphasized with a dictionary, one
foot thick, mounted on a stand to be consulted when an
unfamiliar word popped up in conversation or in a
book: "Don't ask, look it up."

One subject, in books or conversation, was absolutely
verboten in the Conway home. There was no mention
of sex. With an Irish twinkle in his eyes, and a quick grin,
Conway described one brother's way of handling it.
"Our mother would never talk about sex. My brother
Don was amused by this and just to be mischievous,
looked for a way to provoke her. We knew that she liked
to do unannounced room searches. So Don, knowing
she would do the searches, used to leave explicit adult
magazines open, and lay them out in places she couldn't
miss. He knows that she sees them, but also knows that
she won't bring it up. It was a game to see just how far
she would tolerate it before saying something. But she
never would."

When spring thawed the ice on ponds and lakes,
Dennis sought haven from home life through baseball.
In high school, though, he learned the power of polit-
ical connections. At high-school tryouts, he worked
hard in competing to play the third-base position.
Dennis felt certain that he was skilled enough to make
the team and earn the coveted assignment. As a new kid
transferred from a Catholic school, though, he faced certain disadvantages. His father's long hours at work left
no time to attend games, much less observe the tryouts.
Father of Dennis's rival for third base was a local

politician who frequently made his presence known, associating with the coaches, kibitzing, and exerting his local influence. His son was awarded the third-base slot. The experience was among the first of many hard lessons that formed the person Dennis would become.

The most important genetic inheritance for Dennis and his ten siblings was extraordinary intelligence. They were a gifted family, blessed with exceptional brainpower. "Brainiacs," Dennis called them. He thought his older brother Don probably possessed the highest IQ, but all of them were extremely bright. Don was an accomplished chess champion at sixteen, rated among the top twenty-five players in the country for his age group. Particularly brilliant at logic or debate, he also demonstrated excellent skills at playing poker. It took Don a while, though, to decide how to use his intelligence. After he left home under strained circumstances, he spent eight years driving a taxicab in Boston before moving on to Harvard Law School and a successful career.

At first, in this family of remarkable minds, Dennis regarded himself as a lesser star, with no more than average intelligence. It would take years for him to realize that he had also been gifted.

It must be a difficult thing for parents to keep eleven children sorted out. (And even more difficult for a reader.) We shall take a moment here and list them all, in order of birth:

Morgan Patrick (Pat)	born 1951
Donald (Donnie)	born 1953
Joseph (Little Josums)	born 1955
Mary Alice (Mamie, or Malice)	born 1957
Caroline (Kiki)	born 195_

Dennis	born 1959
Martha	born 1961
Susie (Tootie)	born 1963
Elizabeth (Bessie)	born 1964
Andrew (Andy)	born 1965
Francis (Tater)	born 1967

The youngest brother, "Tater," got his nickname from Billy DeBeck and Fred Lasswell's venerable comic strip, "Barney Google and Snuffy Smith." Snuffy was a moon-shine-brewing hillbilly with a bulbous nose and a huge floppy hat. He and his wife, Loweezy, had a baby with a single strand of curly hair, and named it Tater. Dennis recalled that his family must have thought Francis resembled Tater, so everyone called him that for years.

The eldest brother, Morgan Patrick, also possessed superior intelligence, but was an enigma to Dennis. Born in 1951, Patrick developed into a quiet, introspective youth, unlike the boisterous, mischievous personalities some of his younger brothers would later develop. "He was eight years older than I," said Dennis, "very handsome, rail-thin, and soft-spoken. Bullies gave him a hard time in school, and when I was about seven or eight, I could see the devastating effect on him."

By observing what abusive treatment did to Pat, Dennis developed a deep empathy for "nerdy" or withdrawn kids who were picked on in school. Pat, said Dennis, had the vulnerability typical of teenage boys going through physical and emotional changes of adolescence. They grew up in a town populated with people of Mediterranean heritage. The more aggressive ones often teased Dennis and Pat about their pasty complexions and absence of even peach fuzz on their faces. Some of the taunting came from his friends who were shaving by the time they turned eleven.

Their insults to the youthful-appearing Conways were hurtful, but Dennis refused to let it show. Instead, he'd snap back to a tormentor, "I was in line when God was handing out attributes, and he gave me a choice between being a dumb, hairy knuckle-dragger or a smart, handsome, pasty guy, and I chose the latter."

But Pat, Dennis lamented, would take all those things to heart and retreat into himself. He withdrew into books. Pat reflected brilliance in his choice of reading material by purchasing works on calculus and trigonometry at a secondhand bookstore.

Dennis's three closest friends—Dave Losito, Vinny Giannetti, and Tom Shaer—earned his everlasting gratitude for treating Pat nicely without patronizing him. Shaer would eventually gain fame as an Emmy Award–winning sports anchor and reporter for QMAQ-TV in Chicago.

One summer, Patrick demonstrated that he was more than a bookworm. He built a flat-bottomed boat for his family's use, and launched it in a shallow lake, which was formed when beavers dammed a meandering creek about an hour's drive from the Conway home. In winter, the Conway kids ice-skated on the lake; on hot summer days, they rowed around in Pat's boat. But even in that activity, Pat was vulnerable. Once, when three of the boys reached the shore, Pat was standing up in the back of the boat. Don leaped out and jerked the prow up onto the beach. Pat flipped over backward into the water and was convinced that his brother did it deliberately.

A dedicated environmentalist, Patrick worried about the rain eroding the sloping woods behind the Conways' three-story brick residence. He devised a system to curb the erosion by uprooting trees from deep in the forest,

dragging them closer to the house, and replanting
them. Years later, Mary Conway stated that she was glad
her son had such foresight because it saved the whole
backyard right up to the house.

In a home jammed with so many people, synergistic
family dynamics can be formed. Dennis and his siblings soon learned something very useful about their
senior brother. Pat, Dennis found, would eat everything under the sun. Latecomers at the dinner table
would find that other siblings had already hoarded the
more savory courses. The new arrival would sit down to
a plate covered mostly with hated vegetables. If Pat was
there, said Dennis, they could avoid eating the veggies.
"When Mummy turned her back," said Dennis, "we'd
push the cauliflower and stuff we didn't like onto his
plate. As skinny as he was, he'd eat it all. Mother was the
type if you got your broccoli or Brussels sprouts on
your plate, and didn't eat them, we'd have standoffs until
ten o'clock at night. Then she'd put them in the refrigerator and you'd go to bed, and tomorrow you'd have
to go back and eat your vegetables." Without Pat, other
methods were used to avoid the unsavory stuff. "We'd
find ways to avoid swallowing them; spit them into the
napkin, or gotta go to the bathroom with a mouthful and
spit it in there. When Pat was at the table, it was easy.
She'd turn her back and you'd just shovel the carrots or
broccoli onto his plate. And it's like he was oblivious to
this whole thing going on around him. He'd just keep
eating and save us kids from doing it."

Even though timidity kept Patrick from normal socializing, he did have girlfriends, Dennis recalled. But the
relationships were short-lived. Dennis, in compassion-
ate hope, thought that if Pat could find someone who
really loved him, and would do things to reinforce his
ego, that it would change his life for the better. In

Dennis's philosophy, "Some of us need that and some don't." Love is sometimes a fickle island in the stream of life.

One gloomy afternoon, perhaps feeling unloved, Patrick left the house and hiked into the woods, carrying a coil of rope. After tying a noose at one end, throwing the other end over a high branch and tying it firmly down, he slipped the loop over his head and cinched it tightly around his neck.

CHAPTER 3

Matt

Matthew Corbett nearly died twice in his first few days of life. He and his twin sister, Kelly, arrived 2½ months early, on August 8, 1982. Kelly entered the world first, at two pounds seven ounces, and Matt followed a few minutes later, weighing in at two pounds fourteen ounces. They remained in Long Beach Memorial Hospital, Los Angeles County, for two full months.

Nothing could have delighted Jill and Tom Corbett more than being the parents of twins. Vivacious, outgoing, and always ready with a quip, Jill had met her match when she dated and married Tom. His zest for salty humor set a pace few people could surpass, and helped the couple deal with life's dark edges by finding the bright and humorous side. His face deeply tanned by years of exposure to the sun, Tom carried himself with the grace of an athlete. Jill, equally attractive, knew no bounds in energy or social graces. Neither of them feared hard work or shied away from dealing head-on with trouble. So, when the babies emerged too soon, the parents simply gave one another a hug and accepted the challenge.

Jill recalled that daughter Kelly was a real trouper. They had no problems with her from day one, except that she was premature and long—almost twenty-one inches. With Matthew, several problems manifested themselves early. Jill prayed that her infant son, like a cat, would have nine lives. If her prayers were answered, her tiny son used up two of those lives in the first round. Hours after his birth, he nearly expired. Then, a few days later, he barely struggled through another crisis. Little by little, though, his color improved and he began gaining weight. Matt was a survivor.

The pitfalls and financial struggles seemed endless to Jill. "It was tough back then when you're just starting out We'd been married for two years, and we just did what we had to do." Tom labored long hours in the construction industry as a roofer, while Jill worked for the gas company. They barely managed to keep their heads above water each month, and would nearly sink with the added weight of extraordinary medical expenses. Their old, worn-out car couldn't be trusted to make it all the way to the Long Beach hospital. So, for the daily trip to see the twin babies, they struggled the short distance to Westminster, borrowed her mother's car, drove on to Long Beach, stayed with the infants as long as possible, then reversed the process. It allowed only a few hours of weary sleep each night.

When the twins were at last able to go home, Tom and Jill brought them to their rental house in Santa Ana, Orange County. The babies' health improved steadily and they related well to one another. Both of them would later state that it was great fun growing up with a twin.

By the time the pair reached their second birthday,

Tom and Jill Corbett made the decision to buy their own home. They settled on a stylish new tract in Westminster, close to the Garden Grove Freeway (California State Highway 22) to make commuting easier. The ranch-style house featured a large kitchen, four bedrooms, and a river-stone fireplace in the den.

Said Kelly, "We were just really, really close. We always were. When we were little, we shared the same room. We had two twin beds in there. And when we finally got our own separate rooms, at about age seven, every night one of us would call out to the other one, 'Matt (or Kelly), could I come sleep with you?' in the middle of the night. Then we would run in and jump in each other's beds. We just couldn't be apart for very long. This bed sharing lasted until we were nine or ten."

Matt agreed with his sister. "I guess it was just that comfort zone that came from being close together." Until they discovered they were different? "Oh yeah," they proclaimed in unison. According to Kelly, they may have been trying to make up for the 2½ months they would have shared prior to birth if they had not left their mother's womb prematurely. The love and close feelings of the twins stayed intact even when they could no longer sleep in the same room.

Matt developed a social personality first, as well as the typical behavior of a feisty little boy, Jill stated. "I'm going to say that nicely—Matthew was the little devil, Kelly was the little angel. Matthew was very social and he was a jokester. From day one."

Nodding her agreement, Kelly recalled that Jill teased her about being an angel because she cleaned everything in sight, and would do anything for her brother. "We had to eat all of the vegetables on our plates, and I would eat his for him so he could get up from the table. Broccoli—he would not touch it, much less eat it. 'Kel, here, eat my broccoli.' I would do it so he could get up and go hang out, or play." Her comments mirrored the experience of a young boy in Agawam, Massachusetts, who would shovel his broccoli and carrots onto the plate of an older brother.

Looking at Matt for affirmation, Kelly asked, "Remember the shoe races we had? We would get brand-new shoes and race up and down the hallway to see who could run faster." In a high falsetto voice, she mimicked a small child. "My shoes are faster."

It would be difficult to find another family who openly expressed as much sincere love for one another. Even a stranger welcomed into their home felt the radiant affection, and relaxed in a warm glow created by the Corbetts' treatment of guests. Their laughter was infectious. It's no accident that the twins they brought into the world were not only physically attractive, but had personalities that would carry them far in life.

Matt Corbett picked his favorite sport early, just as Dennis Conway had discovered solace in ice hockey rinks and baseball diamonds. Matt Conway also chose baseball. Just a few months after he turned four, he began participating in T-ball, an instructional program teaching children how to swing a bat, how to catch a ball, how to throw a ball, and how to run bases.

He joined a team, and his mother participated fully. With typical self-deprecating humor, she described herself as "the T-ball queen," head of T-Moms for one year. She was also the newspaper mom for another year, writing articles about the team. A third season, she acquired boxes of trinkets from the Anaheim Angels stadium to hand out at parties. For ten years, said Jill, much of her life revolved around baseball.

The first time Jill ever saw Matt play T-ball, he was only five. He managed to whack the ball, scampered to first base, then to second base. For some reason, though, he reversed direction, ran back to first, then to home plate. The other young players were so startled, none of them tagged him out. Jill was in hysterics and other parents in the bleachers joined in the glee. The umpire, also laughing, signaled a fair run. He ruled, "Okay, he got back to home. That's what counts."

Looking back on the incident, Matt said, "Well, I got my picture in the paper."

Unable to resist chiming in with the Corbett humor, Kelly commented, "When he was playing in left field, we'd be yelling to him, 'Catch the ball, catch the ball,' and he'd be out there picking grass."

Coming to Matt's rescue, Jill observed that Matt, with the passage of a little time, made huge strides. He became a skilled pitcher and an outstanding third baseman. "I am not kidding. I'm talking great. He could stretch those legs and make some spectacular catches. You wouldn't believe it."

With appropriate modesty, Matt concluded, "I had a few good picks."

Tom Corbett, likewise, looked back into the past. "We've always been very close and every time I'd get off—I work six or seven days a week, long hours—and when I'd get home, I'd gather up the kids and have some fun. Taught them both how to ride bikes, and took them to the park every chance I got. Matt was the best bike rider, but Kel would do her best to keep up."

In a childlike falsetto, Kelly chirped, "Come on, Kel, let's go." Still giggling, she added, "Remember, Matt, every night, like a routine, we'd say, 'Come on, let's go play with Dad.'"

"Yes," said Tom, "I watched television at night with an arm around each of them, one on each side of me.

When I'd get home at night, and took my work boots off, and my socks, they would start tickling my feet."

Bursting with laughter, Kelly said, "And he paid us a quarter."

"Yeah," Tom agreed. "I paid them a quarter, till they demanded more."

Of course, every family has a certain amount of tension and conflict. Kelly pointed out that, like any siblings growing up together, certain disagreements flared occasionally. Physical confrontations, though, were limited to gentle pushes. Now and then, they would "tattle" on each other. But, both Matt and Kelly asserted unequivocally, they always wound up with expressions of love. Every day they would say, "Love you, Matt," or "Love you, Kel," even to this day.

"They didn't fight that much. They're still great kids or they wouldn't be here. Would've kicked them out years ago," Tom added good-naturedly.

In the early years of school, Kelly and Matt remained together in classrooms. High school was different, but they still shared a few courses and teachers. During that time, Jill found a way to teach her twins how to manage money. When they wanted her to buy them shoes worn by all the other kids, at $140 a pair, Jill searched for the words to say she couldn't afford those kinds of expenses. At last, she decided to teach them about economics. "I'd give them a set amount of money before school started in the fall, and tell them to go buy whatever clothing and shoes they needed, but with a clear warning that whatever they came home with is all they would get for the school year. And they figured out, you know, they needed clothes, not the expensive shoes. They both shopped very frugally, and still do to this day."

Matt found ways to supplement his allowance by finding after-school jobs, just as a young Dennis Conway had in Massachusetts. He mowed lawns and performed other miscellaneous chores for money. And he discovered another talent to help his income. "I would do everything I could in the way of jobs to get some money. I even gambled at school. I was a pretty good gambler. Cards, a lot of cards. I love cards and dice. I love to gamble."

Kelly affirmed his comment, recalling her consternation when he would walk into her fifth-period history classroom, during a break, and casually wave a hello to her. Her mouth would drop open when he sat down with several of the guys and start playing cards. She would ask, "What are you doing here?" He'd say, "Oh, I told my teacher I had to go to the bathroom."

Chuckling, Matt stated that he would sometimes leave the room richer by about twenty bucks. Pretty good "bathroom trip." He admitted that he liked to gamble every once in a while but made it clear he was not addicted. In high school, he noted, he was pretty sly, playing a lot of the time, but his winnings paid for several new pairs of shoes.

Teenagers, of course, begin to think of dating. When Kelly began to show interest in boys, Tom's instinctive caution emerged, as did his son's. Asked if they were protective of Kelly when boys came to the house, Matt replied, "Oh yeah, I still am. When a guy would come around, I'd just stare at him a lot. Give him *the look*."

Kelly nodded. "Oh yeah."

"I'd be the tough guy, like the brother who likes to fight. She'd always say, 'Matt, don't be mean, don't be mean.'"

Tom, too, might tighten his face into a grim mask to test the young suitor's fortitude.

Neither her father nor her brother were really tough on her friends, but were actually nice, Kelly stated.

They liked to tease and make jokes. But she knew that if anyone ever did anything to hurt her, they would pay. "I really didn't bring that many people home. My current boyfriend—we've been together over three years. No, they didn't scare him away at all. Matt was really nice to him. But, after he got to know him, he did say, 'If you ever hurt my sister, I'll be the first one you hear from. Don't hurt her and don't hurt her feelings.' He knows that my boyfriend is a good guy."

Matt and Kelly celebrated their seventeenth birthday in August 1999, three days after a rare solar eclipse. Across the country, people had already started to worry about the coming year, 2000. A panicky rumor spread like wildfire that a "Y2K" glitch might infect computers everywhere and disrupt public utilities, such as electricity, water, and telephone service.

The new year's predicted events were still a few months away and Matt's telephone was working fine in August, when he received a page message that would change his life forever.

CHAPTER 4

Sarah

Martha Rodriquez was rushed to a hospital on January 28, 1982. The emergency trip covered several miles from her home in Lawndale, California, south of the sprawling Los Angeles International Airport complex and adjacent to Manhattan Beach. Her husband, Fernando, drove her into West Los Angeles to the Maxicare medical facility, not far from the old Metro-Goldwyn-Mayer movie studio. After a few hours, the couple was blessed with the arrival of Sarah Jennifer Rodriquez. The infant weighed nearly eight pounds. She was Martha's third child after Javier, age nine at the time, and George, age four.

The first daughter always gets special attention, especially with two big brothers doting over her. Sarah was their little angel. But by the time the baby had passed her twelfth month, her father Fernando, worried about her hair. It seemed so thin and straggly. He had always heard that if hair is sheared off, it will grow back in healthy abundance. So Sarah's dad used scissors and clippers to virtually scalp his little daughter. Martha was horrified when she saw her baby's hairless pate. She gasped, "Oh no! What happened to her?" Later recalling the incident, she said, "I remember my husband chopped her hair really short, made her bald actually, because he believed it would grow out thicker. Her hair was quite thin as a baby. And it actually worked because she ended up with beautiful long, thick, dark brown hair."

Both parents worked full-time, so Martha left Sarah and the boys at the Lawndale home of her parents, Casimiro and Machlovia Ibbara. The grandmother attended to them Monday through Friday. While still in her early twenties, Martha had taken a job as an inspector at TRW corporation, in the firm's huge Hawthorne facility.

She hated leaving her children every day, but she had no other choice. Martha recalled, "Sarah was a happy baby. She loved her little dolls and played constantly with them. When she started kindergarten at Jane Addams Elementary School on 157th Street in Lawndale, she was terrified at first, but adapted quickly to being away from her family and around other children." The campus processed preschool children into kindergarten, then all the way through sixth grade. Their motto, "excellence in diversity," referred to the rich ethnic mix of eight-hundred-plus children in attendance. Sarah's fright vanished when she learned the joy of making new friends. Her social skills became her trademark.

To most young people, their circle of peers takes on extreme importance. But for many, family is equally or more important. Sarah's brother George speaks of a special time during a family outing at the beach. "I remember we were real young, and I have this picture of her in my mind. We were at the beach, eating sandwiches. She was holding hers in her hand, and was just staring off into the distance at the ocean. I don't know why that stands out. I was just looking at Sarah and she seemed so content and peaceful. She was pretty young, just a little girl." He added that he had never seen Sarah in a bad mood or angry at anyone.

Martha's second daughter, Marilyn, arrived five years after Sarah. At first, she was like a new doll to her sister, but with time became her companion and best friend. When Marilyn started school, also at Jane Addams, she stood to the side in awe, watching Sarah demonstrate athletic ability in playing tether ball. Speaking of those skills, Marilyn said, "She was really good at it. She wasn't a girly-girl, but she wasn't a tomboy either."

A few years later, the sisters would experiment with makeup and various clothing. "I always bugged her about makeup," said Marilyn. "She wore very little of it, and I wanted to see her try more. But she wouldn't." Sarah never adopted the contemporary fashion among teen girls in which they hid behind a mask of heavy eyeliner, mascara, and dark lipstick. She preferred the fresh, natural look, and it was perfect for her.

Not all marriages last until the traditional "death do us part." A chasm grew between Fernando and Martha Rodriquez, which finally ended in divorce. Fernando remained on good terms with the family, though, and would later continue close contact with his offspring through teaching Bible-study sessions at the home of his son George.

Martha worked steadily to provide for her household. She left TRW and found a well-paying position with the massive Northrop Grumman Corporation in Hawthorne, where she advanced steadily to become a manufacturing planner. For a time, Martha worked with a lead manufacturing engineer, Bob Dewar. The handsome, bespectacled, soft-spoken, young man impressed Martha as one of the most intelligent and nicest guys among hundreds of employees with whom she interacted. The two worked in close contact for a limited time, but crossed paths occasionally and exchanged pleasantries. Despite bearing four children, Martha maintained a youthful figure and had soft, pretty facial features. Her personality was marked by a vulnerable, shy quality that appealed to men. Bob found her especially attractive. But not until 1990 did he get around to asking her to go out. Before long, they took a day trip to shop in Tijuana, the Mexican border city 125 miles south of Los Angeles. He would later recall, "We kind of hit it off, and started dating after that. I would see her kids quite a bit and we got along fine. I'd go over to Lawndale, where her folks lived, and got used to being around them pretty quickly."

Paths of people who are destined to meet in the future sometimes begin in close proximity. It happened that way with Bob Dewar and Dennis Conway. They began life on the other side of a continent, in the same state, separated by only ninety miles and ninety days. Dennis Conway made his debut in Agawam, Massachusetts, on February 9, 1959, and Bob Dewar was born in Cambridge, Massachusetts, on May 12, the same year.

With an older brother and a younger one, Bob was on the move several times during his first five years. As an infant, he lived near Manchester, New Hampshire, almost two years, then later in Springfield, Massachusetts. During his time in Springfield, only the Connecticut River separated Dewar and Conway. A few months after he started school, in the first grade, his family moved to Belmont, just outside of Boston.

He stayed there until graduation from Boston's Northeastern University in 1982 with a degree in industrial

engineering. Then, like Dennis Conway, Bob migrated
to California. A buddy of his worked for Hughes Helicopter Company in Culver City, so Bob traveled West to
pay a visit. He brought a few résumés with him in case
he liked the area. Eventually he was hired by Northrop
Grumman and decided to make it a career. Dewar's employment with the giant corporation was interrupted
briefly when his facility transferred to Chicago. The
whole staff was invited to go, but he wasn't interested.
So in April 1997, he took a job with Gencorp Aerojet in
Azusa. In an odd twist of fate, Northrop Grumman
bought out the division for which he worked, Electronic Information Systems (EIS), in October 2001,
and Dewar was once again an employee of his old firm.

The real estate market began a long-term boom in the
1990s, and Bob Dewar realized the importance of invest-
ing in a home. He found just the right place in the
Orange County town of Placentia and bought a newly
built, upscale two-story home in October 1993. Established in the late 19th century, Placentia is derived
from the Spanish word "*placento*," and translates to "a
pleasant place to live."

The home stands just over two miles west of the
Richard Nixon presidential library and birthplace and
occupies a corner lot on a hill a few blocks from Alta
Vista Street, meaning "high view" in Spanish. Unlike so
many optimistically named roads, it delivers on the
promise, providing panoramic views of the San Gabriel
and Santa Ana mountains. It is indeed a breathtaking
"high view" of the surrounding area. In the winter, the
scene is dominated by snow-covered Mount San Anto-
nio, known locally as "Old Baldy Peak."

Three blocks from the Dewar home, along Jefferson
Street, is a green belt of athletic fields covering one-
quarter of a square mile, called Placentia Champions

Sports Complex. On the complex's west border, the Village Center mall offers convenient shopping and restaurants. Bob Dewar couldn't have selected a prettier or more comfortable place to live.

Commuting to Hawthorne each day, Dewar continued to see Martha after work and on weekends. On July 9, 1994, they drove to Lake Tahoe for a marriage ceremony.

Martha's oldest son, Javier, decided to stay with his grandparents in Lawndale near the home of his girlfriend, and future wife. George, Sarah, and Marilyn moved to Placentia with their mother and new stepfather. The transition was smooth with only one tiny dispute. George pouted temporarily when Martha assigned him to a bedroom smaller than the one given to Sarah, but he soon recovered.

In his new parental role, Dewar believed that all three kids adapted well to their changed environment and to a new stepfather. Within the first few weeks, he found himself struggling in an attempt to learn a new video game. "You know, one of those complex things with progressive levels, and I couldn't get past a certain point. I asked Sarah and Marilyn for help They really did it well and were happy to rescue a guy in his thirties. They took over the controls, and patiently explained, you gotta do this and this and this. Have you ever seen it when someone knows how to do something and you can't even follow because they are so good at it? But they were both so joyous in trying to help me."

Promoted from a blue-collar neighborhood in Lawndale to the new heights in Placentia, Sarah easily took in stride her new social status. From the first day, her ready smile and optimistic attitude converted strangers into friends at Kraemer Middle School. But she didn't forget her early roots. Visits with her grandparents in Lawndale still lit up her face like a full moon. With obvious pride,

Martha recalled that Sarah enjoyed trips to spend time
with her mother's parents. The older people, she recalled, didn't like having photographs taken of them. For
Sarah, though, they would patiently pose. If it hadn't been
for her, Martha noted, there would be no pictures of
them at all. Sarah loved taking pictures. Sometimes she
would put one arm around Marilyn, then extend her
other hand as far as possible, holding the camera, and
take a snapshot.

When not spending time with friends or siblings,
Sarah enjoyed retreating to her room and writing. She
kept journals, notes, and composed numerous letters to
relatives or pals. Said Martha, "She was always writing
something." Her letters reflected originality and a cre-
ative skill for playing with language. A few years later, one
particular journal would contain haunting predictions
of death.

Bob Dewar warmly embraced his new family, and increased it by one more in 1996 with a son, Michael.

One thing they all shared was an interest in sports.
Sarah's brother George recalled that she was a fan of the
Los Angeles Lakers. They would all get together at
brother Javier's house in Lawndale and watch the games
on television. Baseball, too, inspired debates and took
the family on group outings. Bob maintained loyalty to
his home state's Boston Red Sox, while Sarah and her
siblings gave allegiance to the Los Angeles Dodgers
and the Anaheim Angels. When the Sox came to town
to play the Angels, Bob took his wife and stepchildren
to the games. Martha recalled, "It was so much fun to
watch Bob root for the Boston team while we all yelled
for the Angels."

Martha Dewar eventually left Northrop Grumman
in favor of being a full-time homemaker. When she

eventually decided to find another job, she became a teacher at a Placentia preschool.

In 1996, Sarah entered Valencia High School. According to her mother and sister, she had paid little attention to the opposite sex until then. She earned good grades for three years. Then, at the end of August 1999, she lost her heart to a young man who lived nineteen miles away, in the city of Westminster.

Matt Corbett and Sarah met because she dialed a wrong number. When his cell phone pager buzzed one day, he checked the text message giving the number, but didn't recognize it. He called back anyway. A high, sweet voice came on the line asking for a name he had never heard. Matt kidded her about the mistake. She responded with contagious laughter and her own good-humored teasing. Neither of them wanted to hang up, and the conversation changed to flirtation. Sarah thought he sounded nice, and Matt wanted to learn more about this vivacious character with the voice like honey. "We talked for a long time," he recalled. They agreed to meet. Matt hitched a ride from a buddy to Sarah's home, and love bloomed from that initial day. It didn't matter that Sarah, at eighteen, was seven months older than Matt. They were both entering their senior year in high school, which evened out the age difference.

First dates can be harrowing. Most teenagers know the feeling of nervousness at meeting the parents, and especially in facing big brothers or sisters. "I went to her house and I was real nervous. I met her brother George, and he asked, 'Where are you guys going?'" Matt recalled.

George remembered it too. "I had to look him over, check him out. He looked like a nice guy, as opposed to a lot of other people out there. I would rather not have my sister associate with most of them." Much to

Sarah's relief, he approved of this earnest, good-looking youth.

Sarah's sister, Marilyn, had some reservations at first sight. "He did wear baggy pants and had a shaved head. But that was pretty much the style for young guys."

In defense of his appearance, Matt commented, "It was a fad in high school. Marilyn later went with us on our first movie date. We saw *Dick* (a film satire about President Richard Nixon). I didn't mind that she came along."

The first time Marilyn wanted to accompany Sarah on an outing with Matt, it didn't work out quite as well. Because Matt didn't yet have his own transportation, he arrived at the Dewar home with a friend. The boys invited Sarah and Marilyn to go to Knott's Berry Farm, a popular Orange County theme park that competes with Disneyland.

Martha's warning antenna activated immediately. Protective of her daughters, especially Marilyn, who was only thirteen, she firmly stated, "No way! You're not going anywhere with someone you don't know."

Disappointed, Matt and his friend ended up leaving. Recalling it, Matt reminisced, "I understood. I wanted to go, don't get me wrong, but I understood. I wasn't driving at that time, my buddy brought his car."

Marilyn had a different view. "I was disappointed. I was all ready to get in the car and Mom said no."

In that first year of dating, transportation for Matt and Sarah created a carousel of problems. Not so much for the teen pair, but for the parents. Sarah's mother spoke of it: "Before Matt had a car, neither one of them had transportation. So, between his parents and myself, we took turns driving them. I would take Sarah over there, to Matt's house. Or when they went somewhere local,

I was the driver. I would drop them off, pick them up, and take them wherever they wanted to go."

One of those dates, in Martha's recollection, made her blush. "In 1999, on Halloween, they again wanted to go to Knott's Berry Farm."

Marilyn corrected her. "For Halloween, it was called Knott's Scary Farm."

Martha delivered the young couple, and left them to enjoy the special day of witches, goblins, and haunted houses. A little after two in the morning, they telephoned Martha to pick them up. After they settled into her van, and were en route to take Matt to Westminster, Martha felt the vehicle rocking from side to side. Embarrassed at what she perceived was taking place in the backseat, she turned around and yelled, "Hey, you two, what are you guys doing? Stop it."

Sarah's mouth flew open in horror as her face turned crimson. "Mom!" she gasped.

At that moment, Martha looked up the street and realized that telephone poles were in motion and transformers were emitting sparks, left and right. It dawned on her that one of California's periodic earthquakes was vibrating the area and rocking her van. She recalled, "I felt really dumb. I was so embarrassed and I'm sure Matt was."

Marilyn affirmed Matt's discomfort. "He was staring out the window, like he was thinking, 'Oh my God, Martha thought we were doing something.'"

The commuting problem for a pair of young lovers who lived so far apart also caused problems for Matt's mother, Jill. "Sarah lived all the way up there in Placentia, and we were nineteen miles away in Westminster. They were both in their senior year of high school. He wanted to see her, and so his dad and I put up with this for a while."

They would transport Matt to Sarah's home, drop him off, then go back late at night and pick him up. Sometimes they would trade off with Martha, and she would do the taxi service. Finally, said Jill, they introduced him to public transportation, called "the bus."

According to twin sister Kelly, Matt would catch the northbound bus about four blocks from the Corbett home, on Golden West Avenue, and take it all the way to Placentia, then get off and walk to Sarah's school, Valencia High. He would walk her to dinner or to a movie, then reverse the whole thing. This took place almost every day. "That's dedication," said Kelly.

Matt observed, "It would take about an hour and a half, each way. That went on a year before I got my first car."

Jill painfully remembered that the long-distance relationship seldom allowed her to relax. Matt and Sarah were adamant about their feelings for each other, and refused to consider waiting until they could provide their own transportation. They insisted on being together at least five times a week, if not more. On the days or nights they were apart, Jill noted, the couple talked on the phone for hours. There were several positive aspects to their love, Jill admitted. "They were helping each other in school, which really pleased me."

The interminable conversations by phone put a strain on the family budget, said Jill. "I would get those phone bills. Oh-oh! Sometimes three hundred dollars! I'd say, 'Matt, my phone area doesn't cover Placentia. It's a toll call.' I finally ended up changing my phone company in order to accommodate him."

Long telephone conversations sparked one of the few arguments between Sarah and her sister, Marilyn. They had agreed on a system of sharing use of the phone by alternating time frames. "But she would be on it too long," Marilyn complained. "I'd yell, 'Get off the phone with Matt, it's my turn.' But she wouldn't hang up. I remember one time I was so mad at her, I went to her room with scissors and threatened to cut the cord. She was like, 'Do it then, just do it.' But I didn't, so she hung up and went to the park to use a pay phone." With her big hazel eyes turning misty, Marilyn noted that they ended up laughing about the mild dispute, because they loved one another and never carried any grudges.

Matt and Sarah's long-distance romance continued through the final semester of high school. They attended the Valencia High School prom, even though Matt didn't regard himself as a dancer. Sarah's brother George teased him about it, calling him a wallflower. Matt countered, "I could do okay on the slow stuff, but not the fast dances. I just couldn't make my feet do what I wanted them to do."

During their last few months in high school, classes and homework slipped to second place in priority behind their relationship activities, for both Matt and Sarah. Jill Corbett spoke of it, pointing out that both of the kids had a few academic problems in their senior year. To their credit, though, they recognized the problem, and dealt with it together. Jill said, "If it hadn't been for the two of them assisting each other and talking to each other on the phone, for many, many hours, where I was paying huge phone bills, to get each other through projects, homework, and everything else, I don't think they would have graduated. It was just amazing. It was like they were there for each other. The most amazing thing I have ever seen. Mutual support."

The young couple managed to boost their grades enough to graduate high school in June 2000. To reward them, Tom and Jill Corbett decided it was time to end the long months of providing taxi service. As a gradu-ation gift, they bought a 1986 Toyota for Matt. He soon found a job with an air-conditioning firm in Anaheim, in which he worked sixty-hour weeks, 5:00 A.M. to 5:00 P.M., every day except weekends. The earnings helped Matt start saving money for a different vehicle, one more consistent with the "cool" image of a young man. Later that summer, he traded the Toyota for a "pewter brown" 1997 GMC Sonoma pickup truck.

Sarah also launched a search for employment that summer. Standing just a tad short of five feet, and wear-ing minimal makeup, she looked younger than her true age. That fact struck her hard when she took sister Marilyn along to apply for a job. At the first firm, Sarah asked for an application form. The interviewer pointed to Marilyn and said, "We can give her one, but not you, because you have to be eighteen to work here."

Sarah replied, "Well, I am eighteen and she's only thir-teen." It was one of several places where Sarah's youth-ful appearance was a distinct disadvantage. But she finally found employment with a Montessori school as a teacher's aide.

Within a few months, Sarah saved enough money to buy a car on the installment plan. She picked out a 2001 red Kia Rio. Soft-spoken and shy, Sarah needed help to deal with the auto agency sales personnel. Her stepfather, Bob Dewar, came to her rescue and negoti-ated the deal. He recalled Sarah's overwhelming joy with her new car. Having taken driver's education in high school, Sarah had already obtained her driver's license.

Her sister, Marilyn, flashed back to the special times she shared with Sarah in the red Kia Rio. While riding around, Marilyn would ask to play her favorite CD music in the car. Sarah would say, "All right, but just one song."

When the tune ended, Marilyn would beg, "Let me play it just one more time."

That conversation would be repeated regularly each time they rode together. They would join in singing the lyrics aloud, but, according to Marilyn, Sarah "wasn't really a very good singer." The sisters once used the Kia to travel twenty-five miles south to the golden sand and crashing surf of Huntington Beach. Marilyn remembered: "I went with her one time, but we were afraid of jellyfish, so every time we would try to get in the water, we would just run right out."

Despite Matt's long hours at work, he still managed to spend most of his off-duty hours with Sarah. They found time for movies, miniature golf, and hanging out with friends. Their favorite movie was *Titanic*, with its romantic and tragic story of two young people in love. One dies while trying to save the other.

An activity they both enjoyed took them to a local recreational park known as "Camelot." To this day, Matt laughs when he pictures Sarah trying her best to hit the ball in a batting cage. "She looked like a bobble-head doll swinging that bat around in there."

The park called Camelot no longer exists. Nor does the symbolic image its name evokes in the lives of Matt Corbett and Sarah Rodriquez.

CHAPTER 5

"I Always Got Caught"

Morgan Patrick Conway's attempt at suicide by hanging himself failed. By that same night, he had returned to his home depressed and silent among a noisy herd of brothers and sisters. It wouldn't be the last time he would try to end his life.

Dennis, who always looked much younger than his real age, and still does, later reflected that Pat shared the characteristic that shaved years from their appearance. Visitors to the Conway home were usually surprised when told that Patrick was the eldest sibling.

Just as Pat's age didn't seem to fit him, in Dennis's opinion, neither did his brother's full name. The middle name, Patrick, was okay. But the name Morgan, even though it came from their mother's family, was too strong. "Rich yuppies use it. Morgan sounds like power and wealth. It didn't fit him. He was much too gentle and kind."

The next brother, chronologically, was Donald, six years older than Dennis. He had a more extroverted, maybe even "nefarious personality." The Irish mirth in Dennis's eyes revealed that his indictment of Don was at least partly tongue-in-cheek. "Don was probably the smartest of all, but was also the most devilish."

The primary target for Don's mischief was his sister Mary Alice, or "Mamie." Don called her "Malice." She was the eldest of five girls, born two years earlier than Dennis. A slight speech impediment during her childhood caused her to stammer. So when she addressed her mother, it came out "M-m-m-mummy."

As Dennis recalled, Don would sneak into her room, break into her diary, and write things in it. When she came home, and went upstairs, a terrible shriek would echo through the house. Mary Alice would discover that Don had entered in her diary, "Today I told on Dennis and buttered up Mummy."

Dennis quotes Don's version of a typical squabble with Mary Alice. "There we were, playing Monopoly out in the den, and all I would do is buy Boardwalk or Park Place, and Mamie would be frustrated and yell, 'Donnie!' And from the other room, my mother would holler, '*Donnie*, go to your room.'" In such a crowded household, it's a good bet that none of the children thought they were being treated fairly.

One of Don's escapades landed on the front page of the *Springfield Republican* newspaper. While attending Cathedral High School, Don wrote and produced an underground tabloid called the *Cathedral Chronic*, a parody of the authorized school paper, the *Cathedral Chronicle*. His biting articles reflected a genius for satire and a profound skill with words, but mocked the school, nuns, and Catholic policies. It offended authorities who claimed the *Chronic* had been funded by outside influences. They promptly suspended, then expelled Don, along with four accomplices. The *Springfield*

Republican's headline proclaimed: HIPPIES FINANCED, AIDED "CHRONIC." Of course, Dennis and his brother thought it was hilarious.

Don transferred to a public high school and was evicted from the Conway home by his parents. He moved into an apartment long enough to finish school. According to Dennis, English teachers at the public high school regarded Don as a star for authoring a paper that ribbed Catholic education. Soon after Don earned his diploma, he moved to Boston and started driving cabs.

By the time Dennis completed the eighth grade, he made a major decision. He did not want to attend Cathedral High School, where all five of his older siblings had gone, and where Donald had been booted out. His second reason related to sports. Dennis regard himself as an average athlete. If you picked ten people, he said, he would be number four or five. But he was a kid tough as nails who would never give up, and was not afraid to get hurt. So he played baseball and hockey with Agawam kids who went to public schools. His attendance at the Catholic grammar school was a point of derision and needling from those same boys.

Dennis made a major decision and verbalized it when the monsignor came to his classroom and paternally declared, "Oh, here's another Conway lad, who will soon be going to Cathedral."

Looking up at the black-robed official, Dennis said, "Well, uh . . . no, not really."

By the time he arrived home, Monsignor Kroyak had called Dennis's parents. "In my house, you knew something was wrong when you walked in because all the little kids would be *pre-gloating*. You're in trouble, something's going down, my mother's been ranting, and it's gonna hit the fan. I'm in big trouble. You walk in and they're all like, 'Eeewww!' They watch in glee, this is going to be fun 'cause somebody other than them is getting in trouble."

Mrs. Conway was the primary controller of discipline. Mr. Conway, said Dennis, was a really nice guy who didn't want to work all day, then come home and yell at the kids. But this time both of them had something to say. They summoned rebellious Dennis upstairs and said, "Where do *you* get off deciding your education? Everyone else went to Catholic school, you're going to Catholic school."

Dennis argued, "Why do I want to get on a bus, ride twelve miles to get slapped around by nuns?" In his recollection, he said, "Y'know, I was an altar boy like everyone else, but I just didn't want any more of it."

Talking fast to his parents, Dennis explained that he played sports with kids from the public high school, that his friends all went there, that the school was less than a mile from the Conway home, and that he was having problems with Catholic teachers, the nuns. It took some persuading, but gradually Mary and Donald Conway conceded that their son might have a point. They didn't capitulate easily, expressing worries about his going astray without Catholic guidance, and being exposed to drug usage.

When they at last agreed to let Dennis have his way, Mary laid down a set of strong rules. She had never allowed certain things in the Conway household: no squirt guns, no bubble gum, no comic books, and minimal television. "Okay," she said. "If you go to public high school, no blue jeans, no long hair, no bell-bottoms."

Some of it made little sense to Dennis. He laughed as he related it. "At that time, you couldn't buy any pants without some flare at the bottom, but I agreed. Those were the rules and off I went to public high school. I was the first one, other than my brother Don. Oh yeah, I would take blue jeans in, hide them, and change as soon as I got there."

During summer vacations from school, Dennis landed employment at Riverside Park, Agawam's sprawling answer to Disneyland. Years later, it was absorbed by the mega-theme park corporation Six Flags. The minimum age to be employed there was eighteen, so Dennis, at fifteen, had to lie. He didn't even look fifteen, so the personnel representative must have been preoccupied when he accepted the young applicant.

The boys put in long hours, from noon to midnight, but Dennis thought it was a lot of fun. It gave him boasting privileges that, as a maintenance sweeper, he earned $1.85 an hour, ten cents more than his pals who were paid minimum wage of $1.75.

One of the prized assignments was working midway games, manning booths where customers threw baseballs at bottles, tossed hoops at prizes, shot water guns at miniature race cars, or paid for an "expert" to guess their weight. A couple of the boys running these games found ways to steal some of the money they handled. Dennis at first thought he wanted one of those plum jobs in order to "get part of that take." But he knew that he was one of those kids who, whenever they did something wrong, seemed always to get caught. And something else inside him made the idea seem repugnant. Perhaps the influence of his parents' teaching had much more influence than he realized.

After getting off work late at night, the boys who had squirreled away extra cash often gathered at a nearby VFW club to drink beer. All of them, including Dennis, were under the legal drinking age of eighteen. Dennis recalled, "We thought we were so cool in getting away with drinking at fifteen or sixteen."

The entire experience at Riverside Park was enhanced for Dennis when two of his brothers also landed jobs there. Don was in charge of the Ferris wheel. Dennis described it as a perfect job for his "brainiac" brother because the operator needed to understand load-balancing principles to prevent accidents. With his love for mathematical problems and physics, he was the perfect person for this assignment.

During Dennis's second summer at the park, brother Joe worked the roller coaster. Operation of the ride, with thrill seekers plunging down hair-raising slopes of a classic wooden structure, required extra skill at the manual brake operation to prevent the cars from going out of control. Joe mastered it with ease. A special expression of pride flashed on Dennis's face when he spoke of Joe. "He was the greatest. Really cool, like a philosopher." At seventeen, Joseph built an A-frame cabin up in the woods for himself. The other siblings regarded Joe as their mother's favorite. "She didn't mess him up," said Dennis. "That was her 'Little Josums.'" He put himself through the Massachusetts Maritime Academy and spent a lot of time at sea. Marriage eventually changed that and he undertook the arduous task of earning a law degree at night school and eventually took over their father's law practice.

One of Dennis's favorite memories, and a most painful one, was of Joe's motorcycle. Like replaying a great movie, Dennis could still see himself sitting behind Joe on that bike, driving to Riverside Park. The vehicle would later play a part in separating Dennis from his entire family.

When Dennis at last reached his senior year in the public high school, vague plans started to take form in his mind about leaving home. He still chafed under his mother's strict rules. One of the maternal dictums involved his banked savings. By delivering newspapers, laboring at a nursing home, taking jobs at a golf course, and working at Riverside Park, he had accrued more than $1,500, in his account. But his mother had made certain he couldn't withdraw a penny of it without her cosignature. The requirement was specifically spelled out in his bankbook.

Another rule she had imposed involved motorcycles. "One of the things is, if you have a motorcycle, you can't live in the house. *Unless* you are Little Josums, my mother's favorite son. I could almost understand her preference for Joe. He's great. Tops in my book. She allowed him to break the rule and own a motorcycle."

Joe technically still lived in the house, but as a requirement of his classes at the Massachusetts Maritime Academy, he was away on a training cruise in the fall of 1975. His bike was stored safely in the Conways' garage.

One of workaholic Dennis's first jobs was busing tables at the posh Crestview Country Club restaurant. According to his recollection, the lure of Joe's bike was too much to resist. It didn't make sense to him that he had to hitch a ride or walk the two miles when there was perfectly good transportation sitting unused in the garage. The temptation to use it became irresistible when Mary Conway was confined to a hospital several days for treatment of an asthmatic breathing disorder. He mounted the bike, kick-started it, and drove proudly to the Crestview Country Club, with no problems. The return trip, though, was anything but problem free.

Dennis described it. "Now, since I'm so good at riding a bike, I'm coming down a hill and I hit some water and it slides out and I hop off on the grass and the bike is smashed. I get my friend Vinnie to haul it in his truck over to Popolis Honda in West Springfield. The guy says it's like nine hundred dollars to fix it. I said 'Okay.'

Only problem is, I'm not going to come and tell my mother what I did and take the medicine. It was only later in life that I learned to openly and promptly accept responsibility for my actions. But this is at a point where I'm hiding everything, especially from my mother."

Needing to pay for the repairs, and desperate to conceal the whole incident from his mother, Dennis hit on a plan that seemed a good idea at the time. "I take the bankbook and I dirtied it up, crumpled it, dog-eared it, and made a deep crease on the part where her signature is required. This made it impossible to read that prerequisite. So I go in and take out enough money to pay for the bike being fixed. My mother is in the hospital, so she'll probably never find out. But, you know, for keeping track of all those kids, she was really good at discovering almost everything."

On the day following her release, Mary marched into the garage and asked Dennis, "Where's your brother's motorcycle?"

Groping for a logical explanation, he came up with a reasonable lie. "That guy down the street, you know, the one who's always working on mechanical things, has it to do some repairs."

Mary's face remained impassive, and she seemed to accept the story. Breathing a sigh of relief, Dennis congratulated himself. A few days later, he even managed to smuggle the bike back into the garage.

Joe returned from his maritime duties, took a good look at his shiny motorcycle, and asked Dennis, "Hey, there are new forks on my bike, and new handlebars, new headlight. I can tell. What happened?" Dennis told him the entire episode. With a pained expression, Joe said, "Aww, you shouldn't have done that. It was only worth a couple hundred dollars."

Before the year was over, Joe wound up giving the bike

to a friend, who drove it to Texas. Even with the loss of money, Dennis felt lucky to have escaped his mother's wrath. But he soon found a way to incur it again.

As Thanksgiving approached in 1975, the Conway family looked forward to a rare dinner at which everyone—except the exiled Don—would be present. Joe was on leave from the academy, and two sisters were home from college. Don was still in Boston for having been kicked out of high school. Dennis regretted his brother's absence, missed hearing from him, and wondered how he was getting along as a cabdriver. Much later, Dennis recalled, Don would be admitted to Harvard, at which time his parents would welcome him home like "the Prodigal Son Returns." But during that Thanksgiving season, he was still persona non grata around the house.

Dennis, now a senior in high school, and always disgruntled with his mother, increasingly focused his thoughts on plans to leave home after graduation. Yet, he still looked forward to a festive Thanksgiving.

Early on that Thursday morning, Joe came home from socializing with friends and discovered a roaring fire in the basement. He promptly called 911. The operator would later report that Joe's call was the calmest call he had ever handled.

The entire family evacuated their two-story brick home, but soon discovered that ten-year-old Andy was missing. Mr. Conway ran through smoke and flames, flew up the stairs, found his young son still asleep, and carried him down to safety. Medical technicians arrived and treated the boy for smoke inhalation. He survived with no permanent damage.

Everyone was safe, even their little dog. "We're not a big pet family, but at the time, we had one of those scruffy little dogs that yips all the time, tempting you to kick him across the room. His name was Homer," Dennis stated. The dog and family surveyed the stately brick home, some of them with tears in their eyes.

Flames and water damage wrecked most of the interior, to the tune of $30,000 or $40,000. A major renovation became necessary. When the embers cooled, everyone rummaged through the ruined rooms, recovering whatever property they could, but much of it was burned or scorched. Dennis recalled that his hockey goalie pads survived, but carried a noticeable smoky odor for months afterward.

Newspapers reported details of the fire, and lit a fuse in Mary Conway. The *Springfield Republican* ran a story on the front page, above the fold. When Mary read it the next day, she indignantly marched into their offices, objected to a statement she regarded as an outright lie, and demanded a correction. The reporter had dreamed up a line that gave a leading edge to the article as a clever twist on a Thanksgiving story: "Mr. Conway ran in to save his son Andy and Mrs. Conway ran in to save the turkey." To Mary, this was demeaning. She insisted on, and won a retraction. Dennis noted that his mother wasn't going to allow any embarrassment in their family.

Neighborly response to the emergency warmed the Conway hearts. Everyone pitched in to help with food, clothing, and offers of temporary housing. The kids were farmed out for a short time to various homes. Remarkably, Mary allowed Dennis to camp in the burned house to keep an eye on everything. The opportunity to get into trouble presented itself, and Dennis took full advantage.

In their search for a place to live during the nine months it would take to repair their home, the Conway parents found what Dennis and the kids called "the clown house." It stood on the lot of a local Ford dealer.

At odds with the city over a dispute about billboard advertising, the dealer was denied permission. So in retaliation, he painted the house, which he used as an office, in outrageous, wild, bright colors. Donald Conway negotiated a deal to rent it temporarily, and moved the whole family in, except Dennis.

"So," Dennis recalled, "I'm a senior in a school that is only a mile from our home, and don't have to go live in the clown house with all the little kids. I have a little kerosene heater to keep my room warm, and my brother Pat would come and go, like a spook, a ghost that would just pop in and out. I'm there to keep an eye on the house. I decide one day to take advantage of this independence, and I have a keg party. One thing turns into another, word spreads around school, and the next thing you know, we've got a bunch of people there, drinking, cars parked the length of the block. There's barf, and cigarettes, and joints, and condoms all over the house. Little did I know that every day my mother would come by and check the place out. I had hockey practice at six in the morning, and she comes over and finds the house like this. I was in deep shit. I get a call at a friend's house. 'Your mother is looking for you.'

"I could no longer be trusted, so now I have to go over to the clown house and live with all the little kids. And there's a problem. I had a little stash of weed, and I have to find somewhere to hide it. Down in the cellar, I find what seems to me a perfect place. I stuff my pot, along with my bankbook, in a little bag, and secure it where no one could possibly find it. I come home one day and there's that entourage of little kids with the pre-gloating look on their faces! Somebody's in trouble and it looks like me. So Mummy takes me downstairs, and that yippy little dog, Homer, had somehow found the bag where I had my pot. It was scattered all over the floor with rolling papers. In case you had any doubt as to whose it was, there was my bankbook with it.

"And then my mom opens the bankbook, and what does she find? The money's been cleaned out. And not only that, but the story starts coming out, and she finds out I drove the motorcycle while she was in the hospital. So she climbs up on her cross, 'I'm in the hospital dying, and you're off . . .' The tirade lasted for hours."

As a result of several major infractions committed by Dennis, his parents decided he deserved harsh punishment. His brother Don had been banished from the household, and Dennis suffered the same sentence. He lived in the home of a friend for a couple of months, then moved to the Springfield apartment occupied by another buddy, Steve.

One day, while strolling downtown, Dennis ran into his father. They embraced with affectionate hugs. Donald Conway told his son that he missed him, and promised to speak with Mary to see if he could return home. But the usually lenient father had a word of admonition. He said, "Look, I don't condone smoking pot. I know a lot of kids do it. I think it's dumb, but what's dumber is to bring it in the house for your mother to find."

True to his word, Mr. Conway followed through with his promise, and Dennis returned home for his final two months of high school.

Tension between Dennis and his mother took on a whole new life. His plans to leave home after graduation became even more important to him. California, he decided, would be his destination. His father's sister, Eileen, had settled in the "Golden State," and while visiting Agawam, she spoke of the glorious weather and scenery at San Clemente, an Orange County coastal town. Her daughter worked as an extra on the *Hawaii*

Five O television series. "She was one of those statuesque blondes my brothers and I would drool over. So I got it in my head to go to California."

Dennis struggled through his senior year while working part-time jobs in the evenings. Something had to give, and Dennis decided his English classes were expendable. He skipped all of them. A few days before scheduled graduation ceremonies, Mary Conway received a call from the school informing her that her son had not completed requirements to earn his diploma. She marched Dennis to the principal's office and vented her anger not only at her son, but also at the school administration. "Okay," she snapped. "I'll deal with my boy, but where were you people? He doesn't go to English class for the entire year and you don't try to find out why, or do anything about it?"

Her power impressed Dennis. Arrangements were made for him to take a makeup class that summer. He would be allowed to attend the graduation ceremony, but receive a blank diploma. An official document would be granted upon completion of makeup English.

Dennis's mother took a photograph of him wearing the graduation gown in June 1976. She wrote on the back, "Day of liberty." It wasn't clear whether she meant her liberty or Dennis's.

The following morning, she entered his room to inform him that he would henceforth be required to pay rent or to move out.

"Okay," he said. "I'll pay rent for a couple of months, but then I'm leaving."

"Good," Mary snapped.

The words shocked and hurt Dennis. He would later say, "It hurt, but you see, I got love from my dad. I was one of my mother's least favorite kids, but I was my dad's favorite. My sister Kiki and I were the whipping boys for my mother, but we were my dad's favorites. It balanced out. You have to get love from somewhere."

That summer of 1976, Dennis worked feverishly at Riverside Park, trying to save enough money for his planned exodus. He was allowed to use a battered old Volkswagen his parents had provided for his sisters. He remembered one of the badly rusted fenders falling off while he was driving it. He jumped out, pulled the laces from his hockey skates and used them to reattach the fender. "You had to have the fender because the headlight was mounted on it. We used to take that VW and find a patch of ice and turn it all the way to the left and spin and smash it into a snowbank. We had a lot of fun in that old jalopy." Dennis knew the decrepit Bug couldn't make it to California, so he saved every penny possible in order to buy his own car. He kept his whole plan secret, not even sharing it with any of the siblings.

In August, Dennis finally acquired his vehicle, but not exactly his dream machine. "For two hundred dollars, my brother Pat got me a rusty white two-door '67 Chevy Impala. A guy at work had bought it new but let it sit outside in Massachusetts weather, which had ruined the paint and pitted the metal. Despite the appearance, though, the two-eighty-three engine was in good shape and it ran great."

With the car problem now solved, Dennis began working out details. His friend Jack Harmon (pseudonym) agreed to travel with him. Jack's father was wealthy, so he didn't face financial difficulties as Dennis did. They would caravan to California, accompanied by a big Buick filled with three young women they had met at Riverside Park.

It finally dawned on Mary Conway that something had been brewing for a long time. "She started putting things together. I think it bothered her. Not that I was just getting sick of the treatment and leaving, but that I had planned it a long time ago."

Evidently, Mary realized that Dennis had made a decision to head for California, motivated by the glowing words from his aunt Eileen. But instead of protesting, she simply gave a terse order to her son. "Don't impose on your relatives, or they'll come back here and impose on me."

Dennis recalled his final hours at home in late August. "I packed one of those green army duffel bags, stuffed my clothes in it, grabbed a fishing pole, and tossed a set of golf clubs into the Chevy, and that's it. I was going through the house late at night, kissing my little brothers and sisters good-bye. My mother is yelling at me and probably hitting me on the back or something. I'm on my way out and she tells me that I must not impose on Aunt Eileen."

Her final words to Dennis, though, caught him by surprise. She had never before acknowledged seeing the adult magazines Donald had deliberately left for her to discover during her famous room searches.

"The last thing she said to me before I drove away was 'Go to California. Take your booze and your friend.' And just before she slammed the door she said, 'Well, at least you weren't into porn like your brother Donald.' Those were the last words she said to me when I left."

If Dennis thought life was going to be wonderful out of the Conway home, he was in for a big shock. His troubles hadn't even started yet.

CHAPTER 6

Richard Namey

Six months after Dennis Conway left Massachusetts for his odyssey to Orange County, California, a baby boy was born there, not far from Disneyland. Years later, when the infant reached adulthood, his path would cross with Conway's in a dramatic confrontation.

Richard "Rick" Joseph Namey was delivered to Richard and Dorothea Namey on February 21, 1977. Four years later, Dorothea gave birth to another child, this time a little girl. By the time Richard reached the age of ten, his parents' marriage ended. He and his six-year-old sister were raised by their mother. They lived comfortably in an upscale home close to a freeway in Tustin, which borders Santa Ana, the county seat. He would later say that his home life was loving and supportive. His early education included a parochial school, and graduation from Hillview High School in Santa Ana.

During that period, Namey had friends who attended Foothill High School, a short distance from his campus. He and a small coterie of boys found entertainment by

scrambling down into a drainage culvert adjacent to
Foothill High, and entering a concrete-lined tunnel
that extended miles under the streets of North Tustin.
In the rainy season, gushing water made exploration of
the underground artery impossible, but most of the
time, a stream no wider than two or three feet flowed
through the center of it. The pitch blackness inside required flashlights for fledgling spelunkers to find their
way past several bends. At intervals, strange beams of
light, emanating from small cutouts in manhole covers
above, stabbed the darkness and formed eerie circles on
the floor, the size of shiny compact discs. The walls
were perfect for "tagging" graffiti of every imaginable
style and subject. Timid kids stayed out, frightened of
bats that flitted over intruders' heads. The boys all
imagined that the tunnel would make a great escape
route in case they were ever in serious trouble.

About three years after leaving Hillview, Namey met
a twenty-five-year-old woman who had already moth-
ered two children—an infant and a three-year-old tod-
dler. The relationship evolved to one of sexual intimacy
and Tina Gordon (pseudonym) found herself pregnant again. She gave birth to Namey's daughter on December 29, 1998. The young father celebrated what
some called a "late Christmas present" by having that
date tattooed on his left forearm, and the child's name
on the other arm.

Unlike the industrious kid in Agawam, Rick Namey
had difficulty finding and keeping employment. The few
jobs he held didn't pay very well. At the time of his child's
birth, he was working as a lot boy for a Chevrolet auto
dealer, washing cars and moving them around as
needed. His meager income made it impossible to support a woman and three children, even though they lived

in Dorothea Namey's home. Tina, Richard, and the three little ones all slept in one bedroom.

This difficult existence led to friction between Richard and Tina. After eighteen months, they separated and Tina gave up custody of the baby. She gathered her first two children, all of her belongings, and moved to another state. Richard and his mother kept the little girl.

Apparently depressed, and unable to find a fulfilling job, Namey began experimenting with drugs. Certain sections of Santa Ana are reputed to be areas of easy accessibility for heroin, cocaine, or methamphetamine. Namey found what he needed.

Sometime during this period, Namey visited a tattoo artist. He sat for hours while garish artwork was inked onto the flesh of both legs, above the knees. The letters *S* and *O* decorated his right thigh, and CAL colored the left one. The space inside each five-inch-high block letter was filled with scrolls and geometric patterns. "SO-CAL" is a common abbreviation for Southern California. Are Namey's tattoos gang-related? Probably not, said DA investigator Ernie Gomez, who worked with the Santa Ana Police Department (SAPD), Gangs Unit. His speculation was that Namey only wanted the macho image of gangbanger type inscriptions. Perhaps the tattoos helped in his intercourse with drug dealers.

If he had no trouble finding substances to make him high, he had even less difficulty finding female companionship. His reputation for being well equipped to satisfy a woman's needs made the search for sex fairly easy. His sporadic work pattern included various non-skilled jobs that produced inadequate income to support himself, fund his use of drugs, and pay for raising his daughter. Dorothea Namey acknowledged providing him with financial assistance.

For transportation, Namey chose a distinctive metallic

blue 1964 Chevrolet El Camino. Police are sometimes attracted by this type of "muscle car," but if Namey violated traffic laws in it, he was caught only once. On February 17, 2002, he made a right turn against a red signal, but failed to stop for a pedestrian in the walkway. He chose to fight the citation in court, and agreed to a court date set for the following September, but wound up forfeiting the bail. Perhaps he was more worried about two other more serious legal entanglements that took place in July.

The age gap between Namey and the mother of his daughter had caused problems. In the summer of 2002, he found a new interest in a woman closer to his own years. Andrea Merino (pseudonym), twenty-five, was blessed with an attractive face and a figure that most men would find appealing. She stood about five-four, six inches shorter than Namey. Both had hazel eyes and dark brown hair. The relationship grew close in just a few days and lasted about six weeks. Trouble erupted when Namey discovered that Andrea did not regard it as an exclusive commitment.

They argued, and Namey made threats. His fury intimidated Andrea to the extent that she obtained a restraining order to keep Namey away from her. This act ignited fires in Namey's belly and brain. He fumed about it in cranky despair.

Namey's mother observed his behavior and grew increasingly upset by it. Two days before July 4, she telephoned the Tustin Police Department. She told them her son had been depressed over the difficulties in a broken relationship and that he was also frustrated about his inability to find a job. Reluctantly she admitted his pattern of violent behavior when things didn't go well for him. The mother expressed concern for Andrea Merino's safety. Answering more detailed questions, she revealed that Richard's sister had heard an unsettling comment from an acquaintance who knew her brother. Richard, he said, had been mumbling about killing himself and Merino.

Police attempts to contact Merino apparently failed, as did efforts to find Namey.

On July 6, a few minutes before 6:00 P.M., the Santa Ana Police Department received a 911 call from a twenty-nine-year-old male named Jim Fletcher (pseudonym). A man driving a blue El Camino, he said, had forced his vehicle off the road and into a parking lot. The El Camino had pulled up next to him, and the driver had pointed a gun at him and his companion, Andrea Merino. According to the frightened caller, the individual wielding a gun kept yelling, "I'm going to fuck you up!"

Fletcher reported that he and Andrea had leaped out of his car, whereupon the assailant confronted them, pointing his gun directly at Fletcher's head. "Get the hell out of here," he reportedly yelled. Fearing for his safety, Fletcher took off at a fast gallop, leaving Andrea standing in the parking lot with the furious aggressor. As Fletcher looked back over his shoulder, he saw the man order Andrea into the blue El Camino.

Andrea would later corroborate Fletcher's observation. In mortal fear, she had complied with Richard Namey's order to get into his blue vehicle. She was surprised and somewhat relieved when, instead of starting the car and driving away with her, he remained in the lot. But his next words froze her in dread. She reported that Namey demanded she stay in the relationship, or he would kill her right there and commit suicide. While making these threats, he alternately jammed the gun into his waistband, then withdrew it and aimed it at her.

Trembling and crying, she looked up and saw a police

car entering the parking lot. Namey cursed, apparently believing that Jim Fletcher had called the police. He ordered Andrea to get out. Without a second's hesitation, she scooted out of his car and ran. The El Camino left rubber marks on the pavement as Namey jammed down the accelerator and screeched out of the lot.

The police officer asked Andrea what had happened. During the questioning, her cell phone rang, and Richard Namey's voice came on. He told her he wasn't far away, and advised her to inform the officer that the gun in his possession was nothing more than a toy.

Andrea complied with Namey's request, while revealing to the cop her assailant's name and address.

It took investigators only a short time to set up a surveillance at Namey's residence. When he appeared about thirty minutes after they arrived, he was taken into custody. During questioning, he claimed the gun was only a toy, and showed the officers the "weapon" he had purportedly used in the parking lot. The truth of his alibi was never affirmed. Could he have purchased the toy during the half hour before he arrived home, and hidden a real gun? Perhaps. Or maybe it really had been nothing but a bluff. Later events would cast serious doubt on his story of using a replica weapon.

Charged with violation of California Penal Code 236, false imprisonment, which is the unlawful violation of the personal liberty of another, Namey was confined less than a week before his mother provided bail. A court hearing was set for November.

Andrea Merino never believed that the gun Namey leveled at her face was a toy, nor did Jim Fletcher. Soon after the event, she moved to another city in fear that Namey would carry out his threat to kill her.

It only took two days after being released from jail before Namey found trouble again. This time, right in his mother's home. His sister, whose beauty fueled her ambition to become a fashion model, told acquaintances that Richard had a bad temper and was easily angered. He proved it one afternoon when he interrupted her as she lay on the floor, talking on the telephone. Namey reportedly asked her for money. She ended her phone call and told him unequivocally that she wasn't about to fund any of his needs, whatever they were. His face twisted in fury as he snatched up a little plastic figure of a troll and lobbed it at her face. It struck under her right eye and gouged a two-inch laceration in the tender flesh. At St. Joseph's Hospital, she received the necessary medical treatment. Interviewed by police at the facility, she reported that Namey was the assailant and that he was on bail for kidnapping his ex-girlfriend six days earlier.

Namey explained that she had exaggerated the whole thing. First, he said, she had sustained only a slight scratch when the doll barely hit her. And second, she was conducting herself hysterically, worrying that it might leave a scar and hinder her chances of becoming a model.

This time, he was charged with violating Penal Code 242, battery, which is "any willful and unlawful use of force or violence upon the person of another." Conviction in such a case can be punished by imprisonment for two, three, or four years, or in a county jail, not to exceed one year, or by a fine not exceeding $10,000, or by both the fine and imprisonment. He faced a court date in February 2003.

These pending legal problems didn't seem to dampen Namey's romantic or carnal urges. At the end of July, he met another young woman who would find him interesting. Her name was Sarah Rodriquez.

According to one version of the initial meeting between

Richard, twenty-six, and Sarah, twenty, it occurred via an Internet "party line" Web site. There are numerous Web sites using the "party line" reference, several of them advertising it as a way to meet single men and women.

Another version of the meeting suggested that a friend of Sarah's who also knew Richard Namey introduced them at a party.

In either case, they hooked up in late July 2002, and began a dating relationship that turned intimate, and would eventually end in tragic violence.

Sarah never invited Namey to her home, but did visit his family. According to his mother, Sarah paid her first visit in August 2002. "She had come over to see my son. She and my granddaughter and my son were going somewhere. My son introduced her to me." Mrs. Namey said that Sara visited "several" times that month and continued to do so in September. It appeared to her that her son and Sarah were, indeed, developing a romantic relationship.

She was correct in this assumption. The relationship was not only romantic, it was sexual as well. In September, Sarah discovered that she was pregnant, and underwent an abortion. In a letter to a friend, she confided that Namey was the father.

In early October, Richard decided that he needed a place of his own, where he could not only entertain Sarah privately, but where he could raise his daughter in a separate environment. Mrs. Namey helped him find an attractive apartment in a large Santa Ana complex on Cabrillo Park Drive. On Richard's irregular income, he couldn't afford any monthly payments, so his mother came to his financial aid. She paid not only the rent, but his utility bills as well, including telephone tolls. After the move, she visited frequently and said that Sarah was often there too. "I saw her many times when

I went to the apartment. I went there almost on a daily basis because my granddaughter liked me to fix her hair before she went to school in the morning."

To Mrs. Namey, it appeared that Sarah sometimes spent the night in Richard's apartment. She explained one such sighting. "When I came early in the morning before my granddaughter went to school, Sarah was there, said 'hello' to me, and was getting ready to shower before she left."

Dorothea Namey asserted that she liked Sarah "very much" and thought the relationship was good for her son. If she knew he was using tar heroin during this time, she did not reveal it.

An early sign of trouble for Sarah reared its head in October. Not long after Namey moved into his new apartment, Sarah dropped by. A minor dispute between them erupted, and they argued. Namey's temper took over, and he struck her in the head with his open hand. Later, he apologized, but the blow was something new for Sarah. No one had ever hit her like that before.

It pleased Namey's mother when the couple kept seeing one another into November. "Sarah came by sometimes with my son, because she was driving, rather than him, to drop off my granddaughter while they were on their way somewhere."

The relationship faced a possible interruption that month. Richard Namey was scheduled for a court hearing to face charges of kidnaping Andrea Merino. A stiff jail sentence might very well have ended Sarah's interest in him. But it wasn't to be. On November 12, 2002, in Orange County Central Superior Court, Namey was sentenced to three years' formal probation and ordered to comply with a restraining order by staying completely away from Andrea Merino. Also, he was required to complete an anger management course.

Sarah continued seeing him. According to Dorothea's recollection, Sarah even helped Richard decorate the apartment. She said she knew this "because my son and my granddaughter had told me they had gone shopping. They were looking at accessories for the bathroom. Sarah had picked out something. My granddaughter told me there was a shower curtain and accessories that had ducks on them." The granddaughter was also quite fond of Sarah, said Dorothea.

Another November incident gave Sarah second thoughts about Namey's temper. During an argument, he encircled her neck with his hands and squeezed, his face a grim mask of fury. He backed off before doing any major damage and apologized again.

According to Namey's mother, the romance continued through December. Namey took her to the Spectrum in Irvine, a theater-shopping complex with a carnival-like entertainment zone. Once again, during a disagreement, Namey lost control and angrily threw his cigarette lighter. It struck Sarah on the head, leaving a nasty bump. Fear kept her from walking away from him and the relationship, but the emotional residue was rapidly building up to critical mass.

Sarah's mother, Martha, suspected something was wrong in the young woman's life, but she didn't learn the details until later. It troubled her deeply when she saw bruises on her daughter's neck and arms. Martha also found herself answering phone calls and not recognizing the male voice that asked for Sarah, but would hang up without identifying himself.

In February, the court had another chance to separate Sarah and Namey. He faced one more hearing and possible jail time for assaulting his sister. On February 20, he received an early birthday present. Namey was sentenced to three years' informal probation (remarkable in view of the fact he was already on three years of formal probation for the kidnapping of Andrea Merino) and ordered to comply with a restraining order to stay clear of his sister.

Dorothea Namey, in reflecting about the couple as their relationship entered the new year, recalled, "Sometimes . . . I went over to my son's apartment with my fiancé. [My son] had a problem with his car. It wasn't starting and it wasn't running right, so my fiancé went to help him work on the car. Ricky was downstairs with the phone. He was waiting for a call from Sarah. They had to leave to go get some tools and a part. It could have been the end of February, I know it was around—it was after my son's birthday on February twenty-first. And my son handed me the phone and asked me to please let Sarah know, because he was expecting her to call, that he had to go, and please answer it, and that's what I did. Sarah did call while he was gone."

Namey later confronted Sarah about the late telephone call, demanding to know why she was disrespecting him. During the exchange of words, he gave her a disgusted shove. No physical harm came of it, but Sarah began thinking that he was inevitably going to hurt her.

It is a typical characteristic of men who brutalize women to also exert maximum control over them. Namey began demanding that Sarah call him frequently to let him know where she was and with whom she spent time. He used caller ID technology to verify the number from which she telephoned. He, in turn, barraged her with calls to her home and at her preschool workplace.

Restraining orders apparently didn't mean very much to Richard Namey, and he would prove that again about six weeks after the sentencing.

Just a couple of weeks before Namey turned twenty-six, Sarah had reached the boiling point. She entered the date "2/06/03" on a 5 ½-by-8 ½-inch sheet of paper and began to print in bold, upper case letters, "I HATE RICK NAMEY." She repeated it twenty-two times, filling the page with vitriolic loathing.

CHAPTER 7

Why Did She Stray?

Sarah Rodriquez willingly entered into a relationship with Richard Namey, and kept it secret from Matt Corbett. She certainly must have seen, within a short time, that Namey was a dangerous person. During their time together, she suffered several incidents of physical abuse. Also, he faced two court hearings, one for kidnapping and threatening the life of a girlfriend, another for injuring his own sister. All of this could not have escaped Sarah. Certainly, during intimate times with him, she couldn't have missed the huge gang-style tattoos on his legs. Shouldn't these have alerted her to his tough-guy, gang-wannabe image? Sometimes, though, women find dangerous men desirable.

Dr. Christina J. Johns, Ph.D., criminologist, journalist, author, radio and talk show host, expressed opinions about this perplexing riddle of human behavior, with specific interest in Sarah.

As a criminologist and also as a woman, I can easily identify with, while not approve of, the tendency most women have to be attracted by the testosterone, slightly dangerous, male.

First of all, women are bred and raised with the notion that they can tame the beast. Consciously or subconsciously, she thinks this slightly dangerous man needs nothing more than a good woman to turn him into a virile, sexy, but good husband. Love conquers all and it is the woman's responsibility to bring love to this needy soul.

The woman sees him as something she can control. Yes, he is dangerous, but only slightly, not so dangerous she can't control him and she never feels that he will actually go to the extent of harming her. Nicole Simpson juggled O. J. Simpson's rage and anger in just this way. I have no doubt that she never thought he would actually harm her, mother of his children.

It is the same thing as the rape fantasy. Women do find the rape scenario attractive and appealing and exciting. But, when you get right down to it, this "rape" is a fantasy—not the real thing. Women want to be raped by Robert Redford and in such a way that they feel his power without being really hurt. While feminism thinks this rape fantasy is such a threat it can't be admitted, literature plays with it over and over. That is the nature of the rape in Gone with the Wind. *Raped by Clark Gable is quite a different thing than being raped by a disgusting, foul-breathed ex-con who is overweight.*

But, playing with the fantasy often leads women into the wrong situation.

The woman wants to feel his maleness. I think there is just something innate in the desire to be close to maleness. It is what keeps women coming back to a man for sixty years. Most women don't truly have respect for men who are not male in that sense. But it is a culture that perverts maleness.

Along with this virility is strength. Strength is the willingness to stand up and be counted, to stay when the going gets tough, to be honest and steadfast, to know what's important, to not whine. To say "It's going to be all right" and have everybody believe it even if you don't. It's the ability to say this and sound convincing even when you don't know. It's not contemplating your navel while Rome burns. The buck stops here.

The really powerful man is one with a quiet knowledge of who he is and what is important to him. Weakness is trying to be something you're not, pretending, boasting, posturing.

Women are as confused about what maleness is as men are. And this is reaching a crisis; well, already has. Generations of young minority men are in jail because of perverted notions about "maleness" and what it means. For them, maleness is shooting or stabbing someone who disrespects you by bumping into your shoulder. This is perverted.

There is a great tendency to mistake this intense jealousy and the intensity of feeling displayed in the car confrontation with powerful emotional love. It masks as that. The man thinks it is that. The woman does as well. This is no polite, well-mannered love, but a consuming love that drives one to acts of passion like running the object off the road and threatening both people.

"He loves me so much he can't control himself. He will go to desperate lengths to have me." This is tabloidization of experience going on in our society.

This also explains why a man from a privileged family would adopt such a persona. It's the James Dean persona, the Steve McQueen imitator. But underneath the facade, there is a heart of gold, just like with the whore. Middle-class teen males adopt the gangsta look.

I love this Jekyll and Hyde aspect of Sarah's being. Or at least that's what it seems. She found a guy who might dominate her, and play to the bad-girl side present in many women. Did she play that and then expect to go back to the nice normal guy? Is that what happened?

Perhaps Namey hated everything Sarah (the saint) represented. He could have wanted to defile it, then became enraged because of the defilement. It's the old "hates women, thinks all women are sluts behind the façade" stuff. The man wants to prove to himself that sweet uptight women are all whores, but when he achieves this, he hates them and wants to punish them.

The pattern was present in his previous kidnapping of the ex-girlfriend and threatening to kill her. It's tragic that Sarah fell into the same trap.

This is certainly not to say that Matt Corbett wasn't strong, masculine, and desirable to women. On the contrary, he was that and more. And he was the consummate nice guy. In being attracted to masculine power, Sarah discovered that the real strength, including honesty and quiet self-esteem, was in Matt. With this realization, she knew where she really belonged.

Sometimes, while women truly want the nice guy, they need to experiment with the bad boy before making the lifetime commitment. This behavior didn't make Sarah a bad person either. She succumbed to curiosity, got caught up in it, and found great difficulty in knowing how to escape it.

Los Angeles marriage counselor Cosette D. Case, MSW, LCSW, also suggested reasons for Sarah's affair with Richard Namey:

Why do women often betray relationships with steady, decent men to have an affair with a dangerous, macho-type man as Sarah did?

The absence of logic in a human being's choice for a partner/mate is not infrequent. "I wonder what she sees in him?" is a common enough query. The notion of women being more attracted to the "bad boy" versus the fine upstanding man has certainly been played out in novels, movies, and in real life for hundreds of years. This phenomenon is sometimes equated to the Madonna/whore syndrome in which men engage. In an extreme version of the bad-boy syndrome, convicted murderers are known to have long lines of women begging to marry them. Go figure.

In Sarah's case, societal norms and myths may also have played their roles. Young people are often advised, especially by peers, to play the field, sow your wild oats, or get it out of your system. The unwritten rule that youthful indiscretions are okay, forgivable, or are just a normal part of growing up may have helped Sarah excuse behaviors in herself and others.

One might look at Sarah's choice in terms of infidelity. According to Ruth Houston (2005), until recently more men committed adultery than women, often dismissing steady, decent relationships, but now women are catching up to men in the adultery department. Women state different reasons for betraying men. Women cheat primarily due to emotional need for gratification and men cheat mostly for sexual need gratification. Seventy percent of all married men cheat on their wives; 54 percent of married women cheat.

There does not appear to be any particular profile for women who choose bad boys or who cheat: "I'm bored; there is too much pressure in my social circles to be the perfect *partner or person, I can't keep up; I don't deserve a decent relationship; I can handle the bad boy; he's not that bad; if men can cheat or play the field, why can't I; the bad boy needs me; he's just like my father; I'm not getting much attention from my current partner, etc . . . " are .all reasons given by women for their misguided choices.*

CHAPTER 8

"He Won't Leave Me Alone"

In early September 2002, Matt Corbett received a stunning telephone call from Sarah. "She called me and told me that she had missed her period."

The news jolted him, even though they had slept together. After waiting for Matt to catch his breath, Sarah added that she had taken a test that confirmed pregnancy. At first, he thought she must be joking, trying to lighten up the mood caused by several days of arguing. Her tone soon convinced Matt that she was definitely not kidding about such a serious thing. He told her he would be right over to have a long talk about it.

The conversation changed Matt's outlook. After a levelheaded discussion with Sarah, in which he convinced himself that he was the father, he grew excited about the prospect. And a little nervous. They were young, Matt told himself, and he didn't know quite how they were going to handle the corollary responsibilities. Matt knew that Sarah wanted to have "lots of kids" and thought she'd be happy about the idea of beginning a family.

When he had more time to mull it over, doubts seeped in. "It seemed to me that—I really wasn't quite sure if the kid was mine. I would like to say yes. It's very painful. But I didn't question it in depth at the time."

According to a letter Sarah later wrote to a friend, she felt certain that Richard Namey was the father, so she didn't share Matt's enthusiasm for the pending birth. After more intensive conversation with him, they made a mutually agreeable decision to terminate the pregnancy.

Matt recalled, "About a week after she told me, and we decided to get the abortion, we were on the way to do it, and I was very upset. I began to question it when I found out how long she and the other guy were together. So I couldn't really tell. I never did get a test, obviously. I just went down there and was very upset when I was in the abortion room. Threw a few chairs and kinda got kicked out of the place."

His face growing dark as he looked back in time, Matt said, "I went to use the restroom and I saw Sarah lying there and they were doing their thing. I felt like I wanted—actually just to keep it, I wanted to have it. I like kids, and I'm around kids all the time. It took place in Santa Ana, off of Main Street, I believe, at a legitimate clinic. I paid the three-fifty for it with a cashier's check. They didn't want cash or checks, but accepted a money order. It was a lot cheaper than raising a kid, but I would rather have raised a kid." The operation took place in late September 2002.

Sarah's mother was also bewildered when she accidentally found out that her daughter had undergone the procedure. In a letter Sarah wrote to a friend, she explained Martha's discovery:

Hey, do you remember how I told you that I got an abortion on Saturday? Well, I guess my mom found out because [I] forgot to put the papers away. I left them on my bed and I guess she needed the yellow pages book and that was in my room so I'm guessing that she looked on my bed and she saw the abortion papers and pills, on the bed. When I got home she was very sad with me . . . But you know what? I'm kind of glad that I did have the abortion because it was Rick's baby. I swear to God that I am so scared of Rick.

Even though Sarah was frightened, she continued to see Namey.

She no doubt loved Matt deeply, and began to realize his importance to her at the beginning of 2003, as Namey's dark side gradually exposed itself. Her conscience was stricken about lavish Christmas presents Matt had given her.

On Christmas Eve, Matt arrived at the Dewar home laden with packages. When he had earlier asked Sarah to make a list for him, she jotted down twelve items. Instead of selecting the top two or three, Matt had splurged and bought all twelve. He would later blush about it, though, because when he arrived at the Dewars' front door, it suddenly hit him that he had brought nothing for anyone else in the family. Young Michael, only seven years old, wouldn't understand, and neither would fifteen-year-old Marilyn. Matt had eyes only for his beloved Sarah.

He later described the event. "I loved just keeping her happy. That was fun. About the twelve Christmas presents for her, that was embarrassing. I didn't think about it until I got to the door. Everything for Sarah and nothing for anyone else. My sister, Kelly, had wrapped them all. The gifts included perfume, a bracelet, a calender, clothing, and a little blow-up (inflatable) chair. I don't know why she wanted it, but I actually found it; couldn't believe it."

Gifts and gratitude for them were ingrained in the personalities of both Matt and Sarah. Martha Dewar spoke of how Sarah always expressed her appreciation, even for the smallest thing. She produced a note her daughter had written after Martha had placed three ordinary items in Sarah's bathroom. In the text, Sarah drew a heart shape as substitute for the word "love." It said, "Mom, Thanx for the Shampoo, cond. & Hair Spray! (love) you lots, Sarah." Martha had returned the note after writing across the bottom, "You're welcome! (love) MOM."

Matt's generosity with Sarah was also fondly recalled by Jill Corbett. "He is a very giving person. He has a huge heart and would do anything in the world for anybody that wanted something. He surprised her with a lot of stuff. She'd get flowers out of the blue. That was just Matt."

Did Matt and Sarah have future plans together? "Of course," he said. "Sarah wanted to get married and have a few kids."

How many? "Well, to be exact, seven!" Matt revealed.

Sarah worked with so many little kids at the preschool, Matt observed, it made him wonder if that would satisfy her need for children. Sometimes, during telephone conversations with Sarah, from her workplace, Matt could hear the shrill chatter of young voices. The noise, he said, sometimes gave him a headache. When he had asked her how many she wanted to have, and heard the number seven, Matt reeled. "I said, 'Wheeew,' I sort of had two in mind. I realize how hard it is to raise kids. And we both wanted to go back to school."

As a potential future mother-in-law, Jill spoke highly of Sarah. The young woman had wiggled her way into the Corbett family's hearts with her quiet charm. Jill had nicknamed her "Mouse." At first, when Sarah visited, she would enter as silently as a mouse and manage a nearly inaudible "hi." Later, as she grew to know everyone, Sarah greeted everyone in the room with a fond hug, including Matt's father, Tom. It came as a surprise to Jill that Sarah could cope with Tom's humorous teasing. "She was not scared of him at all. It was hysterical. I loved it. I just thought, 'Oh God, you've met your match.'"

When discussing Sarah, Matt's expression was radiant with love and warmth. But certain memories cause a shadow to pass over his face. In a quiet, somber tone, he spoke softly. "I knew something was going on. I asked her, and we were arguing a little bit. Something wasn't right and I wanted to know what it was and she was too scared to tell me. She was reluctant. Afraid I was going to leave her. She realized the problem and told me, 'You know, I made a mistake.' She admitted that she had met this guy at a party, and he got infatuated with her. I think she was just trying to ease it into me what had been going on. Basically, she just told me his name. Told me that he's just nasty in everything he does; beats her up, follows her, and stalks her, and she's scared. I didn't even wait for her to ask for my help. Even if she didn't want me to, I would have helped anyway. Even though we were arguing, I figured we could settle the differences later. We're young, and everyone can make mistakes. I don't blame her for looking. Even while we were going out, maybe meeting this guy. Y'know, we're young. I mean, people do that. People do that and that's how you learn. She told me she didn't realize what she had until she almost lost it. I don't blame her for that. I feel I'm really a good guy, and at the same time, I needed her as well. I wanted to work things out. And I stuck by her side."

After Sarah's confession, Matt calculated that she had been seeing Richard Namey approximately seven or eight months. But he had difficulty believing that it had lasted that long, or that they had been together very often. "I don't know; I was left in the dark on everything. I was with her every day. Every day, and I don't know how she found time to, or how they both found time. For a while there, we were arguing for about a good month or two. And we kind of had our own space for a while.

"And from what I knew, she was hanging out with a girl-friend of hers I don't like. She was just bad trouble . . . I didn't realize what was going on, wasn't told what was going on, obviously. No one would tell me, that she was meeting with somebody else.

"I really don't want to make Sarah look like a bad person. She didn't want this to happen. The reason is him. I mean . . . people go on dates all the time. It's not a big deal to me."

Matt and Sarah had discussed the problem over a restaurant dinner in early April. She had paused, gazed into his face, holding back her tears, and softly asked, "Can we start over?"

Matt replied, "'Start over'?"

"Yeah, can we?"

With an incredulous expression, Matt had smiled. "Start over? I don't want to start over. Don't you know our anniversary is coming up? I want a present."

In recalling it, Matt explained, "I just kinda made a joke out of a bad situation. Moved on. It's amazing how I thought I would be so mad. And you can't be. Some-one so sweet, I mean, you can't be mad at her, at a person like that. We started with puppy love, and it grew into the real thing. Always together every day. Inseparable, always on the phone, always happy. She would tell me, 'You make me feel so good on the phone. You were just like a little knight in shining armor. Always polite.'"

The young lovers felt the weight of the world had been lifted from their shoulders. Together, they could conquer anything. They had no way of knowing the rage that would grip Richard Namey.

While Matt's love for Sarah allowed him to forgive her actions, Richard Namey reacted with fury when he discovered that she was still seeing Matt. It fanned the flames even higher when she threatened to obtain a temporary restraining order against him for striking and choking her. She might as well have tried to put out the fire by dousing it with jet fuel.

On Thursday, March 27, 2003, Sarah attended a night-school class at the North Orange Community College, Anaheim Campus. She had worked most of the previous evening preparing a poster to fulfill an assignment for an oral presentation, "Early Childhood Development." According to Sarah's reported version of events that night, things turned sour at about 8:20 P.M. Near the end of her fifteen-minute class break, Sarah glanced down the hallway, and recoiled, her stomach contracting in fear. Ten yards away, Richard Namey moved rapidly toward her.

"Where's your car?" he demanded. "I've been driving all over the damn parking lot looking for it."

Biting her lip, Sarah said, "My friend has it."

"Which friend?"

"Jennifer." Sarah knew that Namey disliked Jennifer Vincent (pseudonym), and she wanted to tell him it was someone else, but she wasn't a good liar.

Namey scowled. "If I see her out in the parking lot, I'm going to smash her face in and beat the hell out of her." His jaw muscles twitched angrily while he measured Sarah's reaction. Just to make certain she understood his fury, he added, "Y'know, I've got a gun under the seat in my car."

The exchange went silent momentarily while Sarah's teacher passed them on her way back to the classroom. "Break's nearly over," she said as she walked by. When she was out of hearing range, Sarah locked eyes with Namey, and tried not to let him know she was trembling as she spoke.

"I've got to go back to class," she said, and took a dozen steps toward the entry. Namey walked in lockstep beside her. Sarah's voice cracked. "I've got to. Look, you're just going to cause more problems."

As if she hadn't spoken, Namey barked, "We're leaving right now. Go over there to that public phone, call the bitch, and tell her you want your car. Let her walk home. And I'm going to follow you to make sure you don't pick her up." Sarah had never told Namey that she now carried a cell phone with her at all times. She silently prayed that he couldn't see the bulge of it in the pocket of her jeans.

"I can't do that. It's too far for her to walk, all the way from Anaheim to Placentia." Eight miles separated the school from Jennifer's home.

"You're gonna do it. And you'd better keep your mouth shut about this whole thing, 'cause if you tell anyone and I go to jail, there's going to be hell to pay. When I get out, I'll find you and kill you."

The teacher interrupted again. Opening the classroom door, she said to Sarah, "C'mon, time to get back in class." Sarah obeyed, leaving Namey in the hall, hoping that he would soon leave.

She squirmed nervously in her seat while another young woman made an oral presentation, using a poster that each student had been assigned to prepare. When she finished, Sarah replaced her, displayed her poster, and spoke seven minutes. Upon completion, she signaled to the teacher that she needed to visit the bathroom and exited the room.

To her relief, Namey wasn't there. Sarah dashed to the women's restroom, entered, and withdrew the cell phone from her pocket. She dialed Jennifer's cell number, and told her of the confrontation with Namey. "Don't come over here, I'm afraid of what he might do if he sees you."

Two steps outside the restroom, she almost ran into Namey, who stood near the door, perhaps waiting for her. Sarah jammed the phone into her pocket, hoping he hadn't noticed it in her hand.

"Did you call Jennifer and tell her I was here?" he snapped.

"Yes."

"You have a cell phone, don't you?"

"No," Sarah stammered. "Well, it's not really mine. It's my boss's at work. She let me borrow it." She worried less about the lie than what Namey would do when he realized that she'd been keeping the phone a secret from him. Later, Sarah entered into her journal, "The reason I told him that it wasn't mine was because I knew that he would try and break it if he found out it was really mine."

Sarah's left hand still gripped the tiny instrument in her pocket and Namey reached for her wrist. She would write, "He tried to grab the cell phone, claiming it was his. . . . He then grabbed my arm really hard trying to pull my hand out of my pocket just to get the phone." His angry grip left deep bruise marks on her forearm.

Jerking away, Sarah rushed to the classroom door and tried to pull it open. Namey lunged against it, slamming it shut. Enraged, he circled her tiny throat with one hand and squeezed. Struggling for breath, Sarah managed to twist loose and open the door all in one motion. She fled to her chair, still gasping. In her journal, she later noted, "My classmates saw me. As I went toward my seat to sit down, some girl went to get the security guard."

A burly, uniformed man, Marc St. Lawrence, arrived within ten minutes and escorted Sarah to his office. Namey had vanished.

In St. Lawrence's report, after hearing Sarah identify her assailant as Richard Namey, he noted that he asked if she knew the suspect. Sarah said that he was a guy she used to date, and that she had known him about eight months. They dated for several weeks initially, but she had been trying to end the relationship when he became violent.

Sarah also told the guard that she had not lived with Namey. Reluctantly she added that he had been violent with her on a several occasions, but she had not reported the incidents to police. When asked why, Sarah stated that Namey had threatened her. She told St. Lawrence that she was terribly afraid of Namey, but still planned to ask the court for a restraining order to keep him away from her.

The police showed up at the guard's office and asked Sarah another battery of questions for their own reports. Sarah's mother, Martha, summoned by telephone, arrived within minutes, followed by the ever-loyal Matt. They took Sarah home.

A few days later, on April Fools' Day, Sarah had no time for jokes. Namey continued to make life miserable for her. That morning, Martha received a frantic call from her daughter. "Mom, Mom," Sarah cried, "he's here. He won't leave me alone."

Martha asked, "Who?"

Sarah's voice shook. "Richard Namey. He's here. He won't let me go to work."

Martha realized that Sarah was calling on her cell phone, from inside her car, near the preschool, where mother and daughter both worked.

With her daughter in evident danger, Martha told Sarah she was going to hang up and call the police. As soon as she completed the 911 report, Martha rushed to the site where she met her daughter and a patrol officer who responded. Namey had vanished.

Sarah followed through with her threat to obtain a restraining order on Richard Namey. In her petition, she listed five incidents of physical assault, ending with the one at her night school. A temporary order was issued commanding Richard Namey to stay away from Sarah Rodriquez.

Sheriff's deputies attempted to serve the order on Namey, but they reported that he could not be found. A full court hearing was scheduled for April 22. It would never take place.

During the entire affair with Namey, Sarah had continued to spend much of her time with Matt, especially on Wednesday evenings. Sarah's biological father, Fernando Rodriquez, conducted Bible-study classes at the home of his son George, just a sort distance from the Dewars' residence. They usually met for an hour and ended the sessions at about 6:00 P.M. Matt hoped the Scriptures they examined were helping Sarah cope with the difficulties in her life. "She was really getting into it.

I think she was hoping to find help for this whole Namey situation."

On Wednesday, April 2, Matt arrived at Bible study in his GMC pickup and Sarah in her red Kia Rio. When the session concluded, they kissed good-bye and climbed into their vehicles, each heading toward their respective homes. Matt remembered: "After Bible study that evening, I was going home to Westminster, and she made a left turn on Buena Vista to go to her house. I was going down Tustin to the 91 Freeway and I was on the cell phone with her. She said, 'Okay, I love you,' and all of a sudden, she hung up on me. I thought maybe we just lost the signal and that I'd call back I let it ring, ring, ring. No answer. I thought something might be wrong. But I figured I'd try again in a few minutes."

By the time Matt arrived at the on-ramp to the 91 Freeway, he realized that something must be terribly wrong. Instead of entering the freeway, he made a U-turn and sped back in the direction of Sarah's home. Just a few blocks from her street, he spotted something that made his blood boil. Richard Namey had Sarah cornered.

In a repetition of the incident with Andrea Merino, Namey had used his blue El Camino to force Sarah's Kia over to a curb, stop beside her car, and yell at her through his rolled-down passenger-side window.

When Matt realized what had happened, his wrath exploded. "I was like, 'You son of a bitch.' I wanted to beat the living piss out of this guy. I pulled around the corner and I don't know what felt better, realizing that I had found them, and finally got a look at this creep Namey, or from just being there for Sarah and knowing that I could protect her. I knew what I had to do."

Braking to a halt near the El Camino, Matt heard Sarah scream, "No, no, no, he's got a gun!" Matt didn't care. He leaped out of his pickup, ran to the driver's side of Namey's El Camino, and reached for him through the window. "I apparently scared the hell out of him, because he took off."

In an instant, Matt was back behind the wheel of his pickup in hot pursuit of the El Camino. Both vehicles sped past the sports park on Jefferson and made tire-squealing turns on Alta Vista. The air-ride suspension on Matt's pickup didn't allow for tight turns and put him at a disadvantage, making it impossible to keep up with Namey's car. And when the El Camino flew through successive red lights, Matt refused to endanger other drivers by following. It didn't take long for Namey to disappear from sight.

Realizing that Sarah had gone home, and that she and her mother would be frantic with worry about him, Matt drove to the Dewar residence. He learned that Martha Dewar had witnessed part of the chase and was terrified that the cars would crash.

Matt later said that the police were called, but were unable to do anything about the incident.

If they had, Sarah's life might have lasted longer than two more weeks.

CHAPTER 9

Conway's Odyssey

Dennis Conway and his pal Jack Harmon left Agawam in August 1976. Harmon's father owned large blocks of real estate and a golf course, so Jack regarded the trip as an adventurous exploration, while Dennis saw it as a quest for self-fulfillment and a new life. The three young women who caravanned with them in a late-model Buick simply wanted to see California and Hawaii. They had contracted with a service that connected cross-country travelers and private car owners who need someone to deliver the vehicle to a specific destination.

En route to the West Coast, Dennis encountered the first of a series of crises that would occur with unrelenting frequency during the next few years.

The two adventurers found themselves in the dead of night on an Indian reservation near "Four Corners," the point where the borders of Colorado, New Mexico, Arizona, and Utah meet. The Buick was several miles ahead of them. Stopping for gas at an isolated, rustic station, they were startled when a "tough-looking Indian" stepped out of the darkness. "Hey, can you give me a ride?" he slurred in a whiskey voice. They didn't even have a chance to answer before another man appeared, pointing a shotgun at the Indian.

The drunk opened Dennis's back door and started to climb in as the boys sat frozen in the front seat, dumbfounded. The shotgun wielder yelled, "Don't let him in, he just beat his wife, probably to death. The cops are coming."

Before the Indian could settle in, Jack jammed the accelerator to the floor, screeching away from the gas pumps. The would-be intruder tumbled to the pavement, screaming and cursing.

The boys had traveled only a couple of miles before a pair of headlights mounted on the front of a large pickup threatened to smash through the rear window of Dennis's Chevy. The Indian had leaped into a big pickup truck and followed them. *WHAM!* The noise sounded to Dennis like a train wreck as the pickup slammed into his back bumper.

"Jesus Christ!" he yelled.

In the pitch blackness of endless desert, Dennis and Jack felt the breath of doom. A ray of hope came when they spotted a red flashing light rapidly closing the distance behind the looming pickup. A cruiser siren sounded, and the Indian's vehicle made a sharp turn. Careening over a rocky berm, it sped across the sand and sagebrush, then vanished in the distance.

Jack coasted to a halt on the road shoulder and the police vehicle stopped behind them. The relieved boys learned that the Indian had been living with a woman in a trailer house behind the gas station. He had a habit of getting intoxicated and assaulting her. The station owner had called the cops, then held the assailant at bay with a shotgun until the Chevy pulled in for gas.

The police filled out a report, then let Dennis and Jack proceed on their way to California.

Late on the fifth day of driving, Dennis and Jack, following the three girls, reached Orange County. They pulled up to a house in Westminster occupied by an acquaintance of the female trio, and were given a place to sleep that night. In the morning, the girls left to turn in the car at Panorama City, then departed for Hawaii.

Dennis drove to Huntington Beach to have his first look at the Pacific Ocean. As he recalled it, "I saw it, turned around, and started searching for a job. That night, I was busing tables at the Huntington Inn restaurant."

His mother's training, which left no margin for wasting time when there was work to be done, had been deeply ingrained in Dennis. The very next day, he and Jack found a weekend job at Newport Beach's posh Big Canyon Country Club. They performed grunt labor, cleaning up, raking traps, planting trees, and laying sod. Dennis would later meet John Wayne at the club when the immortal star came in with his Vista Cruiser, a station wagon that he had modified so he could wear his Stetson hat inside. Dennis was particularly impressed with Wayne's "huge hands."

At night, Dennis and Jack slept in the Chevy. A section of the Huntington Inn, a three-story motel on Pacific Coast Highway, was under construction, so the two boys would sneak in during predawn hours to use the portable toilets. To bathe, they would cross the highway to the beach and use outdoor showers. They ate meals at the inn's restaurant where they bused tables. The Huntington Inn, ten years later, would be the site of a grisly murder by serial killers James Gregory Marlow and Cyndi Coffman, in which they kidnapped nineteen-year-old Lynel Murray from a local dry cleaners', took her to a room, sexually assaulted her, strangled her, and left her body in a bathtub.

This rigorous routine of working and camping in a car didn't appeal to Harmon, who was looking for adventure, not meager subsistence. So after a couple of weeks, he talked Dennis into pulling up stakes again and heading north, to Lake Tahoe. Reluctantly Dennis agreed. It took only two days at the scenic mountain lake to discover no one was hiring. September had arrived with a blast of frigid air, typical of the high Sierra Nevada. Sleeping in the old Chevy chilled them to the bone, so they decided to head west again, to Sacramento. After a six-hour drive, they parked in front of California's capitol building, wondering just what to do next. Said Dennis, "We had acquired some camping stuff, a little breakdown stove, pots, and some canned food. We also had fishing poles. In a pinch, we could survive. In fact, we thought like all young men looking for adventure that we could survive in the wilderness if need be. But we noticed this group of people walking toward us. Like tree-hugger types. They see these Massachusetts plates, rusted-out car, and they offer us a meal. Yeah, we're up for that."

The strangers led Dennis and Jack to an old Victorian house near McKinley Park. They provided a meal consisting of "something like zucchini burritos, natural kinds of food." The boys were hungry, so they ate whatever their hosts put in front of them. After dinner, they were led into another room, seated, and treated to a slide show depicting an idyllic mountain retreat. Dennis had always wanted to experience outings in real mountains. In his home state, he had seen the Berkshires, which couldn't compare with the western ranges. "When we saw the Rockies, they were impressive and the Sierras were breathtaking. As a kid, I loved going out in the woods and all that."

Someone in the Victorian house told Dennis and Jack that a group would be heading up to the mountains the next day, and invited them along. The boys briefly talked it over and decided that, since they were out to explore the world, they might as well go up in the woods with these people, even though they seemed a little weird. Dennis assumed they would drive the Chevy, but one of the hosts said, "Oh, no, no, you go in the bus with us."

Shrugging, Dennis parked his car behind the house. He and Jack climbed aboard what appeared to be an old school bus. On the way up, they listened as the group chanted and sang unrecognizable songs. At one point, the boys suggested, "Hey, let's stop and get some beers."

"Oh, no, no, no," said an individual who appeared to be in charge. "We don't do that."

Boonville is a rural California town, population about 1,400, situated in Anderson Valley, a half-hour drive from the coast, roughly 120 miles northwest of Sacramento. It is six miles from Philo, a tiny burg where the notorious serial killer Charles Ng was arrested for theft of military weapons, and sent to Folsom Prison. After his release, he and Leonard Lake began a savage killing spree. Sometimes this rural region has been a refuge for people who didn't wish to blend with conventional society. Outlaw bikers loved the area. The bus carrying a load of "tree-hugger types" and two naive teenagers from Massachusetts halted at a compound a few miles outside of Boonville.

Dennis later described it as "the middle of nowhere." They pulled into a compound with living quarters that resembled chicken coops. A leader separated Dennis and Jack and showed them where they would sleep.

Alarms started to activate in Dennis's mind, but he wasn't quite certain just what to do. Still only seventeen, his limited experiences hadn't prepared him for anything like this. He lay awake a long time that night, wondering just what was in store for them. "We thought we could take off from the group with our backpacks, head for the woods, and rough it. But they wouldn't allow us to do that."

Awakened early in the morning, he was led to a row of tables for a breakfast of hot cereal. Everyone held hands and chanted something, then ate silently. Discomfort turned to anxiety in Dennis and he didn't like being separated from his friend. Nothing was turning out like they had planned, and the freedom they sought had vanished like fog burning off in the morning sun.

Years later, he spoke of it. "I could tell they were some sort of cult. There was a lecture hall and a tent with folding chairs. There was a speaker, like a Berkeley-professor type, talking to these people. What he says is logical, very good talker, condoning love of everyone. Not free love, the sex way, but just love of everyone. They are all your brothers and sisters. All the people there seemed like lost souls and outcasts. I know that's like stereotyping, but that was my impression. They were very strange. I just wanted out. I started yelling for Jack, across the compound, at a logical time like dinner when everyone is gathering in a certain area. He yells back. Some leader types came over. We're saying, 'Let's get the hell out of here.' These guys are big, and acting like they were ready to handle any problems we might cause. Jack is nineteen, but looked older, with kind of an edge to him. I was seventeen and looked about fourteen or fifteen. He wasn't a mean guy, but could bluff like it. He might have scared them a little bit against getting violent with him."

Dennis heard one of the cult members say, in a whiny voice, "He's with the Devil, you're not."

"No, no," Dennis snapped. "I'm going with him."

After a brief confrontation with some elder types, Dennis and Jack said in unison, "We're outta here." Jack growled out loud, "You know what, in a minute, we're going to start kicking the shit out of people."

He apparently impressed their "hosts" as an imposing man. Dennis just wanted them to understand, "Yeah, I'm with him." But inside, he was thinking, *This isn't so cool.*

For a short time, it appeared to Dennis that leaders were going to restrain the boys physically from leaving. But finally they relented and told someone to escort them to the exit. After they grabbed the backpacks they'd brought along, the boys were led along a high fence to a locked gate, laced with barbed wire. Dennis recalled walking rapidly, eager to leave, and would never forget what the escort said to them. "The confrontation had almost turned ugly and physical, and I realized, 'Okay, we don't want it to go there.' So the guy looks over and he goes, 'In my mind, I think you are just a couple of punks, but in my heart, I love you.' I thought Jack was going to pummel him. 'Just open the fucking gate before I rip your head off!'"

Finally the escort unlocked the gate and swung it open. Dennis and Jack wasted no time, practically running down the dirt road, putting as much space as possible between them and the strange compound. But within a half hour, they weren't certain their lot had improved very much. They marched along a narrow road that seemed to be a canyon between tall pine trees. Dennis wasn't even certain which direction they were headed. Lost and more than a little worried, they glanced at one another, mutually thinking, *Okay, what do we do now?*

Typical of Dennis, his troubles only grew worse. If he sought shelter from the rain, he would step into the middle of a hurricane. Less than an hour after he and Harmon escaped the cult encampment, they heard the throttling roar of a half-dozen powerful motorcycles.

In recalling it, Dennis rolled his eyes heavenward. "A bunch of Harleys pull up! Not the bikes they have now, but those original big Hogs." Five or six tough-looking tattooed bikers, some bearded, wearing black leather jackets and Nazi-like helmets, skidded to a halt on the road shoulder. Gravel and dust flew around them. Trashy women, biker mamas, straddled behind their smirking men and glowered with the eyes of predators.

In remembering it, Dennis shook his head. "Now, this is so stupid—we were just kids—but we had our pocketknives out, had them ready." His laughter reflected the absurdity. "I don't know what we thought we could do. They circle around us, gunning the engines, scowling, glaring. One of them growls, 'We're going to butt-fuck you, little boys.' We didn't know how far they were going to go or what they were going to do, but it was scaring the crap out of us."

The next thing that happened, Dennis acknowledged, sounded like it came right out of a movie. A faded red 1962 Chevy pickup skidded to a halt on the gravel. A rifle barrel emerged first, followed by a weathered-farmer type, wearing a faded denim shirt and dusty overalls. He stepped out of the old pickup in full confrontation with the bikers. Dennis had the impression that their rescuer may have known the bikers, especially when he exchanged a few words with them. The benefactor turned halfway toward the frightened young duo and yelled at them, "Get in the truck." He didn't have to repeat it. In less than five seconds, Dennis and Jack scrambled into the safe haven.

The farmer spoke a few more angry words at the frowning bikers, climbed into the driver's seat, and slammed the door. As he shifted gears and stepped on the gas, leaving the gang standing in his dust, he asked, "What in the hell are you boys doing up here?" To no one in particular, he growled, "Goddamn bikers, hippies, and weirdos," then added, "Where were you going?"

Explaining the whole unlikely experience, the boys knew they sounded like lost children.

"Okay," said the farmer, "I'm going to take you to town, to the bus stop."

It took about twenty minutes of travel down a hilly, winding road before they reached a small town. Along the way, Dennis observed an old farm, with a wooden ramshackle house set back off the road, rusting dead trucks, and skeleton cars up on blocks. Noticing Dennis's interest in the place, the farmer explained that it was where the bikers lived. After spitting out the window, he added, "They got a bunch of bodies buried out there."

The earlier narrow escapes had already unnerved Dennis enough. The farmer's comment made his scalp crawl. He thought, *Well, thanks for helping us out, but you don't need to scare us any more than we already are.*

They reached the edge of a town. In later telling the story, Dennis couldn't recall its name. Most likely, their rescuer drove southeast on a provincial highway, 148, to an intersection with U.S. 101 at Cloverdale. He let them out at a Greyhound bus station, waved a friendly good-bye, and took off. Neither Dennis nor Jack had much money with them, but put together enough for tickets to Sacramento. After waiting several hours, they finally climbed aboard a bus and slept all the way to California's capital city. From the station, they walked about ten blocks to the Victorian house and Dennis's car. Just before they drove away, Dennis picked up a handy rock and pitched it through one of the old house's windows.

Back in Orange County, Dennis returned to work at the Big Canyon Country Club in Newport Beach. The companionship with Harmon, though, had run its course. He and Jack decided to go their separate ways. Jack found living quarters with a wealthy family acquaintance at the country club. Now alone, Dennis felt a deep sense of isolation, realizing that Jack, with a wealthy family to help him, could survive easily without working. A few weeks later, Harmon returned to Massachusetts.

Fast-forwarding a few years, Dennis capped the story of his narrow escape. "Much later, I started taking a class or two at Orange Coast College, between jobs—busing tables, barbacking (helping the bartender with everything except mixing drinks) at night, part-time construction in the day. I was taking a sociology class, focused on cults. In researching it, I found articles about a guy who deliberately got himself taken in by Moonies. He was transported to Boonville, sneaked in a camera, and sold a magazine article about his experiences. When we were there, they never admitted what they were, or said, 'We're Moonies,' but it finally hit me that we had been nearly assimilated by them."

"Moonies" refers to followers of Reverend Sun Myung Moon's Unification Church movement. The widespread organization's methods of recruitment were controversial for years, especially at their Boonville establishment. "Unificationists" now regard the term "Moonies" as a denigration of their people and beliefs.

Dennis also found out a little more about the biker episode. While working part-time at a Sears Service Center in Santa Ana, as a parts clerk, he often played poker after hours with fellow employees and some of their friends. One loquacious fellow, who occasionally joined the group, a deputy district attorney from Riverside County, enjoyed telling stories. In one of his accounts, he mentioned indicting some bikers from up north. A body, he said, had been found up there on a farm, but he didn't say exactly where.

Dennis asked, "Was that Boonville?"

The lawyer chuckled, looked at Dennis, and said, "I didn't tell you that. How did you know it was Boonville?"

"Oh, I know a little bit about the area," Dennis replied. He didn't say any more, but it made him realize that there was something to the stuff his rescuer had said about bodies buried there.

After returning to Orange County from Northern California, Dennis was flat broke. He got his jobs back at the Huntington Inn and Big Canyon, but still he found himself consistently short of money. It helped when he found more work at an Irvine factory, where he learned to spot weld their products and earned a princely $2.50 an hour. Yet, it would take a while to save adequate funds to rent a room. Late every night, he drove around to find a safe parking spot and slept in his Chevy. In order to have a place to bathe in the mornings, he paid fifty dollars for a one-year membership at the YMCA (where he is still a member). After the factory shift, he'd go to the restaurant, work, earn a few tips, and eat. This routine—including cramped, uncomfortable sleep in his car—lasted nearly four months.

The police in Orange County coastal cities, particularly in upscale Newport Beach, are not amenable to people camping in cars. Said Dennis, "No matter where I parked at night, the cops would find me. 'Rat a tat tat,' with the Mag-Lite on the window. You know, the wake-up call. Massachusetts plates on an old rusty car with a lot of crap piled up in it, in ritzy Newport Beach, where everyone drove luxury cars. Where I was from, you might see a Mercedes in town, but it was five years old. Here I noticed that even gas station attendants would treat me with contempt because I'm driving an old car, even though I'm making more money than them as a busboy. I'm always fascinated by that phenomenon, people who adopt the attitude of superiority over people they serve."

The police would roust Dennis and occasionally arrest him. Usually though, they would check to see if he had a record, explain that he was in violation of Newport's vagrancy laws, and make menacing comments about throwing him in jail. When his identification showed that he was only seventeen, the officers threatened to take Dennis to juvenile hall and call his parents. Before releasing him, they'd growl, "Don't let us catch you sleeping around here anymore."

To avoid these encounters, Dennis often sought out crowded parking lots, usually behind hotels or around the airport, hoping to blend in with all the other cars. All he wanted was a place to sleep without any danger or harassment.

While Dennis did relish the independence, other feelings began to wear on him. In speaking of it, his face grew somber. "You know, I remember being lonely. First time in my life. I had never been lonely before in a big family. I was always very social. But I didn't know anybody and didn't have any money. I was really lonely."

The experience, as painful as it was, taught Dennis some hard lessons. "Once, I met some kids at the beach and was invited to a party on Linda Isle. I overheard a girl who was complaining to her friend that her father had bought her a BMW for her high-school graduation and she was so disappointed because she had wanted a Porsche. Here I was sleeping in my old car, always cramped, just wanting to stretch my legs. And that's when I understood the theory of relativity. She was unhappy. That is someone, like my mother said, 'who is better pitied than censured.' I felt sorry for her. Her perspective on the world was pathetic. And that's what relativity is. Her situation in her world was as tragic to her as my problems were in my world."

Perhaps seeking relief from feelings of despair and alienation, Dennis drove thirty miles south to San Clemente, site of the former western White House of President Richard Nixon. Dennis's aunt Eileen occupied a stately home in the picturesque beach city. But the visit with her only aggravated his inner conflicts. When she offered him the opportunity to live in her place, free, he declined. "I know, it's crazy, living in my car. I would go down to Aunt Eileen's for dinner and leave to sleep in my car. I didn't tell her why, but she must have thought I was nuts. I just don't like being beholden to anybody or owing anyone money. And my mother's words kept rattling in my brain. 'Don't impose on your relatives, so they won't impose on me.' That just wouldn't go away."

On a subsequent visit to his aunt, she made a prediction. She said, "You're going to go back home, and one of two things will happen. You will either stay there the rest of your life or you will return to California and spend the rest of your life here." Dennis's mother's words—"Time and distance render grand illusions"—rang in his head, but he wouldn't understand them for a long time.

Desperately needing a place to live, but with no credit history or savings, Dennis knew it wouldn't be easy. Scanning newspaper ads, he spotted one that looked good to him, near Newport Harbor High School. A man named Charlie offered rooms to rent in his home, plus a couple of trailers in his backyard. Dennis described him as "in his late fifties, kind of a gross, unattractive person. And he wore a colostomy bag. You could hear the *squish-squish* when he moved." Charlie's fingertips were all missing as the result of a motorcycle accident in which they had been ground off, up to the first joint, by the pavement.

Admittedly naive about sex, Dennis was still a virgin by the time he turned eighteen. He felt that he was "getting worldly," but not in a carnal sense. And certainly, he had never been around a child molester or an alcoholic. Charlie welcomed Dennis to the real world. One night after renting an interior room in Charlie's house, Dennis sat alone on the bed. Charlie walked in, unannounced, carrying a bowl of popcorn and generously offered to share it with his new tenant. Every hair on the back of Dennis's neck stood up. He muttered, "Nah, thanks, just leave me alone, whatever."

The next day, after thinking over what the landlord apparently wanted, Dennis said to him, "Hey, Charlie, I want to rent one of the trailers in the back. I don't want to be in the house." Within an hour, Dennis had moved to the more private quarters.

A man in the next trailer would become a close friend to the young Massachusetts native. Carlos Diaz (pseudonym) worked steadily in home construction as a drywaller. A Vietnam vet, and an alcoholic, Carlos virtually adopted the naive youngster. Dennis recalled that his new pal had stretch marks on his stomach from ballooning up to almost three hundred, then dropping down to less than two hundred pounds. Over drinks, they swapped stories, with Carlos telling tales about combat and other events in Vietnam that "weren't good, really scary, spooky things." Another new tenant, inside the house, befriended Dennis and Carlos. Tall, blond, and well-read, Jim (pseudonym) was a former college basketball player from Michigan. A "very classy guy," said Dennis. They became good buddies. Carlos used his influence to get the two young men jobs in construction.

During the trio's drinking sessions, Charlie was often the derisive subject of their conversations. Carlos informed his pals that the man had been in prison for molesting children. It worried Dennis that little kids would play in the cul-de-sac and interact with all the residents. So, thereafter, at least one member of the group would make it a point to go tell the parents, "Hey, keep them away from Charlie."

Living in the trailer gave Dennis limited separation from his peculiar landlord, but not enough. Being on a sex deviant's property became increasingly uncomfortable for him. By July 1977, he began to wonder if he'd made the right decision in migrating to California. So far, it had not been the Utopia he had imagined. "Time and distance renders grand illusions." Had the whole experiment been nothing but a grand illusion? Perhaps the security and comfort in the Agawam home of his family hadn't been so bad after all.

If he had received a letter intended for him, the decision to return would have been easy. That June, his sister Martha wrote to him suggesting that he come home. She hoped he would just "ignore Mummy" and find happiness with the rest of his family. The letter didn't reach Dennis until decades later, when it was discovered among his mother's possessions after her death. She had intercepted it, and never allowed it to reach her absent son.

Even without the knowledge that Martha wanted him to come home, Dennis decided to make the trip. With only $20 in his pocket, he figured he could make the journey to Massachusetts by hitchhiking. He strapped on a backpack, previously "borrowed" from his brother Joe, and set out.

The first ride came from an older lady, about a hundred miles across the Mojave Desert, on I-15, to Barstow. From there, he was picked up by "some crazy bastards" in a pickup truck, who were giving rides to everyone they saw. Dennis jumped onto the truck bed with three or four other hitchers. At a convenience stop, they all chipped in a couple of dollars each to buy a case of beer. In a wild ride, with the pickup flying through the desert and the bed filling up with people, Dennis decided to check a map to see where they were. It startled him to see the vehicle was headed into Arizona on Interstate 40, parallel to old Route 66, the famous "mother road." He had planned to go north to Interstate 70 and then 80, through the plains states. At the next intersection, he said good-bye to the driver, hopped off, and changed direction by hitchhiking in Arizona.

Within a short time, a Highway Patrol car pulled up next to Dennis and an officer ordered him into the backseat. In Arizona, the Department of Public Safety, Highway Patrol Division, is responsible for enforcing traffic laws on major thoroughfares. They transported him to the nearest town and tossed the frightened teenager into a dusty jail, saying that hitchhiking was illegal in Arizona. Dennis's heart skipped a few beats when he saw a cop emptying his backpack. He held his breath, hoping the officer wouldn't find a joint concealed in the aluminum frame. Fortunately, it remained hidden.

Fidgeting and nervous, Dennis surveyed his surroundings and spotted another young man in the adjacent cell. In an era when long hair was the fashion, it struck

Dennis as peculiar that his fellow inmate's head was shaved. He asked, "What's your deal?"

In a quaking voice, the youth replied, "Well, they found my pot so they shaved my head. And I haven't heard my dog bark for a couple of days."

To Dennis, the comment suggested dark things. Questions besieged him. *Does the guy mean they killed his dog? Are they going to shave my head? How long do they plan to keep me locked up?* He never got any answers about the unfortunate fellow.

After letting Dennis "cool his jets" for about a day, the police released him with a warning. No hitchhiking. Relieved, he nodded vigorously and said he would go right over to the bus station. Happy to be free again, he walked out at a hot pace, rushed to the edge of town, looked both ways, and stuck out his thumb.

Motorists are sometimes wary about picking up hitchhikers, but an eighteen-year-old curly-haired kid who looked even younger didn't represent much of a threat, especially in 1977 when hitching was common. Dennis had little trouble getting rides. It was a relief each time to get out of the daytime August heat, soaring over a hundred degrees in the desert. Conversely, at night, he would nearly freeze before a benevolent driver came to his rescue.

Under a chilly moon late that night, Dennis had trouble keeping his eyes open, and felt thankful when a big Cadillac pulled over for him. He jumped into the passenger seat, spoke a few words of gratitude to the portly, middle-aged driver, then let his drowsiness take over. He had been asleep no more than a few minutes when he snapped awake due to a hand caressing his left leg. Even worse, the car was stopped by the roadside.

It was not often that Dennis lost his temper, or as he stated it, "Let the leprechaun out." But in this case, his anger took over. "It scared me, I never had anything happen like that before." Even old Charlie, the pervert back in Orange County, had never actually touched him. Dennis clenched his fist and slammed it into the driver's face several times in quick succession. It seemed strange to see the man's head bouncing off the window glass. Severely rattled, Dennis reached back and grabbed his pack, lifted the lock, leaped from the car, and bolted into the dark desert. Stopping to catch his breath, he watched as the Cadillac lights went on, and the car vanished into the distance.

After enough time had passed to be certain the molester wouldn't return, Dennis scrambled back to the road and walked until he could stand under a signboard light to wait for a ride. The next vehicle, though, turned out to be a Highway Patrol car. It zoomed by, but Dennis knew the officer had spotted him. The cruiser slowed about a half-mile up the road and maneuvered into a U-turn. This could mean serious trouble as a repeat offender, but Dennis's Irish luck kicked in once more. Before the patrol car finished its turn, a Volkswagen bus pulled over and Dennis hopped in. The occupants turned out to be two brothers driving home to Pennsylvania from college in Arizona.

The final leg of Conway's journey involved numerous short rides before he finally reached Springfield, Massachusetts.

It was the first time he'd been home in a year, and for a couple of days, he was treated like a returned conquering hero. Shortly after that, the old mother-son friction took over again. Even though Dennis was away from the house most of the time, and working again at Riverside Park, he and Mary Conway just couldn't get along.

After two weeks, he moved into an old buddy's apartment in Springfield and found an extra job as a bellman at the local Marriott Hotel. Several celebrities stayed there during that month. Dennis carried comedian Buddy Hackett's half-dozen bags up to his room, extended his most courteous and professional help, only to be disappointed at the miserly tip the chubby comic handed him. Later, though, Hackett kidded the youthful bellman and gave a little more. Other celebrities he met on the job included Leslie West, who sang "Mississippi Queen" with the band Mountain, and the Wilson sisters, Ann and Nancy, who formed the band called Heart.

All the old reasons Dennis originally left Massachusetts began to mount again. His discomfort grew, and the urge to leave once more occupied his thoughts. Reliable Carlos Diaz, Dennis rationalized, would help him find employment again and give him a temporary couch to sleep on.

By early November, he announced to his family, "I'm going back to California."

Mary Conway had been displeased by Dennis hitchhiking across the country. She said, "What we are going to do is buy you a one-way bus ticket." Three days later, Dennis boarded a Greyhound bus for Los Angeles.

Later telling of the interminable ride, he asked, "Have you ever been on a bus for three or four days? Where you are constipated and they stop at every little dusty town? And you can't straighten your legs. I was tempted to cash in the seventy-five-dollar ticket and start hitchhiking again. It was the worst trip of my life."

Back in Orange County again, Dennis found his old pal Carlos, who provided the couch and a job. Crossing construction union picket lines as a scab laborer, Dennis even learned to speak enough Spanish to communicate with coworkers from south of the border. By working construction along with other parttime jobs, he soon saved enough money to start looking for another place to live.

Dennis at last landed on his feet. He found a better situation in Costa Mesa, conveniently located north of Newport, east of Huntington Beach, and just a couple of miles from the seashore. Several young men shared a four-bedroom home on Dogwood Avenue. Dennis would have his own room in a comfortable house. Unfortunately, he would also be arrested and spend more time in jail.

On a bright sunny Friday morning at the end of May, the beginning of Memorial Day weekend, Dennis stood at the kitchen stove, dressed only in a towel, cooking bacon. Someone knocked on the front-entry door, and Dennis answered it. A scowling uniformed police officer asked, "Is Dennis Conway here? I've got a warrant for his arrest." Just a couple of weeks earlier, Dennis had been driving a motorcycle, and was cited for failure to make a full stop at a boulevard stop sign. He hadn't paid the fine or appeared in court to contest it.

Dreading the thought of spending time in another jail cell, Dennis acted on instinct, not intelligence. He casually replied to the cop, "Yeah, I'll go get him." He headed to his bedroom, pulled on a pair of shorts and a shirt, then slipped out through the back window. The officer, realizing he'd been conned, rushed into the house and woke up Dennis's pals. A search of his messy bedroom and chaotic closet turned up nothing. The buddies later told Dennis that the cop, holding his handgun, growled, "Where is that little SOB?"

On Saturday morning, Dennis looked outside and his heart sank. The same cop stood on the porch, motioning for Dennis to come to the door. "The cop is standing there again, really pissed now. I plead, 'C'mon . . . ,' but he's there to arrest me. So he takes me down to the station and books me."

Unfortunately, it had been a busy weekend for the police, and the jail was crammed with everything from hungover drunks to hardened felons. Said Dennis, "It was so crowded in the booking cell that if you fell down, you wouldn't hit the floor." It took seven hours to process him. In his Arizona jail experience, the place had been almost empty. This was different and Dennis felt the rumblings of cold terror.

After what seemed forever, an officer pushed him into the "bull pen" holding cell. Bunks were stacked almost to the rafters. Dennis estimated the count of grousing, angry inmates at close to eighty. He heard cat-calls, whistles, and knew much of the attention was directed at him. Now nineteen, he didn't look any older than sixteen. Dennis had heard stories of prisoners sexually abusing younger inmates, and dreaded the horrible possibility. Luckily, in the restless crowd, he ran into two brothers with whom he had worked on construction crews, a couple of nice guys. They were serving a sentence for some infraction of the law by spending weekends in jail.

Realizing the importance of protection, Dennis attached himself to the brothers as if he belonged to their family. He used the one phone call allowed to reach his roommates and to ask if they could help. Over the noise of a Memorial Day party going on in the house, he heard that they were trying to drum up his bail money, $500. He knew that it was hopeless. It might as well have been $10,000.

Later, reflecting on the experience, Dennis realized what had really caused the police to come after him. It clearly had little to do with running a stop sign.

Instead, it related to a goofy prank in which Dennis had gleefully participated.

Plainclothes detectives often parked across the street from the house Dennis and his buddies rented. A friend of one of the tenants lived just around the corner, a man who also happened to be a drug dealer. "We were smart-asses," Dennis admitted. To give the parked detectives a bad time, he and his pals would go out and put signs up:" NO NARC PARKING BETWEEN 8 AND 5. Adding insult to injury, they donned Halloween masks and jumped around the unmarked car to show off.

So later, when Dennis understood how cops think and work, he knew exactly what had motivated them to knock on his door. "They decided they were going to find out which little assholes living in that house are doing this stuff, and bust 'em. That probably played into this more than a little bit. Anyway, they released me after forty-eight hours in jail."

While living on Dogwood Avenue, Dennis worked a variety of jobs. But the old '67 Chevy finally reached the end of its road, and he needed another car. His friend Carlos Diaz came up with the answer. Carlos's grand-mother owned a '64 Thunderbird, salmon coral in color, with only sixty thousand miles showing on the odometer. It had sat unused for five years. The elderly woman agreed to sell the car to Dennis and allowed him to make moderate monthly payments.

While the car was generally sound, Dennis soon found that the booster pump, which operated the brakes and the power-steering system, malfunctioned due to drying out over a long period of inactivity. The greasy labor of working on cars had never appealed to Dennis, but he tackled the job anyway. He completed the repairs at about two o'clock one morning, and decided to take the car for a test-drive.

Initially he buzzed along the coast highway, up Beach Boulevard, then onto the I-405 Freeway. Since the predawn traffic was light, he decided to push it a little harder. When the speedometer hit 130, Dennis backed off, just in time. A couple of minutes later, though, a California Highway Patrol officer pulled him over because smoke billowed from the T-Bird exhaust pipes. Dennis felt certain he was going to jail again. While writing the citation, the officer mentioned that he knew Dennis had been speeding at over one hundred miles an hour. Instead of trying to make excuses, Dennis told the officer everything, admitted speeding, and apologized, in a sober and truthful manner. The cop leveled a stare at him, hesitated a few seconds, then wrote a ticket for speeding at seventy-five miles per hour. The higher speed would have resulted in a mandatory arrest, but this citation would let him remain free and attend traffic school.

The learning experiences for a young man were gradually building. He later said, "It taught me another lesson about sometimes giving a guy a second chance if he's decent and honest."

The Thunderbird was the first car to give Dennis any pride of ownership. It was salmon coral with a white leather interior. The color embarrassed Dennis. "I didn't want to drive a *pink* car, so I did something that, in retrospect, was sacrilegious. I 'Earl Scheibed' it!" Earl Scheib operated a highly advertised chain of inexpensive auto-painting shops at that time. Dennis later gritted his teeth over the mistake. The original paint was high quality and gave the car its real value, while the new coating looked terrible.

With Dennis's precarious finances, the T-Bird's gas consumption caused problems. "Its three-ninety-cubic-inch engine, fully loaded, made it a real fuel hog and I had it during a gas crunch. I was living hand to mouth and it was sucking gas." He seldom earned much more than minimum wage, and even though he usually worked more than one job, money remained in short supply.

At one place of employment, a factory, he worked with several ex-convicts. As a youngster among such men, Dennis sometimes found himself vulnerable. "I was a kid in that factory with a bunch of thugs, but they were always nice to me." At least he thought they were. One of the men, a biker named Grady Peterson (pseudonym), hailed from Boston, so he had something in common with Dennis. Peterson's claim to fame was having been in jail with an inmate named "Tennis Ball," who bragged about a friendship with Charles Manson. One day at lunchtime, Peterson asked to borrow Dennis's Thunderbird to go buy some food. Always generous, the youth thought nothing about handing over the keys. Peterson drove away and never came back.

Feeling betrayed, Dennis paid a visit to the thief's wife. In the garage of an old farmhouse where she lived, and holding a new baby in her arms, she claimed that she had no idea where Grady had gone. Weeks later, a rumor spread that Peterson had taken up residence in Texas, still driving the T-Bird. But Dennis never saw his car again.

One advantage of living in the house on Dogwood came from the social opportunities it presented. The residents hosted frequent parties, which enabled them to meet local young people, especially girls. One of the men, Scott Farthing, who eventually bought the house, was dating a girl from Newport Harbor High School. She brought other attractive young classmates to the social gatherings. Among them was a vivacious, athletic junior, Lisa Barrett. Dennis felt an immediate attraction to her gorgeous smile, waves of light-brown hair cascading down her back, and effervescent personality. He asked if she would like to go out sometime, and she said yes. Dennis even agreed to take her to her junior prom.

He astonished himself with the offer, since he had never even attended his own high-school prom. Once, it had nearly happened, but it turned out all wrong. In his senior year, he and one of his best friends, Vinny, asked a couple of girls if they wanted to go to the dance. At the time, Vinny was putting his money aside to buy a Triumph sports car, and Dennis socked away as much as he could to buy the Chevy, plus fund his planned trip to California. A conflict arose. They couldn't save money by spending it on dates. Dennis told the girl he had asked, "I can't go to the prom with you." Vinny, too, backed out of his commitment. At school the next day, they suffered the consequences. Dennis said that an eccentric English teacher got on the public-address system and announced, "This song is for Dennis Conway and Vincent Martino, who are too cheap to go to the prom." She sang Art Garfunkel's "I Only Have Eyes for you," apparently to humiliate the two backsliders.

Romantic dates with Lisa Barrett hooked Dennis, and they became a steady couple. He admired not only her attractive features and bubbly happiness, but also her athletic skills as a field hockey player. Lisa's parents, a mixture of Greek and English heritage, became Dennis's California family. He observed that Lisa's four brothers, all good-looking guys, got away with more than she could. She was the good girl and had to maintain that image. Her father, said Dennis, was a "Ronald Reagan" type of man.

Perhaps the ecstatic feelings of mutual affection came free, but if he planned to continue seeing Lisa, Dennis once again needed a car and more money. He had been working four shifts of busing tables at the Spaghetti Factory, but increased his load to seven. It bothered Dennis that he was forced to compete with the offspring of wealthy residents who took restaurant jobs for "work experience" when indigent kids really needed them. "Mummy and daddy," he complained, "wanted them to pay for gas in their gift BMWs. But they were constantly taking vacations and time off, so I'd pick up their shifts. I was a shift whore." He worked every night at the restaurant and spent days on construction jobs. Dennis took pride in being a hard worker, probably a subconscious result of the values his mother tried to teach. He admitted having a problem with punctuality, and wearing his hair too long, not shoulder-length but thick and curly. His uniform was often messy, and the "ministerial" things went astray. "But I was a really good worker. I set a record for making fifty dollars one night as a busboy by working so hard."

In need of transportation, Dennis acquired a rattle-trap 1962 Ford Falcon for $150. It was a magnet for police attention. Routinely, when he drove to Lisa's upscale Newport Beach back-bay home, the cops would stop him. He knew the drill, learned it by heart: *Make sure the tires aren't bald, the windshield is not cracked. Have my license and registration ready, they're going to make up some reason for pulling me over in that car. I'm a kid and I'm not going to protest to a cop, "What's your reason for stopping me?"*

Even this seeming harassment made an indelible and positive impression on Dennis that would serve him in the future.

No matter how hard he tried to avoid it, though, trouble would always find Dennis, sometimes with a little help from him. One night, leaving Balboa Island after a few drinks, he sideswiped a parked truck. Dennis got out, examined both vehicles, and decided that nothing more than a "little paint transfer" had taken place. His own car was such a junker, it couldn't be damaged any more.

Back in his car, he headed for the only exit from the island, the Jamboree Road Bidge. As he reached the other side of it, flashing cruiser lights lit up his rearview mirror. He pulled over and was surrounded by three or four Newport Beach patrol cars. As soon as he rolled down the window, officers barked, "Get out."

Standing in the beams of flashlights, Dennis slumped his shoulders and decided the only logical course was complete honesty about the collision. He volunteered a complete account of it. One of the cops examined the new dents and "paint transfer" on the Falcon. "We heard about that," he said. "The truck owner was out smoking a cigarette and saw you."

Once again, Dennis felt certain the cops would take him to jail. But the lead officer amazed him by saying, "You've been up front with me, so you know what I'm going to do? I'm going to write you up for a hit-and-run misdemeanor and follow you home."

Relieved and grateful, Dennis knew he had escaped serious consequences. But he still faced a court hearing, and needed legal assistance.

Lisa and her parents helped Dennis find an attorney. It warmed Dennis's heart that she and her parents gave him such affection and respect. Not only his first real girl-friend, Lisa was also his best friend in the world.

The Falcon soon died, so Dennis bought a motorcycle. Within a few weeks, while riding it to work, a car struck his bike and sent him spinning onto the pavement. A woman jumped from the vehicle, tried to help him up, and profusely apologized while choking back tears. Dennis felt sorry for her and said he was okay. His motorcycle was operable, so they exchanged insurance information and departed. By that evening, Dennis realized he was not okay, and lost a couple of weeks of work due to contusions and sprains.

The accident gave Lisa's mother reason to worry and she forbade her daughter to ride on the bike with Dennis. Parents' orders, of course, are meant for teenagers to ignore. It wasn't long before Mrs. Barrett spotted the bike headed up Irvine Avenue, with Dennis gripping the handlebars and Lisa astraddle behind him, her arms around his waist, their hair flying in the wind. No helmet law existed then, and of course neither of them even owned one. Dennis wore shorts, a T-shirt, and rubber flip-flops instead of shoes. Lisa was dressed in shorts and a halter top.

Dennis caught sight of Lisa's mother at the same time she saw them. He thought, *Oh no, Mrs. Barrett is going to kill me.* Dreading the probable wrath he faced, Dennis took his girlfriend home. "Her mother gives me *the look.* Later, she chastised Lisa, 'There you were and your butt hanging out of those shorts. . . .'"

Dennis fondly recalled, "Mrs. Barrett was really a great lady. And Lisa was really, really sweet, an all-around good girl. We went to two proms at Harbor High school."

The happiest times that Dennis could remember, in that period of his life, took place during his relationship with Lisa. But unforeseeable events would soon send him into a tailspin of despair.

CHAPTER 10

Five Bullets

For Sarah and Matt, the turbulence of recent months seemed to have calmed like the blue Pacific after a storm. On Tuesday, April 15, 2003, Matt presented Sarah with a very special gift, intended to celebrate hope for better times in their patched-up relationship.

In Matt's memory, one of their best moments ever was the day he bought her the top-of-the-line stereo for her Kia Rio. When Sarah ended her work shift that day, Matt drove her in the Kia to a stereo shop, keeping their destination a secret. At the store, he announced the surprise, and Sarah danced with delight.

Matt had saved his money for months to purchase the gift, but still didn't have enough, so he paid half in cash and the balance with his credit card. The store manager, a friend of Matt's and an admirer of Sarah's, said, "You know, man, she's worth it." He gave Matt a discount and installed the whole thing for free.

It put a huge smile on Sarah's face and she screamed,

"I got bumps!" She especially loved the booming bass thumping from the high-quality speakers.

The happy couple drove back to Matt's Westminster home where his mother, Jill, couldn't miss the couple's effusive mood. Sarah rushed into the house shouting, "Jill, Jill, Jill, you gotta hear it."

Ordinarily, Jill Corbett would avoid going anywhere near a thunderous stereo because she was constantly after Matt to turn down the volume of his music. Subjecting herself to earsplitting noise from Sarah's new system wasn't high on Jill's list of priorities. If the so-called music was the mother of all sound to Sarah, it was the spawn of misery to Jill. With patient understanding, the mother who had dealt daily with teenage twins smiled at Sarah. "Okay, hon" she said, and walked out with the beaming young woman.

The precious memory brought laughter to Matt's lips. "She was just—I have never seen her smile that big. I had bought a lot of nice stuff for her before that, but this was something she really wanted. And she was just so—that smile from ear to ear, I couldn't get it off of her. I said, 'Well, calm down.' She was going home, and she called me when she got on the freeway and asked, 'Can you hear it from your house?'"

When Sarah arrived home at about nine-thirty that Tuesday night, she rushed inside, still radiant with joy. "Mom, Mom," she yelled, "you gotta hear my new stereo."

Her mother, Martha, smiled, but said, "Not right now. What will the neighbors think with that loud music? I don't want to bother them."

"Aw, come on, Mom," Sarah pleaded.

Martha replied, "I'll hear it tomorrow." Later, she regretted the decision and wished she had humored her excited daughter.

On the following morning, Sarah wrote to a friend:

Today is Wednesday (Bible Study) night and Rick hasn't bugged me at all, thank God! I am so happy, you don't even know. It's been like 2 weeks since he has bugged me, seen me, or called me. I don't know if he drives by my house, but he better not! I told you that I got a restraining order on him, huh? I don't know if I told you that I didn't have anyone to give it to him, so I had a Sheriff serve it. Well, I called on Monday and some lady told me that it has not been served yet and that it is still out in the field. I was like, damn! O-well—hopefully it will be served to him real soon!

Attempts to serve the restraining order failed. And Sarah's letter was never mailed.

Sarah completed her duties at the preschool by three o'clock that Wednesday and left. On her way home, she used her cell phone to call a young male friend in Yorba Linda, David Mendoza. They spoke almost daily by telephone, e-mail, or cell text messaging. Sarah asked, "Hey, are you going to be home for a while? I want to come by and show you the new stereo Matt gave me."

Mendoza said he would be there. Sarah arrived at 3:25 P.M., and Mendoza, seventeen, greeted her in the driveway. She grinned and turned the music volume up. They listened for a few minutes, moving to the beat, before she turned it down. Beaming with pride, Sarah chatted with her buddy until about 3:40 P.M. She said, "I've gotta take off. I'm meeting Matt at my house and we're going to Bible study." As she backed out of the driveway, she waved and yelled, "I'll see you later."

When she arrived home, Sarah greeted her mom, then rushed upstairs to ready herself for Matt. She looked forward to the classes conducted by her biological father, Fernando Rodriquez, just a short distance from the Dewar residence.

That morning, Sarah had looked at her mother's hands and playfully suggested a manicure. Martha gave herself one, and made a point of showing it to Sarah that afternoon. "Look, I did my nails."

Sarah teased, "Oh, you really messed that one up." She giggled, then went into the kitchen and washed the dishes. Afterward, she bent over Martha's chair and gave her a kiss before she and Matt left to go to Bible study at George's house. They went every Wednesday night. Martha was concerned about the Namey situation and worried that he still might be stalking Sarah. Each day, after leaving work, Martha made a habit of circling the neighborhood in her car to make certain that Namey wasn't hanging around to cause trouble.

Matt arrived and parked his GMC pickup at the curb, near the Dewar driveway. He and Sarah embraced before Matt climbed into the passenger seat of her red Kia Rio. Sarah, wearing white sports shoes, blue jeans, and a loose white T-shirt, gave him one of her trademark glowing smiles. They decided to grab a snack at McDonald's before going to George's home. To pay for the food, they needed to visit an ATM first. Sarah drove, with her new stereo blasting their favorite CD.

They left the tract via Hill Street, breezed past the sports complex, and headed to Rose Street for the Quaker City Bank. From the ATM, Sarah withdrew $20 at 4:55 P.M., leaving an account balance of $62.17. She turned in the direction of a McDonald's restaurant on Chapman, not quite two miles away.

Using the drive-through service, Sarah ordered a Big Mac with no onions, and Matt requested a double cheeseburger with no onions or pickles. Running a little late, and needing to return to Sarah's house to pick up something she had forgotten, they decided to wait until they arrived at Bible study to eat the burgers. At 5:10 P.M., they exited the McDonald's parking lot. Sarah turned from Alta Vista and drove north on Jefferson Street, passing the greenbelt sports complex, aiming for Hill Street, the entrance to her tract.

From the opposite direction, they both noticed a black Nissan Sentra as it apparently pulled away from the curb and barreled toward them at a high rate of speed. It stunned the pair to see that Richard Namey was driving.

Neither Sarah nor Matt had ever seen him in that vehicle before. She twisted the wheel and made a right onto Hill Street, with Namey in close pursuit. In a flash, he pulled alongside. Through his rolled-down window, he yelled, "Hey, what's up, dog?" Namey accelerated, jerked his steering wheel to the right, and edged toward Sarah's car. His action forced her to brake and stop about eight feet from the curb, approximately 120 paces and around the corner from Sarah's home. The Nissan angled in and halted in front of her Kia, blocking any possible forward movement.

Namey jerked the Nissan door open, jumped out, and circled in front of it. Holding his left hand down at his side, as if concealing something, he strode full-tilt to the Kia's passenger side, then switched the object in his left hand to the right. It all happened in a few brief seconds.

The sequence of events was an incredible repetition of Namey's actions the previous July when he had forced another vehicle into a parking lot, then threatened Andrea Merino and Jim Fletcher with a "toy" gun, despite a restraining order issued against him.

Sarah pushed her door open and yelled to Namey that she had a restraining order, and that he'd better leave or she was going to call the police.

Matt sat in the passenger seat, ready to spring out and defend Sarah.

Halting at Matt's open window, Namey snapped, "How do you like me now?" Before Matt could react, Namey raised his right hand up to Matt's eye level. His fist gripped a .357-caliber stainless-steel Charter Arms revolver, aimed directly at Matt's face. As Matt raised his right arm and twisted to one side, thinking only of Sarah's safety, an explosion shattered the silence. The bullet entered the back of Matt's head, just below the right ear, ripped through his nasal cavity, and exited through his left eye, taking out flesh, the eye, and bone fragments from the socket. Namey pulled the trigger at least twice again, maybe three more times. The second shot put a crease at the back of Matt's skull, glanced off, and pierced Sarah's body below her right arm. It tore through her rib cage, mangled a lung, grazed her spinal cord, and stopped inside her body. Another bullet tore into Matt's shoulder blade, then struck his spine and lodged against the spinal cord. His entire body went numb. One slug bore into his left arm.

Matt recalled it: "As I leaned down, I remember the first shot hit me and all I could hear was Sarah screaming. I fell down to the gear shift, trying to hold Sarah, and then I tried to get up and look at him. And I remember Sarah screaming, 'No! Stop! No!' Screaming. Hysterical. I was just gushing blood out of my eye. I could still move then. The second shot hit me in the back of the head. It flashed through my mind that maybe if I just lay still, he would leave us alone; if I act dead, he would just leave."

In Matt's memory, he speculated that the second shot, which glanced off his head and struck Sarah, may have killed her. "Before that, she was screaming. But after the second shot, I didn't hear her anymore."

Richard Namey had at least one round remaining in his five-shot revolver. He deliberately walked around the Kia and stopped at the driver's door, which Sarah had opened. He extended the weapon into the car, aimed at the left side of Sarah's head, just in front of the ear, and pulled the trigger.

The short life of Sarah Jennifer Rodriquez, age twenty-one, ended in those few violent moments. Matt Corbett, twenty, lay curled over in the Kia, blood spurting from his back, arm, and mutilated eye socket, his body numb from a damaged spinal cord. Every muscle from the upper chest down was completely paralyzed.

CHAPTER 11

Crime Scene

Megan Gilbert (pseudonym), fifteen, stood before a mirror in her parents' second-story master bathroom, pulling a brush through her long brown hair. Shortly after 5:15 P.M., she heard a commotion coming from outside, on Hill Street. A male voice shouted words that sounded to Megan like, "Get out! Get out!"

Startled, she spun around and peered out a window adjacent to the bathtub. Across the street and a few yards down the block, she could see a red compact car parked about eight feet from the curb, and a black vehicle angled in front of it. A man stood at the passenger door of the red vehicle, pointing something at the person seated inside. Megan drew a sharp breath when she realized the object could be a handgun.

A sudden muted pop, much like a distant firecracker, followed by more identical bursts, verified Megan's fears. In movies and television programs, she had heard gunshots, but these real-life explosions weren't nearly as loud. She rushed into the adjoining master bedroom, where the view was better through a partially open sliding glass door to a balcony. From a position next to her parents' bed, she was transfixed by the drama being played out on the street below.

By this time, the agitated gunman had circled to the other side of the red car. Megan guessed he was the one who had been doing the yelling. He stopped just outside the driver's open door.

The crack of yet another gunshot, perhaps two, reached her ears.

Megan felt that she couldn't catch her breath as panic and fear gripped every fiber of her body. She turned away from the horrifying sight, rushed to the other side of the bed, and grabbed a telephone from the nightstand. Just as she dialed 911, she glanced outside again and saw the black compact car accelerate west on Hill, toward Jefferson Street, then disappear as it exited the residential tract.

While speaking to the emergency operator, Megan said she could see a person sitting in the driver's seat of the red car. The youngster couldn't tell from that distance if the driver was male or female, but the individual seemed to be making an unsuccessful effort to sit upright in the seat. Then, said Megan, she saw the figure slump over toward the passenger side and disappear from view.

A radio call was sent out by the 911 dispatcher at 5:23 P.M. "Possible shooting in the fourteen hundred block of Hill Street. Two reported victims down."

Placentia Police Department (PD) detective Gene Stuckenschneider and his partner, Detective Cory Wolik, received the radio call. They happened to be less than one-half mile away, waiting at a traffic signal on Jefferson Street. Because they were preparing for an undercover operation, on a special enforcement detail, they wore civilian clothing and occupied an unmarked brown Nissan Pathfinder. With Wolik driving, they arrived at the crime scene within two minutes.

Stuckenschneider described it: "Traffic was light. When we got actually onto Hill Street, it was almost like an eerie feeling, 'cause there was nobody out on the street at all. It was just like a ghost town out there."

Detective Wolik parked their Pathfinder well behind Sarah's red Kia. The two detectives cautiously walked toward the still vehicle. Stuckenschneider approached the passenger side, and Wolik the open driver's side. At first, they could see only one person in the Kia—a female in the driver's seat. As soon as they looked inside, though, they saw a male victim slumped down across the center divider. Wolik checked on the young woman and quickly realized that she had expired. Stuckenschneider hovered over the male victim's motionless form and spotted nearly imperceptible signs of breathing.

The detective described Matt Corbett's condition. "At first, I didn't know if he was alive or dead. He was semiconscious, making almost like a gurgling sound. And he was bleeding from his mouth and his head area. He was leaning over to the left, almost—I would put it on her right shoulder area. Just leaned over."

Wolik put out an immediate call for paramedics and an ambulance. Stuckenschneider understood the importance of not moving the severely wounded young man. "Due to his injuries, I didn't know what actually he had sustained. . . . I didn't want to worsen his condition."

Also recognizing the possibility that the youth hovered near death, in which crucial information might be lost forever, Stuckenschneider bent close to the young man's face and asked a few questions. The detective's efforts focused on trying to get the victim's name and attempting to keep him conscious. The bleeding youth seemed to be fading rapidly. Stuckenschneider asked, "Do you know who shot you?"

Barely gasping, Matt tried to answer. It sounded like he said, "Richard Navies or Richard Davies." The officer couldn't clearly understand because of the amount of blood in the victim's mouth. Matt did manage to say that the shooter was driving a black vehicle and that he lived in the city of Santa Ana.

It was a superhuman, courageous effort by Matt, considering how grievously he had been injured.

Stuckenschneider watched over Corbett until emergency medical technicians (EMTs) arrived a few moments later. They quickly concluded that Sarah Rodriquez, identified by a driver's license in her purse, was beyond earthly help. Working desperately to stabilize Matt, they transported him to Western Medical Center in Santa Ana.

Other Placentia PD officers arrived, secured the area, and set up a crime scene perimeter within the surrounding neighborhood.

A giant full moon loomed on the horizon, washed in a bloody orange color.

Two blocks from the tragic site, Sarah's stepfather, Bob Dewar, walked down the street from his home to chat with a landscaper who was working on a neighbor's yard. Dewar wanted to find someone to hire for similar work on his property.

A few minutes earlier, as he arrived home, Dewar had noticed Matt Corbett's pickup parked near the driveway. Since Sarah's red Kia was gone, Dewar subconsciously noted that the couple had gone somewhere together, probably to Bible study, since it was Wednesday.

Later, Dewar recapitulated his experiences of that

day. "I got home from work about five-twenty that afternoon. I heard a lot of sirens going on, the whole time I was walking down to see the landscaper and coming back, more sirens." His first thought was that something had happened over at the sports complex. Every now and then, kids get hurt over there and need emergency care. But when he returned from chatting with his neighbor, another man pulled up in his car after passing near the crime scene. He told Dewar that all the emergency activity was just a block or two away. He was going to walk over there and Dewar decided to join him, curious to see what was going on.

The two men rounded the corner and saw yellow police tape almost up to Hill and Granger. A group of people stood twenty or thirty feet down the street. Dewar couldn't see anything yet because his view was blocked by the crowd. Someone said that there was a shooting; three or four shots had been fired, and there was a little red car down there.

"Little red car!" Those words made Dewar's breath catch in his throat. As soon as he heard the chilling words, he moved quickly to the middle of the street and ducked under the tape barrier. He spotted the red Kia parked out on Hill Street, with the driver's door standing open.

"I knew right then and there it was Sarah's car. Instantly I just knew that something terrible was wrong. Although I had heard hints of some problems during the past couple of weeks, I didn't know any of the details. Just that some guy had been bothering her and she had been trying to get a restraining order against him. But never having met the guy, or heard Sarah talk about him, I really didn't know much about it, and I certainly didn't know that the severity of it was anywhere near what it actually was."

Dewar walked toward the detectives and police officers near the Kia. A couple of them glanced up, their expressions warning him not to interfere. He approached one of them and said, "That's my stepdaughter's car."

Now close enough to see everything in detail, Dewar's eyes stopped on a yellow tarp covering something on the pavement behind the Kia. In a flash, he knew it was Sarah's body.

An officer asked Dewar his stepdaughter's name and he told them it was Sarah Rodriquez. He figured they knew the name already, and were probably verifying his statement. They had looked at her driver's license in her purse.

As the nightmare continued to unfold, a plainclothes officer asked Dewar if he had any idea who might have done it, and the name just came immediately to him. His quick recollection of it even surprised Dewar. "I said there is someone named Richard Namey. She was having problems with him."

One of the men requested that Dewar lead an investigator back to his house so they could search for any evidence to connect Sarah with Namey. He nodded and escorted the detective to his home.

As they approached it, Dewar saw Martha outside in the driveway near the open garage. He assumed that she had just arrived home from work and might have been there for a few minutes. He stepped over to her, his face ashen, and spoke softly. "Martha, something bad has happened. There was a shooting around the corner. I think it involves Sarah and Matt."

He added, "Sarah's gone."

A look of confusion and disbelief creased Martha's soft face. As comprehension set in, she insisted on going to the scene. Dewar recalled that she didn't scream or anything, but appeared kind of frantic, like she had to get to her daughter. It seemed impossible that Sarah could really have been shot and killed. The detective didn't want her to go, but she wouldn't be denied. She was a mother going to her child. She left immediately, walking rapidly toward the corner, then to the site of her daughter's death.

The detective asked Dewar to stay at the house because another investigator was coming to ask questions and look for information on Namey. He waited about ten or fifteen minutes and no one else showed up. The neighbor who had walked with him to the crime scene returned and said, "Bob, you need to go over there." Dewar knew that he meant Martha was obviously under terrible emotional stress.

Forget these people, Dewar thought. *I can talk to them later.* He rushed back to the site of the car to be with Martha. The police and investigators paid little attention to them. Dewar found his wife in the driveway of the house directly across the street, sitting on the concrete, leaning against the garage door, sobbing. Her son George stood next to her. Police officers had kept her away from the tarpaulin covering Sarah's body.

The minutes passed like hours. The family could only watch in helpless despair. Reporters showed up, but officers kept them at bay, and away from the grieving relatives. The owners of the property where they stood invited Bob and Martha to sit on a sofa in their garage, giving them a bit of comfort while they watched and waited.

Dewar couldn't recall whether the coroner's van showed up before they finally trudged home. Dewar recalled, "There was really nothing we could do at the scene and I wanted to get Martha back into the security of our home. I'd rather do that than just have her sitting there with Sarah out there in the street." In his best estimate, he figured they had stayed at the horrible scene about two hours. Concerned neighbors who had heard the sad news began dropping by to see if they could help in any way.

Retracing the ghastly events, Dewar said that he never saw Matt, and guessed that he had already been transported by ambulance. While Dewar was waiting initially for the detectives, Martha called, using her cell phone, and told him that Matt had been taken to the hospital, Western Medical Center. She asked Dewar to call Tom Corbett.

Martha's chin trembled as she revisited the terrible memory. "Bob came with a man to the door. The man said I shouldn't go there, but I had to. I walked over there and saw the yellow tarp. All I could see of Sarah was the back of her arm. I wanted to go to her, pick her up, and bring her home. Matt was already gone to Western Medical. Bob called Matt's parents to let them know what was going on. . . . All I could do is sit there and cry helplessly knowing there was nothing I could do to help my daughter. Then, to find out that Matt was critically wounded—everything just went dark. Who would do something so evil?"

In the Corbett home that evening, Jill answered the telephone. She recognized Bob Dewar's voice, but was confused by his solemn tone, which she interpreted as short and abrupt. Without any greeting, Dewar said, "Let me talk to Tom."

With a feeling of consternation, Jill handed the phone to her husband on the front porch. He barely said hello before Dewar spoke the stunning words, "Tom, Matt's been shot. He's alive, but I don't know how well he's doing. He's at Western Medical."

Tom Corbett would later describe it as the worst day

of his life. There are no words, he said, to describe it, especially for a parent who is "as close to their children as we are. To hear your son and his girlfriend have been shot brings unimaginable pain."

Jill remembered fear and confusion along with the pain. It took nearly twenty minutes for them to find out which one of two Western Medical Centers Bob meant. One was in Santa Ana, and one in Anaheim. Several telephone calls finally answered the question. As they sped along the freeway toward the Santa Ana hospital, Jill gently told her husband, "If you continue to drive like this, we won't be alive to see him. Please calm down. We'll get there and find out."

When they arrived, Tom sprinted from the car into the emergency care unit to see Matt. But he was still undergoing intensive efforts to save his life. Jill paced nervously in the waiting room.

In emergencies, communications often fail. Tom had recently acquired a different cell phone and Kelly didn't have his new number. She arrived home and called a cousin, only to hear him crying on the phone. Kelly asked, "What's wrong, what's wrong? I don't have my dad's cell phone number and he didn't tell me. What's wrong?"

The relative could only say, "Call your dad, you need to call your dad."

Her patience strained to the breaking point, Kelly yelled, "*Tell* me what's wrong."

The words sent Kelly reeling in disbelief. "Matt's been shot. And you need to call your dad right away." She felt herself falling to pieces, screaming and crying. It took several more minutes to learn Matt's location. Kelly rushed to the hospital, ran into the waiting room, spotted her mother, and rushed over to embrace her. Tom was at Matt's bedside. Mother and daughter waited, still uncertain about the horrendous events. They did learn that Sarah had not survived the attack.

Said Jill, "We didn't know a whole lot then. Even the doctors didn't. They told us originally that Matt had five bullet wounds. We thought, 'Oh my God, he got shot five times.' Eventually, through deduction, we started to believe that he was shot four times, but one grazed his head and hit Sarah. They were looking at entrance holes and exit holes. You really couldn't tell right away because there was so much blood."

It took over eight hours, long after midnight, for surgeons to operate on Matt's wounds and stabilize him. His parents and sister waited all night. When the grievously wounded victim was finally brought into the critical care unit, they were allowed to visit him. Jill recalled that the first words out of Matt's mouth were questions about Sarah. Unsure about what to say, Jill whispered to her son, "We don't know yet, we don't know." At that point, she could not tell him the truth. Not until the next day did Matt learn, from his father, that Sarah had been killed. Emotional agony compounded the excruciating physical pain he was suffering.

The family had one more jolt to bear. "We gradually found out that he was going to make it, but that he would be paralyzed." Although intense feelings, like electric shock, coursed through his arms and legs, he could not move any of the limbs.

At the crime scene, investigators continued their meticulous work of gathering witness statements and physical evidence.

Officer Ben Yamaguchi noticed a teenager among the bystanders who seemed especially interested in the event. Yamaguchi asked the youth his name and why he was there. David Mendoza told the officer that he was a friend of the girl who had been shot and that he had seen her just a few hours earlier when they listened to Sarah's new stereo. Answering Yamaguchi's questions, Mendoza described the visit by Sarah that afternoon. He said that later, he'd been watching the six o'clock news on television and had heard the report of a double shooting involving a female victim in a red compact vehicle. When the reporter said the incident had taken place on Hill Street in Placentia, Mendoza realized it might be Sarah. He called a buddy and they rushed to the scene. As soon as he saw the Kia Rio, and a white sports shoe protruding from under a yellow tarp on the pavement, he knew Sarah had been killed.

Since Mendoza seemed to know the victim so well, Yamaguchi asked if Sarah had ever mentioned anyone harassing or following her. "Yes," replied the youth. "About two weeks ago, she told me that a guy named Ricky followed her to night school and gave her some trouble." Mendoza could offer no more details about the confrontation.

After completing the interview with Mendoza, Yamaguchi paid a call at the home of Megan Gilbert, the young girl who had observed the shooting from her parents' bedroom and had made the initial 911 report. Megan, rattled and nervous, had difficulty with Yamaguchi's first few questions. Even though she had seen a man fire a weapon toward someone in the red car, she could not provide a description of the shooter, nor would she be able to identify him in a lineup. She could only remember that the suspect was a male, maybe six feet tall, medium build, brown hair, and wore a dark-colored short-sleeved shirt and long denim pants.

The investigators located another witness, who lived closer to the shooting site. Jeremy Chiong, eighteen, said that he had arrived home close to five o'clock. According to Chiong's recollection, he followed his usual custom of backing his car into the driveway. When he switched off the ignition, he turned his attention to several text messages listed on his cell phone. Because cell transmission was inconsistent inside his home, Chiong remained in his vehicle to return calls.

In his peripheral vision, said Chiong, he was aware of two compact cars moving along Hill Street. The black one swerved at an angle in front of the red one and both of them came to a screeching halt several feet away from the curb. The red vehicle was "sort of trapped." But the witness still didn't pay full attention to them until he heard a sudden shriek, even though his windows were closed. "The girl in the driver's seat of the red car was screaming. It appeared like something was really wrong. She had her hands up, and it was a high, shrill scream."

The next action stunned Chiong. "I saw the man in the black car get out with a gun, and he held it sort of down by his left side. I focused in on the gun, because that's when I got worried, and I noticed the gun was right by his hip, by his pocket. He walked around the front of both cars to the passenger's side of the red car and started shooting." Chiong realized that the couple in the red car may not have seen the weapon until it was too late.

With his heart racing, and concerned for his own safety, Chiong had moved quickly, exiting his car and running through the open garage door, then into his kitchen. During this movement, he heard more gunfire. After locking the door behind him, he raced to a telephone and called 911. Immediately after hanging up, he bolted the front door and waited for the police to arrive. But curiosity took over, and he had to take another peek outside, through the living-room window.

The black vehicle had vanished, but the red one remained. "I remember the driver's door standing open, and the woman in there was sort of like bent over in the seat, motionless." Within moments, Chiong heard the police sirens.

The crime scene team worked late into the night, Wednesday, April 16, to search for evidence. Not until dawn did they tow the Kia Rio away, and clean up the street, leaving no reminder of a stunning tragedy in the upscale, quiet neighborhood.

In the late afternoon of Thursday, the Placentia PD received an anonymous tip from a female caller, who gave only a first name. With a quaking voice, she said that she was a friend of Richard Namey, but asserted that she didn't see him very often. She provided his address on Cabrillo Park Drive, and said that she had last visited him two weeks earlier. At that time, he had confided in her that he would be going to jail soon for violating his probation. The reason, he told her, was "beating up" Sarah at the college she attended. He had "slapped her and grabbed her arm" before the incident was interrupted by a school security guard.

The informant also wanted to report that she had seen Richard Namey's blue El Camino parked at his mother's house in Tustin, which meant he would probably be driving a black Nissan, which belonged to Namey's sister.

One final bit of information the caller volunteered regarded a handgun. She said that more than a year ago, Namey had shown her a small black pistol that he had brought out of his mother's house. The police report noted that the informant refused to divulge anything further and ended the call.

Investigators made a note to pursue the identity of this mysterious woman to see if she could provide any more information about a man who was now a suspect in a murder case.

That same evening, April 17, one of the Placentia PD investigators, Sergeant Daron Wyatt, visited Matt Corbett at Western Medical Center in Santa Ana. He took with him a "six-pack," police vernacular for a photographic lineup of six mug shots. The object was to see if a witness could identify the person they saw at a crime scene. This particular lineup consisted of Orange County Jail booking photos of various arrested men who bore similar physical characteristics. Richard Namey's photo was in position number six.

Sergeant Wyatt first spoke with Corbett's male nurse, Vivencio Reyes. Reyes said that Corbett had suffered "several" gunshot wounds, including one to the left orbit (the bony cavity in the skull forming the eye socket and containing the eye), one to the midface area, one to the cervical/thoracic spine, one to the scapular (shoulder) region, and a wound to the left upper arm. The patient had lost his left eye, and was paralyzed from the neck down. The nurse added that it couldn't yet be determined if the paralysis was permanent, or if Corbett might regain any use of his limbs. He had already undergone extensive surgery to save his life.

His survival was nothing short of miraculous.

Several questions occurred to Wyatt. "Were any bullets, fragments, or other evidentiary material collected during the surgery?"

"Most of the gunshot injuries appeared to have been through-and-through wounds," said Reyes. "There are some bullet fragments lodged in the patient's cervical spine, and these were not removed." One more larger fragment had also been left in his left shoulder.

"Is Corbett coherent or able to talk to me right now?" Wyatt asked.

"Yes, he can speak to you."

"What kind of medication is he on?"

"Well, he's receiving various antibiotics, and morphine for pain. His last dose of morphine was two milligrams at four o'clock. It shouldn't have any effect on his ability to be interviewed."

Wyatt entered room 17, where Matt lay, hooked up to tubes, the left side of his face heavily bandaged. Speaking softly, Wyatt asked Matt, "Do you know where you are?"

"Yes, in the hospital," Matt replied in a weak but clear voice.

"Do you know why you are here?"

"Yeah. I was shot."

"Do you know who shot you?"

"Richard Namey."

"How do you know that?"

"Because I saw his face."

Confident now that Corbett clearly understood what was taking place, Wyatt dug a little deeper. He asked Corbett if he knew Namey personally. Matt answered that he had seen Namey on one prior occasion. What were the circumstances of that meeting? Matt closed his remaining eye for a moment, as if summoning the memory, then told Wyatt that he and Sarah had been in a relationship about four years. They met as the result of a wrong-number telephone call, and ended up dating for the next few years. He said they had broken up for a "very short time" a few months ago. Matt's next comment shook Wyatt. "We *are now* back in a dating relationship." Matt's use of the present tense made the sergeant wonder if Matt knew that Sarah had died in the attack.

Matt spoke more rapidly in retracing his version of the broken triangle of romance. According to Wyatt's report,

Matt said that Sarah was introduced to Namey at an unknown time, through a mutual female friend. Namey wanted to date Rodriquez, but she repelled his advances because she was already dating Corbett. This angered Namey and he began harassing Rodriquez. Corbett went to visit Rodriquez at her Placentia house one night, and when he drove into the neighborhood, he found that Namey had blocked Rodriquez's vehicle in the street, preventing her from driving away. He said he approached and confronted Namey, and that Namey fled the scene. It was the only face-to-face meeting Corbett had with Namey prior to the shooting. A restraining order had been acquired, Corbett told the officer.

Answering Wyatt's questions, Matt led the sergeant through events of the previous day, Wednesday. He had parked his pickup at Sarah's home, they went to McDonald's, and sighted Namey driving a black Sentra. After Namey made a turn, caught and passed them, he forced Sarah to stop her red Kia. When Corbett saw Namey exit the car, "he realized that Namey probably had a black handgun. . . ." As soon as the bullets struck him, said Matt, his whole body went numb.

After the shooter moved to the other side of Sarah's car and shot her, Matt recalled, he tried to talk to her, but she did not respond. He couldn't say what Namey did afterward, and he thought the police had arrived "within seconds."

With the nurse Reyes as a witness, because Matt couldn't sign papers, Wyatt held up the six-pack for Matt to view. Wyatt recalled, "Within thirty to forty-five seconds, he stated, 'Number six.'" As a precaution, Wyatt asked, "What about number six?"

Matt replied, "It is Richard Namey, the guy who shot me." With the help of Reyes, Matt loosely gripped a red pen and circled the number six photograph. Wyatt noted, "He was not able to write his initials or anything else on the lineup, but the identification was recorded on audiotape."

For the Placentia Police Department, which numbered only about sixty employees, approximately half of whom worked patrol duties, homicide rarely happened. Just a few weeks before Richard Namey shot Sarah and Matt, an opening had existed in the Crimes Against Persons Unit, and the commander selected a man to fill it who wasn't very exited by the idea. Detective Chris Stuber had been successfully working to bust drug dealers. By wearing his thick black hair in an unkempt shoulder-length style, and a rough beard cascading down to his chest, he had infiltrated the dark world of narcotics easily. When he was appointed to the Homicide Unit, forcing him to shave the beard and get a haircut, he reluctantly accepted.

A little over six feet tall, bespectacled, with intense hazel eyes, smooth features, and a masculine, articulate voice, Stuber could fit easily into any male organization. He had no trouble sailing through the Robert Presley Institute of Criminal Investigation (ICI), a private training organization available to smaller police agencies to improve the effectiveness of investigators. Core course exercises include: 1) interrogating or interviewing an actor playing a specific role in a criminal investigation, 2) searching a simulated crime scene, 3) surveillance under controlled conditions, 4) writing a search warrant, and 5) presenting a criminal case in court. All of the exercises pertain to a criminal case that participants solve during the course.

Stuber's career as a police officer would never have happened except for a recent development in surgically correcting eye problems. Nearsightedness had ended his military career early and threatened to prevent Stuber from holding any job with high vision standards.

Born and raised in Wisconsin, Stuber joined the navy in 1975, at age seventeen. Somehow he was accepted despite his poor eyesight, but navy doctors caught up with him in the middle of basic training and promptly sent him back to civilian life with an honorable discharge. In Michigan, he applied for a police department job, but was rejected again due to vision problems. So he decided to seek an education. Attending Oklahoma State for a year, then Humboldt State University on the Northern California coast for three years, he studied biological oceanography. In 1985, with a new bride, he moved to Southern California and found employment with a fledgling discount department store called Price Club, which is now Costco.

A news article about radial keratotomy, an eye surgery technique to reduce nearsightedness and astigmatism, caught Stuber's attention and he decided to give it a try. The procedure, performed in 1992, improved his sight enough to qualify for police work. He attended the academy in '95 and was soon employed by the city of Placentia. After a three-year stint of patrol duties, he filled a vacancy in the Narcotics Unit, and worked there until the beginning of 2003. His assignment, the commander said, was temporary until a few personnel problems were solved. Stuber accepted the new duties with a promise that he could return to drug busts as soon as a replacement could be found and trained. He cut his homicide investigation teeth on the Richard Namey case. Sergeant Scott "Scotty" Audiss, Stuber's partner for three years in narcotics, would team up with him again. With nearly two decades of experience in several phases of police work, including five years of robbery-homicide investigation, Scotty's help would be invaluable.

In the evidence room at Placentia PD headquarters, Detective Stuber examined the contents of Sarah's purse taken from inside the red Kia. He listed several items, including a small, orange photo album, a blue information card for victims of domestic violence, an Anaheim Police Department (PD) information card with notations "assault and battery," and a small spiral notepad. Opening the notepad, Stuber read Sarah's entries. On one page, she had printed the Lord's Prayer. On another, she had entered nine phrases, separated by horizontal and vertical lines:

> *I am scared to die—Why am I going through this?—I just don't understand—I'm very sad—And I am depressed—Why do I feel like this?—Or should I say, why do you want me to feel like this? Please come into my life Lord Jesus—Please be my savior.*

On the opposite page, she had printed:

> *I live in a world*
> *all of my own*
> *no one to talk to*
> *no where to go.*
> *No need to live,*
> *no need to die,*
> *no need to cry.*
> *The only thing*
> *left for me*
> *to do is die.*

Stuber paused to reflect on the emotions a young woman had experienced just before her life ended. He carefully placed the notebook into an envelope and marked it for future use.

The evidence chain was growing, all with meticulous documentation for a possible murder trial. Now, the question remained, could Richard Namey be found and arrested?

CHAPTER 12

The Search

Richard Namey seemed to have vanished. If anyone, including his friends or relatives, knew anything about where he might be hiding, they kept it to themselves. Police agencies issued bulletins advising that Namey was wanted in connection with a homicide and warning that he was "armed and dangerous."

Placentia PD investigator Brian Perry drove to the Orange County Crime Lab on Thursday morning, April 17, to witness the processing of evidence taken from the red Kia Rio. Forensic scientist Liz Thompson, from the Orange County Sheriff's Department, snapped numerous photos of the vehicle before touching anything. Then, wearing latex gloves, she carefully removed Sarah's remaining personal possessions from the vehicle. Among the items tagged and bagged was the temporary restraining order, issued on April Fools' Day, 2003, commanding Richard Namey not to "harass, attack, strike, threaten, assault (sexually or otherwise), hit, follow, stalk, molest, destroy personal property, or disturb the peace of Sarah Rodriquez." In addition, he was ordered not to "own, possess, have, buy or try to buy, receive or try to receive, or in any other way get a gun or firearm." The document seemed profoundly toothless and impotent in view of the previous day's tragic events.

Liz Thompson completed her work on the Kia by applying black powder to various surfaces and lifting any latent fingerprints. The California Bureau of Criminal Identification and Information would later report that several of the prints belonged to Richard Namey. Of course, there was no way to determine when he might have been inside the vehicle.

That same morning, the body of Sarah Rodriquez was taken from a refrigerated compartment in the coroner's office for autopsy. Dr. David Katsuyama performed the operation witnessed by investigator Perry and Liz Thompson. The doctor concluded that Sarah's death was caused by massive injury to the brain combined with exsanguination, or loss of blood, from the gunshot wounds to her lung and head.

On Friday, April 18, two days after Namey shot Sarah and Matt, Placentia investigators visited two residences in their quest for potential evidence.

First, in the early afternoon, they arrived at Bob and Martha Dewar's home and asked for permission to search Sarah's room. Sergeant Jerry Zamora and Officer Brian Perry explained that they would be looking for items that could "describe the relationship" between Sarah and Richard Namey. They also hoped to find anything that might provide clues to his current location, plus names and phone numbers of possible witnesses who would have "pertinent information."

Among more that a dozen items they discovered and later booked into evidence were a restraining order, dated April 1, listing Sarah as the protected person, two letters composed by Sarah, and a spiral notebook in which she had made startling entries.

Sergeant Zamora felt pity when he picked up and read the letters she had written, actually hand-printed, one of them dated April 16, the day she died. In the half-page note addressed to a friend, Sarah said that it had been two weeks since Namey had stalked her and that she had learned that the sheriff's department was unsuccessful in serving the papers. In the second letter, undated but apparently written months earlier, Sarah revealed to a male friend that she had undergone an abortion and stated that Namey was the father. She noted that "I swear to God that I am so scared of Rick," and expressed hope that the correspondent might one day beat Namey so badly that "he won't be able to walk."

Although most cops develop an armor against emotions in their work, it is sometimes impossible to completely shield their own feelings. When Zamora and Perry picked up a spiral notebook in which Sarah had filled eleven pages laying bare her innermost thoughts, both men shook their heads. In the private journal, Sarah spelled out her fear that Namey was going to kill her. The first four pages detailed the incident at night school where Namey had accosted her. On page five, Sarah described another incident:

> On Friday, March 28th around 10:30 A.M., while I was at work, he . . . called. As I was on the phone with him he was telling me that I had better not [have] pressed charges because he is already on probation. He also told me that I had better not get a restraining order on him because then I will be making a big mistake. He also told me that nothing better happen to him otherwise he was going to kill me when he gets out of jail.

Sarah also used three pages to record the April 2 encounter with Namey, which involved Matt Corbett. In the first few lines, she told of driving home from her brother's house while speaking to Matt by cell phone.

> *I had turned left onto Buena Vista and I saw Rick's car parked on the street. . . . I hung up on my boyfriend, Matt, because as I passed Rick he made a U turn to get behind me. As I turned into [my neighborhood] he of course started to follow me and he was trying to stop me by almost hitting my car on the side. So I stopped. . . . He started talking to me and I had told him that I got a restraining order on him and I didn't want nothing to do with him. He then told me that I didn't know what I was doing, that I am making a big mistake and that I just made things worse for myself. I told him to do what he's got to do and that I did what I had to do. Just then my boyfriend comes from around the corner and gets out of his truck and just starts to yell at Rick. Rick then takes off all fast and leaving tire marks on the street. My boyfriend starts to follow him. I was going to follow too, but I saw my mom outside of our house and she calls me telling me to park my car in the driveway. I parked there and got out. My mom gets in the driver's seat and I get in the passenger seat and we take off looking for my boyfriend. My mom then calls the cops telling them that this guy Rick won't leave me alone, that he keeps on [stalking] me. Well I called my boyfriend on the phone asking where he was and he told us that he was in front of our house waiting for us. I asked him what happened to Rick and he told me that Rick kept on running every red light and that he (my boyfriend) was not going to follow him any more because he didn't want to run any red lights. My mom and I went home and just waited for the cop to arrive. The cop came and I told him everything that happened.*

Pages six and seven in the journal contained Sarah's account of yet another threat by Namey and spoke of her decision to obtain a restraining order:

> *On Tuesday, April 1st 2003, as I was leaving my house on my way to work I saw him down the street . . . He then started to follow me almost hitting my car so I stopped . . . I then started to drive away because he had gotten out of his car to come . . . talk to me. He got back in his car and started following me again. I stopped because I thought he was going to crash into me. He was yelling, telling me that I am going to be making a big mistake, so then I called my mom on her cell phone telling her that he was by me and that I was scared that he would hurt me again. So my mom called the cops and told them that this guy Richard Namey was following me. Richard then took off in his car. I went to work and the police called my mom wanting to talk to me. I talked to the police and they [asked] me if I wanted someone to come by my work. I said yes. 20 min. later a police officer came and I talked to him telling what had happened. He told me to go to the courts to get a restraining order on Namey. So, that same morning (around 8:30 A.M.) I went to the court in Orange to get a restraining order on Richard Namey.*

A document was issued by the office of Michael S. Carona, Orange County Sheriff, on April 17, the day after Sarah was shot to death by Namey. It stated, "I, the undersigned, Sheriff of the County of Orange, State of California, do hereby certify that after due search and diligent inquiry, I have been unable to effect service of: Temporary restraining order . . . on Richard Namey." The actual order had been issued by Orange County Superior Court on April 1, 2003. April Fools'

Day. It set a hearing date for Namey to appear at a hearing on April 22.

It is unclear exactly what efforts were made by the sheriff's department to find Namey and serve the court order. Namey's harassment and lethal attack of Sarah certainly verified his knowledge that she had, indeed, obtained a legal order by the court for Namey to stay away from her.

Recent studies examining the effectiveness of court-ordered restraining orders find that the majority of victims report a significant decrease in the risk of violence reported to police when the orders are *effectively enforced.*

The National Institute of Justice concluded that the criminal record of the abuser is an important factor in predicting whether or not the abuse will continue in violation of the order. A longer criminal record correlated with a greater chance the abuser would continue the pattern despite the restraining order. Sixty-five percent of men named in protection orders had an arrest history. The mistreatment of women by these men consisted of injury with a weapon in 37 percent of the cases, beaten and choked in more than 50 percent, and threatening, stalking, or harassment in 99 percent of the reported incidents.

Sarah's decision to appeal to the court for help may have been the catalyst that resulted in her death. Detective Chris Stuber later spoke of it. "The most remarkable thing in this case was this restraining order business. People seem to think that a restraining order is a bulletproof shield. It does have an important use, but too often you see cases where the RO is what sets the guy off. I don't want to discourage people from getting them, because they do provide a reason to arrest a bad guy when he violates a court order. But sometimes, it's the catalyst for more violence. Guys like Namey, you can't predict. That's what set him off, that restraining order. It's the 'I own you, I tell you what to do, and you aren't telling me what to do, you're not rejecting me, I'll reject you' kind of a mentality that some men seem to have, including him. He had a lot of issues with women and you just never know. From the day that first order was signed, his bad behavior just escalated. He did the exact same scenario with his previous girlfriend."

In the ongoing investigation, Stuber's partner, Scott Audiss, drove to Tustin to interview a woman who had been a mystery, but only temporarily. On Thursday, one day after the shooting, she had called the police anonymously to report seeing Namey's El Camino, and suggest that the shooter was probably driving his sister's black Nissan.

It had taken only a short time to identify the mystery caller as Carliss Tate (pseudonym), who lived a short distance from the residential units where Namey lived. As Detective Audiss arrived at her apartment, he spotted her getting into a vehicle parked a few stalls away and persuaded her to stay for an interview.

Tate told him that she had known Namey approximately one year. They had been casual acquaintances for about six months before becoming "good friends," which had blossomed when she returned from the market one day and Namey offered to carry the groceries into her apartment. A few months later, Tate discovered that Namey was dating someone else, a girl named Sarah. She had been surprised to learn that it was a serious relationship. Tate admitted to the detective that she had "romantic" feelings about Namey, but claimed that she never revealed them to Namey until after the fling with Sarah had ended. At least she thought it had ended.

Tate described Namey as being "calm" during the relationship with Sarah, but all of that changed after the night-school confrontation. He admitted "putting his hands" on Sarah, said Tate. He appeared to be consumed with the girl, could speak of nothing else, and spent all of his time trying to figure out how to get her back. Tate commented, "Even when he's not talking about her, I can still see the wheels turning in his mind. When we were alone, he would start talking about what he and Sarah would be doing if they were still together."

Audiss asked Carliss if Namey had told her about the school incident. No, she replied. She found out about it by mentioning to a security guard at the apartment complex that she hadn't seen Namey around and wondered why. The guard told her that Namey was in trouble and was hiding from the police. In the guard's account, Namey had gone to Sarah's school and entered into a verbal altercation about Sarah's possession of a cell phone. The dispute escalated, leading Namey to put his hands on her, knocking her down, or maybe pushing her. The guard was unclear about the details, said Tate.

When she again saw Namey, Tate said, she asked him what had happened. In his version of the events, Namey explained, he had gone to the school to talk to Sarah. He admitted "putting his hands on her," but refused to add any details. It was true, he admitted, that he hadn't wanted to hang around his apartment, or his mother's home, because he believed that Sarah's family, or schoolmates, had probably called the police and they would be looking for him.

"I think the cops did come to his apartment, looking for him," Tate said.

The next statement from Tate seemed strange to Audiss. She said that Namey asked her to call Sarah and apologize for him. Tate had tried, but was unable to reach Sarah.

"I told him that Sarah probably hated him after the first time he was mean to her, and was probably sitting around the house kicking her own ass for not breaking up sooner."

Audiss asked, "Were you aware that Namey got physical with Sarah on prior occasions?"

"All he told me was that he had put his hands on her before. But I don't know when or any details about it." In the days following the incident, Namey had been upset because Sarah would no longer accept any calls from him. "That's when his behavior turned obnoxious."

"What do you mean, 'obnoxious'?"

"Don't get me wrong. I really liked him. When it seemed all over with Sarah, I thought he was back in the game and available. What I mean by obnoxious is that all he could talk about was his ex. He was totally consumed with her."

Scott Audiss wanted to know if Namey had ever done anything to make Tate believe he might harm her. She replied, "Not really. He told me he was in some sort of an anger management program because he'd been mad at a couple of other girls. And I knew about him doing something to Sarah. I guess it was possible that he could have hurt me, but he never did. I guess it's possible. I don't put violence past anyone." Tate paused as if troubled about expressing what was on her mind, then added, "Rick did mention to our security guard that he sometimes didn't believe that he had normal thoughts or rational thinking." She also wondered aloud about Namey possibly wanting to hurt himself.

"What do you mean by that?" Audiss asked. Tate said the security guard had spent quite a bit of time with Rick and suggested that someone needed to keep an eye on him. According to the guard, Namey had recently spoken of shooting himself, and speculated about a self-inflicted gunshot to the head always being fatal. In addition, Namey had asked the guard for paper and envelopes, leaving the idea that he might want to write suicide notes.

"Is there anything else?" Audiss inquired.

"Well, lately Rick's been kind of preparing his daughter to live with her grandma."

"Just one more question," said Audiss. "Have you ever seen Namey with a gun in his possession?"

"No, not personally. The guard said that Namey told him about once owning a gun. So I asked Rick about it and he said he had gotten rid of it."

Tate glanced at her watch and said she had engagements at her son's school and needed to leave. Audiss wrote down a telephone number where she could reach him, expressed his appreciation, and left.

At Western Medical Center, Matt Corbett lay in a bed, paralyzed and suffering from excruciating pain.

The family of Sarah Rodriquez, heartbroken, prepared to attend her funeral at Memory Garden in the nearby city of Brea.

Richard Namey remained at large, armed and dangerous.

CHAPTER 13

Tailspin

In the spring of 1980, Dennis Conway still faced a court hearing related to the incident on Balboa Island when he had collided with a parked truck. He had seen that it was nothing more than a "paint transfer," panicked, and driven away only to be stopped by the police. Fortunate to avoid immediate arrest, he was issued a citation that required a court appearance.

In desperate need of a lawyer, but with no money to pay legal fees, Dennis sought advice. One evening at his newest place of employment, the Red Onion Restaurant in Huntington Harbor, he spoke to the bartender about his problem. The older man said, "Well, there's this guy I used to know in San Francisco. He has a law firm here now. You might want to contact him." Dennis thanked his coworker and jotted down the name.

The mother and father of Dennis's girlfriend occupied a special place in his heart. "The Barretts were really nice people and like second parents to me," Dennis recalled. On the day after he received advice from the bartender,

Dennis mentioned his dilemma to Mr. Barrett. With a paternal nod, Barret said he knew just the right lawyer to help, and recommended a firm he knew and trusted. Dennis couldn't believe it. It was the same name given to him by the bartender! To Dennis, the coincidence was an omen. He called for an appointment.

Dennis arrived promptly and the receptionist ushered him into the office of a young, well-dressed attorney, a former deputy district attorney. The lawyer listened to Dennis's narrative about the incident and confidently said, "We'll do a civil compromise. You pay for the damage. When we go to court, because you don't have any rap sheet, except for the traffic things, we'll be able to get the charges reduced." As if the whole thing was already settled, the lawyer asked Dennis how he planned to pay for the legal bill.

"I don't have any money, so I guess I'll have to make some monthly payments," Dennis offered.

A frown darkened the lawyer's face. "Well, it probably won't cost more than a couple grand. Don't you have someone who can give you the money?"

"No, I really don't. And what money I had was used up when I lost a couple of weeks from work after a car hit my motorcycle." Dennis described the incident and said he had never pursued any compensation for it.

A happy glow replaced the lawyer's scowl. "Oh! Well, I'll be able to work something out. We can collect enough from the insurance to take care of your legal fees."

Unhappy with the whole process, Dennis told Lisa that he didn't like the lawyer's ideas and thought the fee was ridiculous. He decided to work it out himself. He and Lisa drove to Balboa Island, and after a little searching, he found the truck and its driver. The good-natured man said, "Hey, I was just out having a smoke, no big deal." Dennis offered him $50, which he happily accepted.

At the court hearing, he explained to the judge that he had settled the matter to the other party's satisfaction. The judge asked a few questions, examined some papers, and dismissed the case. Elated with the outcome, Dennis felt encouraged that the system could be fair. The lesson would find an indelible place in his store of knowledge.

But it did not end his goofy brushes with the law. A few weeks later, while riding a bicycle to a new job, he was stopped by a patrol cop. The officer said he had seen Dennis run a traffic light. Frustration boiled inside him and he struggled to keep cool. "I was really fed up with always being hassled by cops, so I gave him a fake name and phone number."

The officer ordered Dennis to wait while he called the phone number. He came back shaking his head. Dennis knew he had erred and decided to face up to it. "Okay," he said, "I lied to you. I finally cleaned up some warrants and I just didn't want another ticket. You guys have been so heavy-handed with me." He apologized.

Unimpressed, the cop said, "Okay, let's go to the station and talk about it."

Pleading, and giving his real name, Dennis said, "Look, I'm supposed to start a new job right up the street. C'mon, this is my real name and this is why I lied to you."

His contrition did no good. At the station, Dennis was arrested and spent two days in jail. The phony name he had given was recorded as an *aka* (also known as).

In recalling the event, Dennis's face turned crimson. He said, "I don't even want to tell you the name I used." Urged to reveal it, he reluctantly gave it up. "Okay, it was Al Sapelli. Because I grew up in a small town full of Italians. So it was the only name I could think of on the spur of the moment. The cop is looking at this little red-faced Irish kid. I'm sure he thought, 'This is no friggin' Al Sapelli.' I used to do the dumbest things."

Adding insult to injury, someone stole the bicycle a few days later. He had bought it in Massachusetts before entering high school, by saving money earned on his paper route. The Bianchi ten-speed had cost a small fortune, $350. After selling his motorcycle, and needing transportation, he had arranged for the bike to be shipped from his hometown to California. Within three weeks of its arrival, someone broke into the garage of his rented quarters and snatched the bicycle.

So far, 1980 wasn't going well for Dennis.

In June of that year, he looked forward to Lisa's, nineteenth birthday. Maybe he would even be able to afford a little party for her. However, he probably wouldn't invite one of Lisa's friends, a wealthy girl named Gail Kendall (pseudonym). Dennis didn't like the way Gail treated Lisa. It really offended him when he learned that Gail was hosting a party, while her parents were in Palm Springs, at her lavish home on the back bay of Newport Beach. But she hadn't invited Lisa. And, to make matters even worse, Gail had asked Lisa if she could come over to help with preparations, and to stop in later to help clean up after the party was over. Even Lisa's mother had advised her to ignore the requests, but the good-natured teenager couldn't refuse a friend.

On the night of June 14, Dennis worked a late shift at the Red Onion restaurant as a barback and later cleaning up after closing time of 2:00 A.M. He didn't arrive home until 3:30 P.M., three hours before sunrise. The phone rang at 6:30 A.M. and Dennis answered, so groggy he could barely open his eyes. It was Lisa, asking him to give her a ride over to Gail's home to help clean up from the party before her parents returned home from Palm Springs. Dennis mumbled, "Okay," and immediately collapsed back into a deep sleep.

At 7:00 A.M., she called again. "C'mon, Dennis," she pleaded. "I need a ride."

"Okay, I'll be right there," he croaked again, not even conscious of what he was saying. Again he surrendered to the overpowering urge for sleep.

Lisa called three more times, and Dennis was still unable to drag himself out of bed. Finally, a little past 7:30 A.M., even without the jangling phone to wake him, his mind cleared enough to understand that she needed him. "I'm going to go pick her up," Dennis told himself. He pulled on his pants and shoes, slipped into a T-shirt, and headed toward her house in his latest hulk of a car, a 1964 Dodge Dart.

Almost by habit, he steered the route, up Riverside, right on Fifteenth, turning on Irvine Avenue, toward Newport Harbor High School. Countless times he had glanced up at the big school clock and this time was no different. He noted that it was ten minutes before eight o'clock. That moment was branded into his brain, never to be erased.

At Lisa's home, Dennis was met with devastating news. Gail had driven over in her Toyota Celica and picked Lisa up shortly after seven-thirty that morning, but the two girls had never arrived at Gail's place. Near the intersection of the 55 Freeway and Fairview Road, a driver returning home from a party broadsided Gail's Toyota on the passenger side. In the grinding crash, Lisa was killed instantly. Gail survived.

Lisa died at exactly ten minutes before eight o'clock,

the very moment Dennis looked at the school clock about two miles south of the accident site.

Still pained decades later, Dennis choked up in speaking of the tragedy. "Lisa was in the passenger seat and was killed in the collision. We were together every day, my best friend. She was the Barretts' only daughter. I was depressed, angry, bitter. People would avoid me because they didn't know what to say. I was from the old school where you wouldn't go get help or try to find some kind of support group. If I had, it might have expedited my recovery process. But I was from an era in which you didn't do that. And I wouldn't have known where to find one. She died right before she turned nineteen."

Dennis suffered what seemed like unendurable pain; from one extreme of walking around in a numb lethargy, to the other extreme of feeling as if he had fallen into a stygian scene painted by Hieronymus Bosch.

Trying to shake off the nightmare, Dennis would tell himself that it's all relative. There was turmoil all over the world—in the Middle East and in Ireland, people were dying needlessly. Their relatives suffered as much grief. He ordered himself to stop being such a baby. The horror just wouldn't recede.

Yet, it marked a profound turning point in his life. "After that, I would never leave reality anymore. I've never been drunk or touched any type drugs since then. You know why? Because it conjures up all those really horrible, scary feelings deep down inside you. Those were a couple of very tough years. I'm pretty much a glass half-full person, make the best out of things. Part of me has blocked it out."

The relative who had lived in San Clemente, Dennis's aunt Eileen, wanted to help. She made him an offer few people would be able to refuse. She had relocated to

Florida, and told Dennis by telephone that he could have the two-bedroom beach cottage for free and rent out the main house. He refused, "I stubbornly maintained that I don't want my mother to have anything to hold over my head. I know it's crazy, but I just don't like being beholden to anybody, owing anyone money."

Another family member came to Dennis's rescue before 1980 ended, while consuming grief still racked his daily existence. His sister Martha flew from Massachusetts to visit her absent brother. She saw his disconsolate mood and persuaded him to return east with her, to Boston, where she was influential in the Church of Scientology. Across the country they went in his 1963 Comet (she called it "the vomit") through pounding rain and snowstorms.

Of course, Dennis could not freeload on his sister, so he immediately sought employment and found two jobs within the first few days. At a restaurant in Boston's landmark Faneuil Hall Marketplace, he bused tables. A few blocks east, a brand-new Marriott opened in the Longwharf waterfront district and needed young bellhops.

Lisa's death had sparked in Dennis a search for philosophical answers. He had been pondering the importance of honesty. "Remember, I said I used to lie to my parents, do stupid things, shoplifted small stuff. I'm a kid who, whenever I did something wrong, got caught. Some of my friends seemed to be able to escape no matter what they did, but not me. It taught me lessons. I was a pretty honest guy who just got caught up in some silly, wild stunts, but nothing ever really bad. Ratholing change at Riverside Park, shoplifting a few music tapes, but I was a fundamentally honest kid and believed in Karma and consequences I'd suffer for making bad decisions. I don't want anything that's not given to me, that I haven't worked for."

On day while sweating through his busboy duties at the restaurant, still living hand to mouth, the honesty question confronted Dennis head-on. Rushing to a table where two women had left after finishing their meals, Dennis was in the middle of picking up dirty plates and wiping the table clean, when he noticed a thick envelope lying on the booth's seat. He picked it up, took a look at its contents, and sucked in a quick breath. It contained $2,700 in cash and another $1,500 in traveler's checks.

Without hesitation, Dennis turned the envelope over to his supervisor. But misgivings raced through his mind. "He's one of these coke-snorting, arrogant guys who drove a Porsche. I realized exactly what he was going to do with the money."

Only one course of action was correct, Dennis knew. He raced out the front door to look for the two women. As usual, though, mobs of people milled through the Faneuil Hall environs. For the next fifteen minutes, Dennis zigzagged through the crowd. At last he spotted the two women. "They were probably in their fifties, two sisters, one from South America. He told them about finding the envelope and giving it to his boss. As he escorted them back to the restaurant, the grateful woman who had left the package told Dennis about herself. "Her husband had died, and she sold everything to come to the U.S. Every penny she had was in that envelope."

As they entered the eatery together, Dennis later recalled, he could see the disappointment in his supervisor's face. I said, "'This is the lady who lost the envelope.' My instincts told me that even if they remembered where they had left it and called, they never would have seen it. I was so glad for what I did."

After more than a year of living in Boston, Dennis, though still melancholy, felt he had healed enough to face life again in California. Another adventurous driving trip in the ravaged Comet, with a stop at the World's Fair in Knoxville, Tennessee, brought him back to Orange County. Still facing the need to survive each day, he returned to work. Over the next few months, moving around to several jobs, Dennis found it difficult to concentrate on any of them. In 1982, he labored at cleaning swimming pools, but had little respect for the tight-fisted business owner, called Jack, who constantly found ways to cut expenses, even resorting to dangerous methods involving unconventional uses of chlorine. Still struggling with lingering anguish about Lisa's death, Dennis had just begun to make some progress when fate struck him another devastating blow.

He received word in November that his eldest sister, Mary Alice, had suffered a fatal asthma attack. This was Mamie, once called Malice by her brother Don. She had put herself through Massachusetts General Nursing College, then Wellesley, with minimal help from her parents. Not long before, she had met a man she planned to marry, a doctor at Massachusetts General. She collapsed in his living room. Though brain dead, her body was kept on a life-support system to allow her loved ones to see her before surgeons harvested her transplantable organs.

With little money, and only a junker car to drive, Dennis decided to head for Massachusetts. He cornered his parsimonious boss to ask for overdue pay. When the man expressed reluctance, Dennis explained that his sister had passed away in Massachusetts, and he needed the money to travel there. Decades later, still fuming about the employer's insensitivity, Dennis said, "This guy had tons of money squirreled away and was one of the most angry, negative, bitter people I have ever met."

Snarling, as if he were granting a special favor, rather than paying what was owed, the tightwad pulled a roll of cash from his pocket, peeled off a few bills, and handed them to Dennis. Furious, Dennis almost lashed out, but controlled himself with the recollection of his mother's admonition, "Better pitied than censured."

Convinced that his jalopy wouldn't make it across the country, Dennis flew to Massachusetts. At his parents' home, he watched friends and relatives gather for services. A sense of detachment made him feel more like an observer than a participant. Some of the people, he mused, played the role of victims. He made a mental note about real victims of tragedy—that some suffer quietly with dignity, while others fall to pieces.

Happy to see his brother Don again, Dennis marveled at the sudden contrast in how Don was treated. He had been evicted from the home, and ignored while he drove a cab in Boston for eight years. But Don had finally found his place in life, gained acceptance to Harvard, and was working toward a law degree. Suddenly Don was their mother's hero, the prodigal son returned. She had posted a letter from him on the refrigerator. Dennis wondered: did love and respect hinge on family ties, or on achievements and success?

When the family lined up for the wake, Dennis broke ranks to greet old friends. His mother chastised him and demanded he show respect by standing still and quietly greeting guests in traditional formality.

While viewing his sister's body before life support was disconnected, something happened to Dennis. Enlightenment seemed to flood his mind. "I realized, looking at my sister, all she had done with her life. I basically had a talk with myself, to stop sitting around feeling sorry, moping in self-pity. To follow her example and do something with my life. To be a bitter, cynical, depressed person, who wasn't going anywhere, was just a horrible waste. I'd been working crummy jobs, living hand to mouth, taking a class here and there, but usually dropping out before completing them. In California, I could attend night school at minimum cost. Try that in Massachusetts where college costs generally exceeded two hundred fifty dollars a unit."

He made himself a promise. He would return to California, earn a college degree, and turn his life around. Perhaps it would help earn a little respect from his mother.

It soon became apparent that Mary Alice's death also profoundly changed Mary Conway. She had vicariously lived through her favorite daughter's attendance at Wellesley College. The loss seemed to have worn her down, softened her attitude, and caused her to ease her restrictive ways. Mary turned her lost daughter's bedroom into a shrine. Dennis later heard from his sisters that their mother made frequent trips to the cemetery to visit Mary Alice. For the rest of her life, a part of her still grieved.

After the burial, Dennis was ready to head west again. He used every remaining penny to buy a cheap airline ticket. At the last minute, though, his family granted him Mary Alice's automobile for the return trip. The journey, as usual, did not go well.

It began with Dennis getting lost and finding himself in upstate New York, where mechanical troubles with the car plagued him. He struggled through to Pennsylvania, but the vehicle quit for good with a malfunctioning clutch and worn-out brakes. He coasted to the roadside, got out, and considered his options. With no money, no maps, and no transportation, Dennis decided to use the airline ticket, still in his pocket. He flagged down a cab and negotiated a deal—giving the driver the car in exchange for a ride to the airport.

At the airline counter, agents didn't seem to know how to deal with the ticket he had previously purchased to fly from Boston to Los Angeles. For some reason, they put him on a flight to New York, where other agents shuttled him back and forth between LaGuardia and JFK airports. He spent two days, with no sleep, trying to get the problem straightened out. Finally, trying to reason with another counter agent, he croaked, "I'm going to throw myself in front of a subway train or a bus. I'm going to kill myself. I've been up for two days and you've bounced me around all over the place. Just put me on a plane anywhere. Anywhere."

They did. To Atlanta! Finally he found someone who understood the problem and managed to place him on a California-bound jet.

Keeping his self-promised commitment, Dennis enrolled at a community college. He could only attend part-time since daily survival required continuation of minimum-wage jobs to pay rent and living expenses, plus the newly added school costs. Dennis found the classroom work relatively easy, and he understood why. His mother had kept him away from the idiot box by emphasizing the importance of reading. The lifelong habit, and love of books, eased the way for him in school.

With money so tight, Dennis seldom used any for conventional entertainment. He found more interesting things to do. One rainy afternoon, in Santa Ana, he needed to find a dry place to sit and while away a few hours. He chose the Central Superior Court building on Civic Center Drive. It was a perfect place to escape his humdrum daily routine, relax, and watch real human drama rather than some artificial, dreamed-up theatrics on television or movies.

Dennis took an elevator up and walked the halls until he found a courtroom in which a trial was being conducted. He silently entered and took a seat in the gallery. A young prosecutor, who would later become an important part of the state governor's staff, was presenting his case. Dennis watched at first in detached lethargy. After a few minutes, though, the complex interplay sparked his interest. He found himself vicariously participating in the legal give-and-take. His interest grew minute by minute.

Staying longer than he had intended, Dennis tried to guess what questions would be asked by the prosecutor and by the defense attorney and how they would be worded. Sometimes the interrogator seemed to miss the point, and Dennis had to suppress an urge to shout, "No, no. Ask it this way."

Slowly something dawned on Dennis. An epiphany! *I can do that. I can do it and way better than these guys. I can do that!*

The thought embedded itself in the psyche of Dennis Conway. When he walked out of the courthouse that day, the rain had stopped and fresh breezes cleared the blue sky. A renewed sense of self gripped him. He realized he had been wallowing again in self-pity and was sick of it.

Since his 1976 arrival in California, Dennis had bounced around almost seven years, and accomplished little. At the age of twenty-four, the time for a major change in his life had arrived. Although his father had been a lawyer, and his brother Don was putting himself through Harvard Law School, Dennis had never even given serious thought to entering the profession. Now it caught him like a giant Pacific wave under his surfboard. An exhilarating feeling floated him right to the top of the curl.

In making the decision, Dennis faced some hard facts. "Becoming a lawyer seemed to be a remote goal because I thought I would have to get a B.A. degree first. I've always had to work at least two, sometimes three, jobs, living hand to mouth." Somehow he had managed to save about $2,000, which would come in handy for the added expenses of education.

He had earned a few units by sporadically attending college classes. To complete a four-year degree, then law school, would take about seven years, full-time. Realistically, though, due to working odd jobs and attending classes part-time, a twelve-year plan would probably be more viable.

In September 1983, Dennis took the first steps by entering Orange Coast Community College. Still working various jobs, he resisted the temptation to reduce the number of classes. No more drinking and absolutely no drugs. Just a daily grind of working, studying, and reminding himself that he had been wasting a great deal of potential that he knew lay deep inside him. "Things weren't easy, but I think part of me likes the struggle, likes the sacrifice. Maybe part of the martyr syndrome that goes with being Catholic. I kept my nose clean, wasn't getting arrested anymore."

Within a year, still short of an A.A. degree, he had accrued enough units to qualify for entrance into the University of California at Irvine. A few weeks after enrollment, though, he reassessed the long-term plan. The attainment of a law degree was like a mirage in the Mojave Desert. It would take so many years. Dennis decided to search for a shortcut, and soon found the perfect one.

In nearby Fullerton, the Western State University College of Law, established in 1966, offered a special program of admission without a bachelor's degree. Dennis applied, took a battery of tests, sat through interviews, and was accepted.

The $2,000 in Dennis's bank account seemed paltry when he tallied the costs at Western. He needed to find more money in a hurry and adamantly refused to seek a loan. With a close friend who bartended with Dennis at the nearby Marriott, he hit on a way to pad his nest egg. The two men began betting on basketball games. As happens with most amateur gamblers, their schemes failed miserably. Dennis lost his entire bankroll and his car. Broke again, he doubled up his workload, but was forced to postpone entry into Western law school for at least one year. By bartending at night, doing construction framing part-time, and working as a parts clerk at an appliance store in the remaining hours, Dennis gradually regained his footing. A pal at the appliance firm liked Dennis and knew of his bartending skills. Through a network of connections, he managed to get Dennis a job at the trendy Studio Café near Newport Beach. It would turn out to be an important link to profound future events in Dennis's life. He started there in August 1984, on the very day that relay runners carried the Olympic Games torch along Pacific Coast Highway en route to the Los Angeles Coliseum.

It was at the Studio Café, in 1985, that Dennis met a woman who would give him a son.

Chapter 14

The Chase

Alberto Zavala (pseudonym) steered his red '99 GMC Safari van into a strip-mall parking lot on Saturday afternoon, April 19, 2003, a little after four o'clock in the afternoon. Darting his dark eyes back and forth, he surveyed the block-long parking area, seemingly in search of someone. At age fifty-one, Zavala knew his way around the neighborhood, and knew many of the underworld inhabitants by their first names. Driving slowly, the overweight, balding man, with a face ravaged by years of sun and cigarette smoke, crept along in front of yellow, Spanish-style storefronts. He repeatedly passed the hub building, a budget grocery market. Mall shops generally catered to the predominantly Hispanic population of the Santa Ana community.

Later, Zavala would claim he was searching for a parking place during the five or ten minutes of cruising among scattered cars. People familiar with the mall knew that all the parking spaces were seldom, if ever, full.

As he pulled to a stop near a main exit, a young man,

white, medium height, with a shaved head, approached the van's passenger side.

In a subsequent complaint to the police, Zavala claimed that the black-clad youth strolled up to the van's open passenger-side window and asked for a dollar. Before Zavala could answer, the bandit pointed a pistol and motioned to unlock the door. He leaped in, sat down, and ordered Zavala to drive east on busy four-lane Seventeenth Street. When they reached the next intersection, Zavala obeyed instructions to turn south, proceed to a quiet, residential street, turn west, then pull over to the curb. They had traveled only four blocks, almost circling back to the mall. All the time, the driver stated, the gun was pointed at his stomach.

Inside the idling van, the youth snarled that his gun was real and that he wasn't afraid to use it. He ordered Zavala to put the vehicle in park and hand over all his money.

"I was afraid for my life," the victim stated, "but I jumped out of my car without giving him the money, and I ran as fast as I could." He galloped thirteen blocks, he said, until he reached his home, then called the police to report a carjacking.

Santa Ana PD officer R. L. Tanksley drove to Zavala's residence and took the report, noting detailed information about the hijacker, the weapon, and the van. Within minutes, the information was dispatched to a state computer and to all patrol cars working the late-afternoon shift.

Skeptical police officers, who suspected Zavala of dealing drugs in an area well known for illicit transactions, wondered if the alleged carjacker was in fact someone who wanted to buy drugs but decided to take everything from the dealer.

Zavala had recently purchased the red van. He

thought he knew all of its extra equipment—the stereo system, burglar alarm, power seats, and other comfort items. But he was completely unaware of one very special feature. The previous owner had installed a LoJack system, which emits an inaudible signal when the vehicle is reported stolen. As soon as the law enforcement agency enters the vehicle identification number (VIN) into a state police crime computer, the LoJack transmitter is automatically activated, and can be tracked by police receivers, including aircraft.

Four hours after a thief carjacked Zavala's van, a pilot at the controls of an Orange County Sheriff's Department helicopter, an airship code-named "Duke," heard the familiar LoJack signal. He reported by radio that it emanated from a red 1999 GMC Safari van. The vehicle was in the area of McFadden Avenue and Standard Street, about two miles from the site where Alberto Zavala claimed he had fled the commandeered van. It was also about two miles from the apartment complex where Richard Namey was living before he shot Sarah Rodriquez to death. He had been on the run three days.

Santa Ana PD officer Ernie Gomez, in his patrol vehicle, received a radio call to assist in responding to the report from the helicopter. His smooth, friendly features, with piercing brown eyes, crowned by a coal black buzz cut, could turn grim when bad guys tried to play games. As soon as Gomez learned the details of the so-called carjacking, including the location where it took place and the victim's name, his intuition, enhanced by extensive street experience, kicked in. He had grown up in Santa Ana and had spent years working the Gangs Unit with the SAPD. Nothing about the local drug scene fooled Gomez, and this incident smelled like a drug deal gone sour.

Born in 1970, Gomez learned the ways of gang members from neighbors and even a few relatives. But he rebelled against the idea of conforming to the code of criminal conduct. At age fifteen, to demonstrate his antipathy toward that lifestyle, he joined a Special Interest Explorer Scouts Post sponsored by the Santa Ana Police Department. Gomez maintained his membership until 1990. Santa Ana first employed the intelligent, powerfully built youth in other capacities, and accepted his transfer to the police department in 1992. From patrol duties, he moved to a variety of assignments. "Initially," he recalled, "I thought I might have problems dealing with gangs I had grown up around, but it never turned out that way. The highlight of my career was going to the Gang Homicide Unit for three years. I think Santa Ana is the only city that has such a unit."

While responding to the radio dispatch of a carjacking, Ernie Gomez had an idea. Messages from the Duke helicopter led him to believe he knew where the van was heading. Gomez drove directly to a motel, a spot he knew to be a favorite loitering center for gangs and druggies. As he turned into the parking lot, a half-block from the 55 Freeway, the Duke pilot advised that a red van was leaving a nearby Mobil gas station, only yards away from the motel, and entering the northbound 55, known as the Costa Mesa Freeway. Gomez had hit a bull's-eye.

Within seconds, he sped to the same on-ramp, flipped on an overhead red light and siren, accelerated onto the freeway, and caught sight of the van. In his rearvew mirror, the flashing lights of another black-and-white appeared. Because officers patrolling the community were now communicating on the special "red channel" reserved for unusual situations in which all Orange County patrol cars are tuned in, other units heard and joined the chase. At 8:23 P.M., the race was on.

In Southern California, television viewers love watching when station directors cut away from regular programming to show police cars chasing scofflaws at high speeds. The pursuits sometimes last for hours, and are free of commercials. They are true "reality TV" shows, which sometimes end in bloodshed, and are irresistible viewing.

Five miles into the pursuit, where the freeway passes over Lincoln Avenue, Ernie Gomez clocked the van at one hundred miles per hour. At that point, the 55 ends in a transition with the east-west 91, or Riverside Freeway. The van driver's reckless lane changes endangered other drivers as he swerved right and left to pass slower vehicles in the relatively light Saturday-night traffic. A few angry horns and high-beam headlight flashes protested his dangerous maneuvers. Curving eastward onto the 91, the van sped over a bridge crossing the Santa Ana River and proceeded another mile before exiting on southbound Tustin Avenue. Its tires squealed in protest as the driver rounded a full-circle transition ramp, which took him back onto the Costa Mesa Freeway.

Now headed in the reverse direction, back toward Santa Ana, where the chase began, the fugitive again jammed the accelerator up to ninety-five miles an hour. At Seventeenth Street, not far from the strip mall where he had first jumped into the GMC van, the driver exited again, with Ernie Gomez in hot pursuit. Four other police cars had joined the chase and caravanned eastward behind the lead cruiser. Under the dim glow of streetlights, they passed within a block of Richard Namey's apartment residence. Gomez later described the race along Seventeenth Street: "The driver showed a wanton disregard for public safety, running numerous red lights in this residential area. He was almost colliding with vehicles between Prospect Avenue and Newport Avenue." In that one-mile strip, the van rocketed along, sometimes hitting120 miles an hour.

At an intersection with Newport Avenue, which angles northeast, the wild driver turned left and soon passed Foothill High School, adjacent to a drainage tunnel that runs under the residential neighborhood. His headlights probed the dark street that bends and twists in broad curves through an area called Crawford Canyon. To Gomez, right behind the van, the speeding vehicle seemed to be on the verge of sideslipping out of control at any time on the sharp curves. But the driver controlled it for two miles of frantic steering before turning right on the upslope of Chapman Ave and rising toward the foothills of Cleveland National Forest.

Instead of trying to elude the police in mountainous terrain, the van driver chose to remain on Chapman less than a minute before twisting the steering wheel into a risky right turn south of Jamboree Road. On the unlit country thoroughfare, the driver continued at breakneck speeds past the greenbelt of Peters Canyon Regional Park. Gomez observed that he continued to disregard the danger to other drivers, and forced several cars into skidding off the road, winding up on the shoulder. At least nine times, the van nearly caused collisions and potential fatalities.

After seven miles of hair-raising near misses along Jamboree, the van swerved right, westbound, on Irvine Boulevard. At this point, Gomez obeyed a radioed directive to let another Santa Ana PD officer take the lead. It had been decided at headquarters to let Officer Mike

McCarthy and his K-9 partner, named Chris, assume the point. The strategy was simple. When the driver finally abandoned the van, which was inevitable, the dog would be released. Chris would have a far better chance of finding and subduing the fugitive in the dark of night.

Mike McCarthy, known for his smooth good looks, muscular build, and ready grin reflecting an imperturbable personality, enjoyed his role as a K-9 officer. His sincere affection for his partner, Chris, a Belgian Malinois breed, was evident in their easy communication and teamwork. As Mike passed Ernie Gomez near Irvine Boulevard to be first in line behind the fleeing van, he could feel Chris's excitement escalate in the backseat. The speed again reached one hundred miles per hour.

Once again the van turned northeast on Newport Avenue, reaching 120 mph, and crossed Seventeenth Street against the red signal. It could only be termed miraculous that an explosive, metal-grinding, lethal collision did not occur. The van finally slowed and swung left at Dodge Avenue, where Foothill High School occupies several acres in the northwest corner. The driver bumped over a curb, shot through a parking lot, barely avoiding one of several stately pine trees, and screeched to a sudden stop. The right front wheel came to rest within inches of a chain-link fence separating the lot from a culvert, a drainage canal that fed into the underground tunnel.

The black-clad driver pushed open the van door, leaped from the driver's seat, and headed for the fence.

McCarthy simultaneously halted his cruiser a few yards back, jerked open the rear door, and released Chris with a command to get the bad guy. Chris reached the suspect in time to embed his fangs into a white sports shoe and pull it from the evader's right foot. At that moment, the fugitive jumped onto the van's hood and used it as a platform to launch himself over the fence. Scrambling down a slope lined with rough chunks of concrete and stone, he sloshed through a shallow channel of water about two feet wide, and jumped down a slight drop to the entrance of a drainage tunnel. Ten feet wide and about six feet high, the tunnel led underneath Dodge Street into pitch darkness. Without a flashlight, it would be necessary for the fugitive to guide himself by dragging a hand along the concrete wall as he rushed into the murky black gloom. His presence sent dozens of resident bats fluttering from their hiding places.

McCarthy and Chris vaulted over the fence and stopped at the black, foreboding tunnel entrance, while Ernie Gomez and four other officers gathered at the van and held a quick conference to determine the best course of action. After the long, perilous chase in which the fugitive had deliberately endangered many lives for his selfish flight, none of them were willing to let him get away. Yet, they were faced with a problematical situation. They had all heard the warning about the man being "armed and dangerous." If the officers rushed into the pitch-dark tunnel after him, they would be perfect targets as they entered, silhouetted against the ambient light at the entrance. The use of flashlights would make it even easier for the runner to take potshots at them. And there was no time to call in the SWAT team with their armor, helmets, and special equipment. Each of the seven officers realized the danger. To continue the chase could jeopardize each of their lives.

In unison, they forced open a gate in the fence, scrambled down the slope, joined McCarthy and Chris, then took the first cautious steps into the black void.

Mike McCarthy later described it: "As we go in the

tunnel, we're kind of going in a diamond formation, knowing that the walls are solid concrete in there. Ricocheting bullets could end up hitting us even if he didn't aim at us. So we were worried about that. I sent Chris, my K-nine, up ahead to probe for scent. He's tracking him, his nose to the ground, working the scent inside the tunnel. All we had was our flashlights."

Another problem popped up just a few yards inside the tunnel. The concrete walls, about eight feet apart, and the ceiling, a little over six feet high, blocked electronic communications. Each man carried a radio, but they wouldn't work. McCarthy explained, "We know this because they are programmed to deliver a warning tone when they can no longer send or receive signals. So we were concerned if someone got hurt, we couldn't call in for help. If someone were to get injured or shot, we'd have to carry him all the way back and who knows how bad the wound is. But we couldn't let this guy go. He might find an exit along the way, crawl out into a dark city street, and escape."

Within the first few yards inside the tunnel, the cops modified their formation to help provide some slight element of safety. Three men moved forward to form a front rank and four men followed close behind. If gunshots came from the darkness in front of them, the leading three officers would drop to their knees. In this position, when the second rank fired back, they would be shooting over their colleagues' heads. They all wore the standard protective vests, but had no helmets.

With flashlights aimed low to minimize making themselves perfect targets, all seven officers moved with care, their adrenaline pumping full blast. A stream, two to three feet wide, ran along the tunnel's center. Along the dryer shoulders, the officers could see prints left by the fugitive, one made by a shoe and the other by a sock-covered foot. No doubt existed that he was ahead of them, but they could hear nothing to verify it. The sounds of their own footsteps echoed along the concrete walls, and bats made a soft whirring noise as they flitted in erratic patterns between the hunters and above their heads.

Even in the blackness, the officers realized the tunnel was making a long, gradual curve to the left. About 150 yards into it, where the ceiling was almost seven feet high, McCarthy saw that his dog, Chris, was picking up a scent. "I could see his body posture changing. Things are getting real tense for us. The lead guys are hunkering down because they can see Chris putting his nose in the air and following the fugitive."

In the tense situation, McCarthy knew that his own emotions and apprehension could be felt by his K-9 pal. "He would run back to me to check on me to make sure I was okay. He'd nudge me, a little probe, and then head out again. I think that's one of the reasons he did so well because he could feel my stress in trying to find this guy, who is armed and has the advantage. We had our flashlights on, creating the danger that the guy could hunker down and shoot at the light beams. We were vulnerable. It was so eerie and dark in there. We could tell when we went under intersections because you could hear the cars rumbling overhead, driving over you. I had no idea where we were in this tunnel."

The squad had covered nearly three-quarters of a mile when they noticed a round hole in the left wall, about three feet from the floor. It was just large enough for a man to crawl into, and it angled upward. A shallow ribbon of dark water ran down and dripped onto the tunnel floor.

At the sight of Chris tensing his body and staring at the

yawning circle, all seven officers halted, their handguns at the ready. The dog vocalized his excitement with raucous barking. Flashlights aimed into the tube revealed only its upward slope and what appeared to be a point where it divided into two shafts.

Without a doubt, the fugitive had crawled into the tube. It wasn't going to be easy to get him out of there. But it would be a cinch for Chris, unless the man crouching up there opened fire.

The sergeant in command yelled up into the tube, "Santa Ana Police . . . we have a police dog. Will you surrender or shall we send the dog?"

He was answered with silence. Wooding signaled McCarthy to release the dog. Chris easily leaped up into the tube, crawled toward the divide, and disappeared from sight. Then came another round of hoarse barking. McCarthy recalled it with a smile: "He's telling me, 'Hey, Dad, I have a scent.'"

Finally all seven officers heard the voice of the man they had been chasing. He yelled, "Hey, okay, call your dog off. I give up!"

McCarthy shouted a command for Chris to retreat. To the suspect, he yelled, "Okay, since we can't see you, not only are you going to come out with your hands up, but you're going to talk to me the whole way out to let us know exactly where you are. We'll know by the echoes too."

The indistinct voice muttered words suggesting he was surrendering, but the cops realized it was becoming more distant. The fugitive was crawling away from them, farther into the tube. McCarthy recalled, "After conferring with the guys—it's too dangerous to crawl up in there and make the turn. We are thinking he could just shoot down at us through the smaller tunnel now. Water is coming down. The bottom surface is covered with a bunch of slippery algae. We're nearly a mile into the main tunnel. I have no way of measuring how long the tube is, in which I would have to crawl on my hands and knees. So I send Chris up again."

The fear could be heard in the fugitive's voice as he screamed, "I can see your dog. I'm coming back. I give up."

Once again, McCarthy ordered Chris to back away and shouted to the suspect, "Come down here and let me hear your voice while you do it." Nothing could be heard except the echo of McCarthy's words. It was time for positive action. McCarthy gave Chris the order to attack. The Belgian Malinois obeyed and leaped toward the hand holding a gun, consistent with a year of training, and clamped his jaws around that wrist. When the revolver landed on the cement, the man continued to struggle, and Chris bit his lower leg. He wouldn't be able, though, to drag the criminal back down the tube by himself. Help from the officers would be required.

Mike McCarthy scrambled into the tube first. "I had to crawl on my hands and knees to them. It was impossible to do that and have my gun out too. So another officer came in behind me. The plan was, if the bad guy started shooting, I would lay flat and my cover officer would shoot over me." His words carried a clear implication that if gunfire struck and disabled him, his body would serve as a shield for the officer behind him.

As McCarthy reached the sharp turn, after crawling about forty yards, blood flowed from his hands and knees, both lacerated by concrete and debris lying on the tube's bottom. He aimed a small flashlight at the dark figures of his dog and the outlaw, still wrestling. "There was no way for me to take Chris off the bite, 'cause I'd be down tunnel. And no way to get the crook past me—I'd have to back up while holding the dog. So I had to crawl over Chris and the guy as they continued to fight. He sees me and starts reaching for the gun. I could see his hands go out. So I end up in a little struggle with him." McCarthy snatched the weapon and tossed it behind him, then convinced Chris to "release." The officer directly behind McCarthy moved forward and snapped handcuffs on the suspect. It took several minutes to drag him back down the tube into the main tunnel. They also retrieved the fully loaded weapon, along with a black leather-bound Day-Timer planning calendar and a handful of drugs.

Now the officers could put their flashlights to full use. They examined the wounds inflicted on the bad guy by Chris's teeth, and discovered they were superficial. Injuries to McCarthy and the other cop, sustained from crawling and struggling inside the narrow tube, were painful, but not serious.

In the long walk out of the tunnel, they could see a variety of graffiti on the concrete walls. Among the scrawled figures and words, they noticed one prophetic proclamation. It announced, "YOU LOSE!" Ernie Gomez chuckled at the interesting prophecy for the man who had led them into the dangerous pursuit.

One other inscription also had a certain significance, but since the officers still didn't know the identity of their captive, who was at that point only a carjacker, it didn't register on them. Someone had printed with black paint, "Love Is Death."

Outside the tunnel, Gomez put the groaning, perspiring suspect into his cruiser's backseat. Another officer picked up the white shoe Chris had ripped from the runner's foot.

A crime scene investigation (CSI) van arrived and technicians performed a thorough search of the red Safari. They collected loose rounds of ammunition from the floor, along with a red-and-white box of bullets. Also included on a list of evidence confiscated from the vehicle's interior were "Forty-two (42) brown plastic bindles containing tar heroin with the weight of 41.6 grams, and sixty-six (66) white and brown plastic bindles containing cocaine hydrochloride with a total weight of 13.7 grams."

During the CSI team's search, another black-and-white patrol car rolled to a stop near the cruiser in which the carjacker sat. He was ordered to step out and stand by the door. A spotlight beam focused on him. In the passenger seat of the newly arrived car sat Alberto Zavala, the red van's owner. An officer asked if the "subject" standing outside was the person who had taken his vehicle. In a calm, unwavering voice, Zavala growled, "Yeah, yeah." Asked if he was certain, he answered, "No doubt. That's him."

As soon as the CSI team completed their work examining the Safari's interior, Zavala was allowed to take possession of it and drive away.

Ernie Gomez also headed out of the parking lot, with the still-unidentified captive seated in the back. En route to a medical facility, where the suspect and wounded officers could be treated for their injuries, the youth spoke. He seemed idly to wonder if California had a death penalty. Then he said that he didn't know the dog would be that fast, and admitted that he thought about shooting the K-9, hoping that it would slow the officers down and let him escape. The suspect muttered, "I'm probably going to do life in prison."

Gomez, still under the impression they had bagged a

small-time thief, thought his passenger was overreacting. Then the suspect said, "Well, I guess you know who I am."

Gomez said, "No, who are you?"

From the backseat came chilling words: "I'm the one who killed those people."

CHAPTER 15

Redemption

Diana Wheeler (pseudonym) walked into the Studio Café one warm night in the summer of 1985, and bartender Dennis Conway couldn't keep his eyes off her. She ordered a drink and flashed a flirtatious smile in his direction. Bartenders learn to be great conversationalists, whether they are truly interested in the customer or not. In this case, Dennis was more than interested. He learned that Diana was an attorney, which gave them important common ground. Dennis told her of his plans to enter law school soon. She had attended Pepperdine University in California, then earned her law degree at Regis University, Denver, Colorado. Having passed the bar there, Diane was not licensed to practice in California.

Impressed with Diana's beauty, Dennis was even more enchanted with her intelligence. "She was probably the smartest person I ever met, next to my brother Don. Not only that, but she had a quick wit, great sense of humor. Half Italian, half German, with olive skin, dark eyes. And an athlete, too, who regularly kept in shape by running. I met her at a time when I was feeling better about myself; I'm back with the living," He would soon discover that this marvelous creature was not perfect.

Assessing his status at the time, Dennis said that even with all the crazy things going on in his life, his experiences with women had been quite limited. Lisa Barrett had been his true love, but they were like kids together. "So, when I settled down, I began to think about having some relationships." Diana filled the need nicely.

"We start dating and she told me she couldn't get pregnant. That old story. Because she was a runner and didn't menstruate regularly. Of course, that turned out not to be true. How blue does that test have to be, right? I dated her about four or five months and she got pregnant."

Even though Diana carried Dennis's baby, he knew that marriage was not going to be part of the plan. She agreed. They talked about a possible abortion, but rejected the idea. Dennis envisioned shared custody of the child, but they delayed a final decision.

From the beginning, Dennis knew that Diana liked to drink. That's how they met. But it took some time for him to recognize her serious problem with alcohol. Her need for a constant liquor buzz led to arguments. He warned that booze consumption could harm the fetus, but she shrugged it off. Dennis also disliked Diana's tobacco habit. When he'd catch her drunk and inhaling cigarette smoke, he'd growl in frustration, "What is wrong with you?"

Hoping to keep a closer watch on her, Dennis rented an apartment near the Studio Café and moved Diana in. In a patient voice, he told her, "All you have to do is stay sober." But a realization dawned on him that he really didn't know this woman very well. Even though Diana's problems doubled the burden, he remained true to his plan to become a lawyer. He enrolled at Western State University in 1985 while continuing to work multiple jobs; law clerking for different firms part-time and bartending at night. He hoped that Diana would accept more responsibility as her belly expanded.

Instead, she grew more irresponsible and spent much of her time in the apartment watching soap operas. In the early months of her relationship with Dennis, she had worked as a cocktail waitress, but gave that up when the pregnancy became obvious. With no savings or assets, she depended entirely on Dennis's meager income.

The baby boy arrived on September 10, 1986. Dennis insisted on naming him Donald "Donnie" Joseph Conway, after his own dad and brother. Soon after, to Dennis's astonishment, his mother traveled from Massachusetts to see her new grandson. Younger brother Andrew accompanied her and decided to stay in Southern California. Dennis later would summarize Mary Conway's short visit with this impression of her attitude: "She assessed the situation I was in: working two jobs, attending law school, coping with an alcoholic woman and a crying baby. She said, 'You've got some real adult problems, son. Good luck to you.'"

While Donnie's birth was a welcome event, it marked the beginning of even more stress for the new father. "I'd be at work and would get an emergency call to come home and attend to him. The baby was colicky and would be up all night. I'd sleep with him on my chest. I didn't get any real sleep for what seemed like months. She'd be drunk, passed out. I'd wake up with her pouring a half-gallon of milk on my head, arguing with me. In the mornings, she wouldn't remember any of this. Just to get some peace and quiet, I'd take him and go sleep in the car, put him in a little basket. He was small, and could only eat a couple of ounces at a time. I couldn't get much food in his belly. I realized that for every ounce I could get in his stomach, I could get an hour of sleep. I'd walk him to stop the crying. In that environment of mental torture, I can see where that governor in our brains can malfunction and a person can lose their cool with a screaming baby."

Meanwhile, Diana reeled completely out of control, having no idea how to cope with a baby. In her drunken stupors, she would call 911 because little Donnie was crying. Or she'd call Dennis at the Studio Café, yelling that it was an emergency. He would rush over to the apartment only to find that nothing was really wrong. Suppressing the urge to lash out at her, he would feed the baby, change his diaper, and put him to bed.

On one mind-boggling occasion, a buddy called Dennis. He said, "Hey, I was going down the peninsula to go surfing, and I see a baby crawling along the shoulder of Balboa Boulevard. I pull over and look around, and there's a house with the door standing open. I carry the baby in and there's two women passed out. I shook one of them awake and ask if either of them knows that baby. One of them said, 'Yeah, that's my baby.' I ask, where's the father? The mother mumbled that his name is Dennis. I told her I know Dennis, give me his number. They said they had been partying all night."

Embarrassed and furious, Dennis hurried to the site, thanked his friend, and retrieved little Donnie. He could think of only one person, someone he loved and trusted, to ask for help. He went to Lisa's mother, Mrs. Barrett. On that terrible day, and many more times in the following months, she assisted in caring for the baby.

To Dennis, that year was one of living hell. His emotions were ragged and his finances a disaster. At least he could sometimes use his brother Andy as a sounding board. Dennis had helped him find a job in a valet parking lot.

Problems with Diana only grew worse. The more money he gave her, the more she spent. It stunned Dennis to find that she had cleaned out the last $500 from his checking account. She had written a check for the entire balance to pay for baby pictures. More than once, Dennis nearly dropped out of law school, but gritted his teeth and kept going.

Years later, Dennis painfully recalled that period. "I was at my wit's end. That was the most difficult couple years of my life, notwithstanding the depression I had gone through with my girlfriend dying. A couple of friends had told me over the years that I was like an island. I probably should have reached out for help, but I didn't. Part of it is embarrassment. I had never been with an alcoholic before. I began to realize that I was living with a drunk and it started to dawn on me maybe this is what alcoholics are; the more you give them, the more they take and the worse they get. It's my problem. I was always like, don't impose on people. And that was the worst I have ever been through. I'm in the middle of law school and other people there were talking about all the money they're gonna make. I thought, 'I wouldn't do this just for money.' For what I need, and what makes me happy in life, bartending was paying three thousand dollars a month, I was doing fine. It was all I needed. Riding my bike, reading a good book, go body-surfing, go play some Scrabble, I mean I'm happy. I don't need a lot of money. I can drive old cars and don't have to have a lot of stuff. I wouldn't put myself through all that crap for money. It wasn't for me. I just decided

I wanted to make something of myself. I just felt inside that this was something I needed to do. I knew I had more potential than to keep working at dead-end jobs.

"Those were two of the most difficult years of my life. I almost quit law school several times.

"You know what inspired me? I brought this up to my dad and I said, 'You went to law school when you had four or five kids and more on the way. And you were working full-time. If you can do that, I can do this.'"

His father replied, "I had a woman who loved me and helped and supported me." The sagacious words struck a deep chord inside Dennis. He flashed back to a wish he had made for his brother Patrick: *If Pat could find someone who really loved him, and would do things to reinforce his ego, that it would change his life for the better.* Somehow Dennis had never thought of his mother as giving that kind of support. He even began to feel a little grudging respect for her.

Diana's behavior changed—from bad to worse. She spent most of her time in an alcoholic stupor, which rendered her incapable of tending to the baby. She needed a full-time caretaker herself, with constant observation and therapy. Dennis simply could not do it all. He decided to move her to Grand Junction, Colorado, where Diana's reliable sister could provide guidance and care. He packed all of Diana's possessions into his 1977 Plymouth Volare and told her, "This can't continue. I need you out of my life. I'm moving you and the baby to your sister's place."

The night before their departure, Diana insisted on visiting some friends. Dennis agreed to pick her up there. "Of course, she's drunk. Donnie was sitting in the middle. She gets in and she's hammered. We're driving down the freeway at seventy miles an hour and she starts an argument. She's trying to get the car door open. You know, I'm tempted to just let her. Really. What would they find? Her lying on the side of the road. She had once been cited for a DUI with a blood alcohol level over three times the legal limit. I really came close. 'Hey, Officer, she opened the car door and fell out.' Of course, I didn't do it. I reached over and pulled her back into the car. I took her to Colorado, visited a couple of times, got to see Donnie, and this helped my frame of mind."

Diana lived with her sister for a few months, then moved to Denver. She met another man, a law enforcement officer, married him, and had another baby. Her parents kept in communication with Dennis and would paint rosy word pictures of her progress.

With his burdens lightened, Dennis focused his full attention on law school. Weeks, and months dragged by, filled with drudgery, working two jobs and forcing himself to stay awake during classes.

Death had already struck several times in Dennis's life and eroded his emotional stability. He thought he had developed a tough shell until it paid another unwelcome call to his family. In January 1989, his mother passed away at age sixty-two after a long battle with asthma. Dennis reeled with mixed emotions. Conflicts had forged a gap between them, but familial love also existed. Deep inside, he knew that her influence had developed valuable strengths in him. One of them was persistence. He grieved over the loss, but realized that he must continue to pursue the dream.

Eking out a 2.5 grade point average in law school, he pecked away at the required classes. Likening it to filling a bucket one drop at a time, he agonized over the slow progress. It took four years, including summers and every weekend. Later, in retrospect, Dennis noted that his life at that time was so different from what other people experienced. "It was a grind. They would be going on surfing or skiing trips, enjoying life. Me, always working and studying. But it paid off."

In 1989, he finally reached the long-sought pinnacle, graduating with a law degree.

Now, facing one of the toughest bar exams in the country, Dennis needed time and a place to concentrate. "The Barretts, Lisa's family, let me have a room in the back of their house. I sold everything I had and just studied for the bar a couple of months." Blessed with inherited intelligence and a superior work ethic engendered by his strict mother and inspired by his understanding father, Dennis passed the California bar exam on the first try.

In postassessment, Dennis observed, "It's not how smart you are, it's how badly you want it. I figured that even if I didn't pass the bar, I had made the transition from being a bartender with no degree to a graduate with a Juris Doctorate, thereby dramatically improving my future prospects. I don't mean to be cocky, but I was fairly certain I had nailed the bar exam. And since only forty or fifty percent of the applicants pass it, that would put me in the top half. That's not bad when you look around at all the clowns who are lawyers and judges."

It was time for a break. During the next few weeks, Dennis saved every penny earned from part-time jobs, and in the summer of that year, he gave himself a well-deserved trip. "I bought a Eurail Pass and went to Europe, staying in youth hostels. Thirty days on the cheap."

Refreshed and finally ready to join a law firm to "make something of himself" as his mother had always demanded, Dennis ran head-on into a brick wall. Without the networking benefits usually associated with attendance at a four-year college, then law school at the University of California, Harvard, or other top-ranked institutions, job placement was sometimes difficult. For Dennis, it seemed like the impossible dream.

Once again tending bar at the Studio Café, Dennis also performed law clerk duties, mostly with little or no compensation. He worked at various times for First American Corporation, at the National Fair Housing organization, for two different lawyers specializing in property and insurance. None of these internships resulted in finding regular employment. His real goal was to do trial work. But, at age thirty-one, he began to wonder if his future was going to be an extension of his past.

Sometimes serendipity intervenes with remarkable results.

At the Studio Café, bartender Dennis met people from all walks of life, but mostly from the upper crust of South Orange County. One patron brought back old memories of anger. The former swimming pool service employer, who had reluctantly handed Dennis overdue back pay a few years earlier, came into the bar and recognized him. Trying to be civil, Dennis mentioned that he was attending law school. The oafish miser stayed true to form, asking, "Why would you want to be a lawyer? Don't we have enough lawyers?" Dennis didn't dignify it with a response.

Other customers made the job a pleasure. Among them was a legendary retired judge named Robert Gardner.

One of the most colorful, intelligent, and respected judges ever to wear black robes with the Orange County Superior Court, Gardner commanded respect on many levels. Born in 1911, he earned a law degree at USC, joined the Orange County District Attorney's (DA) Office, then served as a lieutenant commander on

Admiral Chester Nimitz's Pacific Fleet staff during WWII. He was appointed to the bench by California governor Earl Warren, later chief justice of the U.S. Supreme Court. Governor Ronald Reagan elevated Gardner to the 4th District Court of Appeals, in 1969. After retiring in 1982, at age seventy-one, he was named chief justice of American Samoa, where he wore a lavalava (skirt) and honed his skills as a champion surfer. He described the time in Pago Pago as "sort of like being a king."

Known for praiseworthy decisions as a judge, his rulings were often quoted in law books. Dennis Conway's studies at Western often took him to Gardner decisions, many of which were laced with humor. In one opinion, the esteemed judge cautioned lawyers to give jurors' intelligence the weight it deserved. "A juror is not some kind of a dithering nincompoop brought in from never-never land and exposed to the harsh realities of life for the first time in a jury box." Another Gardnerism, issued in a divorce case, noted that the law "may not be used as a handy vehicle for the summary disposal of old and used wives. A woman is not a breeding cow to be nurtured during her years of fecundity, then conveniently and economically converted to cheap steaks when past her prime."

In addition to being a master jurist, Gardner authored several books, including *The Art of Bodysurfing,* published in 1972. Other judges who followed Gardner in Orange County regarded him as an idol. Donald A. McCartin, a legend himself, characterized Gardner as "Roy Bean reincarnated or Solomon with a sense of humor"; he emulated Gardner and spoke of him as "my mentor and role model." At McCartin's retirement party, he beamed with pride when Gardner delivered a complimentary speech.

Dennis knew Judge Gardner by reputation and felt honored to chat with him when the stately, white-haired icon patronized the Studio Café. "Gardner would come in after he got back from American Samoa. He wasn't a big drinker, but would gather with cronies after a game of golf. He used to bodysurf the wedge (a surfing Mecca in Newport Beach) when he was in his seventies. And he would say, like most people being polite, 'Oh. isn't that nice you're going to law school.' So I got up my nerve because I was so desperate for a job. I called Gardner and asked if he could put in a good word for me with the district attorney."

With the same tenacious drive that propelled him to finish law school, Dennis set his sights on becoming a prosecutor with the district attorney's office. After all, his visit to a court one day, and observation of a prosecutor's work, had been the major inspiration to enter the law profession. Now he applied that personal resolve to his new objective.

After Dennis submitted his written application, a series of interviews followed. At the end of the second session, Assistant District Attorney (ADA) Brent Romney asked, "Is there anything about yourself that you want to tell us?"

"Yes," Dennis replied. "You are going to look in my background and see that I had some arrests for some low-grade stuff as a kid out on my own, but in the last seven years, I haven't even had a moving violation. I've straightened my life out. This is the reason I got a law degree, and I'll be good at it. But if you are not going to allow me to work here because of that, then I guess our conversation is over. But to make you feel better about my past, I will give you fifty references."

Romney, without changing expression, leaned forward,

locked eyes with Dennis, and said, "This is Friday. I want those fifty references by Wednesday."

On the following Wednesday, Dennis delivered a stack of papers to Romney's office—exactly fifty written recommendations to employ this bright, hardworking lawyer.

"I brought them to him. I called the hiring secretary every day. This is the job I wanted. The investigator checking on me said it was the most extensive background investigation he has ever done. He called people I went to high school with, that I hadn't seen in fifteen years. He called neighbors where I had lived ten years earlier. People told him, 'good worker, good guy, honest.' He even mentioned that he knew I had registered as a Democrat, which probably wasn't a great help in predominantly Republican Orange County. They really checked."

The investigator became one of Dennis's backers, and confided, "Dennis, I admire you. I went to law school a couple of years and quit. I really want you to get this job, and they really like you. But I'm nervous. So I'm doing this detailed check to help you. I like your story, but it would really help if you had a connection, an 'in' with someone."

Offering thanks for the extra support, Dennis mentioned that he knew a judge who used to come into the Studio Café in Coronal Del Mar, where he worked—Bob Gardner. His voice incredulous, the investigator croaked, "Bob Gardner?"

The next day, according to the investigator, ADA Maurice Evans sprinted down the hall to District Attorney Cecil Hicks's office and said, "You know who just called me? Bob Gardner." The living legend had honored Dennis's request for putting in a good word.

He got the job. From his first assignment in the

Family Support Unit, he would progress to the Gangs Unit, and eventually into handling homicide cases.

For taking a chance on him, Dennis would always be grateful to the people who were instrumental in the process. One of the interviewers, John Connelly, a New Englander who knew the environs of Agawam, and had earned his degree at Yale, became a supporter. He later commented, "Dennis, my colleague Ed Freeman told me, when I started doing interviews of people to hire for our office, that I needed to keep something in mind. He said, 'Occasionally you want to hire at least a couple of people who have hardscrabble backgrounds because they make great trial lawyers.'"

If rough-and-tumble experiences made great trial lawyers, Dennis was the perfect selection. He certainly possessed more than his share of such practical knowledge. But one aspect of his previous horizons reemerged during his first few months with the DA's office. The troubling problem demanded an immediate solution.

Two years after Diana, the mother of Dennis's son, had resettled in Colorado, Dennis received a vexing phone call. A new crisis had erupted in her life. Diana was under investigation and a child services protection agency had discovered serious problems with little Donnie's care. They had taken the child, now three years old, into custody, and wanted Dennis to come get him.

While Dennis now had a good job, he hadn't yet pulled himself out of the financial hole dug by education expenses. He still harbored a deep-seated prejudice against borrowing money, keeping with the belief that "if you can't pay for it, do without."

Desperately needing a miracle to help him rescue little Donnie, he found it in a colleague prosecutor who would one day be married to the Orange County district attorney Tony Rackaukas. Kay Anderle was a good and true friend. She used her credit card to pay Dennis's airfare to Denver, and to return with his young son.

Because Dennis had made a few visits after taking Diana and their son to Colorado, the child knew his father well enough to greet him with the precious word "Daddy."

"I brought him home to my one-bedroom place in Huntington Beach." Bringing his son to Orange County did not end the problem for Dennis. Within a short time, Diana tried to regain custody of Donnie. She filed lawsuits against the social services agency that had released the boy, and against Dennis for taking Donnie to California. Technically, she was on firm legal ground. The organization should have placed Donnie in foster care until the case was adjudicated. Diana's family, though, helped Dennis, knowing that Donnie would be in better hands with his father. Facts came out that stunned Dennis. Donnie had once fallen out of a car moving at nearly forty miles per hour, due to Diana's carelessness. Another time, he was found at midnight standing beside the road, wearing a messy diaper, throwing rocks at cars while his drunken mother lay passed out.

Eventually Diana gave up. Dennis gained full custody of little Donnie. "Diana, like many alcoholics, was fundamentally a good person but couldn't get a handle on her disease. We had a pact to never say anything disparaging about each other to our son, and we both kept that promise."

Years later, Diana died from alcohol-related organ damage. Said Dennis, "She drank herself to death. She broke her mother's heart. Her family members are wonderful people who have always been there for me and my son."

Upon returning to his job, Dennis saw the irony in his duties. "I worked in the Family Support Unit, and put every bit of energy I had into it. In that assignment, I saw way too much unnecessary damage inflicted on children of estranged parents. I was raising my son and chasing after deadbeats who couldn't accept responsibility for their kids. My son is the best experience of my whole life."

As a single parent, Dennis sometimes considered getting married, but it "just didn't happen. I once told my mom I wanted a traditional marriage, family, and house. I came close a few times." Among his several girlfriends, one also became a lawyer, and would one day represent the family of a man Dennis would send to prison for murder.

Death had crossed Dennis's path several times in his journey, but it still struck him hard when he received news of yet another family member's life coming to an end, in 1994. His older brother Patrick had tried suicide by hanging himself years earlier, but failed. This time, after methodically destroying all photographs of himself that he could find, the depressed senior Conway sibling obtained a shotgun. He walked into the woods in Connecticut, sat down, put the muzzle in his mouth, and pulled the trigger. Patrick finally left behind a life he had never really enjoyed.

The deep empathy Dennis had always felt for his lost brother, and the sorrow, lodged in his psyche among a host of experiences that provided a deep understanding of human nature.

When talking about the roller-coaster years before law school, Dennis saw the silver lining. "I loved bartending for the experience of meeting so many people. It led to me having a son, and to Judge Gardner helping me get my job. I talked to my Harvard brother, Don. He wondered how I could get through law school with no prep degree. Law school isn't how smart you are; it's how hard you work. And the reading, pushed so hard by my mother and father, turned out to be huge in my life. When I talk to high-school classes, I emphasize that. I think it was the basic reason I could go from no degree to the law school environment. When I was in high school, I wasn't a very good student. Maybe I have some natural wattage. And you know, I'm glad I went through all those tough times because it makes me really appreciate where I am now."

CHAPTER 16

It Was Her Fault

A welcome telephone call came to the Placentia Police Department night shift watch commander at 1:00 A.M., Sunday, April 20. A Santa Ana PD dispatcher informed him that a 1997 black Nissan Sentra, wanted in a homicide case, had been towed from a strip mall parking lot, near a budget market, and stored in a police impound lot.

A quick check showed the vehicle was owned by Richard Namey's sister. He had been driving it on the day Sarah Rodriquez and Matt Corbett were shot, and he had abandoned it in the parking lot, where he had met Alberto Zavala, carjacked his red van, and sped away.

According to three letters seized by police in Namey's apartment, he had not planned to survive when he left his mother's home in the Nissan on that deadly Wednesday. The first letter was addressed to Namey's mother. In it, he acknowledged being nothing but trouble to her, expressed love for his daughter, and said she would be better off living without him. Asking his mother not to be sad, he said he would finally be at peace. He had never been happy, he noted, and speculated that he never would be in this world, which he hated. The letter ended with an expression of perpetual love for her, no matter where he wound up.

Letter number two, addressed to Namey's daughter, also affirmed his love while telling the child that she should not bear any fault for his actions. In a strange comment to a young girl, Namey said that he was far from perfect, and was "all fuct [*sic*] up" in the head, which made him do strange things. He hoped she would be happier living with her grandmother, he said, and reminded her that when he was gone, he still would be watching her from the sky. With a caution never to "do drugs," or be negatively influenced by her friends, and to always do the "write" thing, Namey signed off with another expression of love.

The third letter, to Namey's sister, apologized for the way he had treated her. He had just wanted to give her his love and protection. Since she was now a woman, he said, she could probably take better care of herself than he could of himself. Namey repeated his assertion of being "fuct up" in the head, and admitted being a terrible brother, son, and father. Since he doubted his ability to improve, he had decided to go away forever. With an appeal for her to help his daughter grow up, Namey ended with a promise that if he found the ability, in the afterlife, to make things better for his family, he would do it with love.

At exactly the same time the watch commander received a call about the Nissan, 1:00 A.M., Richard Namey walked into the tiny cubicle used by the Placentia PD as an interview room. Handcuffs encircled his wrists and he wore a white hospital gown, with a sheet wrapped around his midsection. He plopped down in a chair next to a small desk, his back to the wall.

Detective Chris Stuber seated himself at the desk and spoke into a microphone to record the date and time. His partner, Scott Audiss, sat nearby. Both men knew that a video camcorder was switched on to record the entire session.

Stuber turned to Namey and stated, more than asked, "You know why you're here, right." Namey ignored him, choosing instead to focus his eyes on the handcuffs as he pulled his wrists apart, snapping the connecting chain.

In a calm voice, Stuber said, "Just go ahead and relax, take a few minutes to think about what you want to tell us. I'm interested in listening to your side of the story. Okay?"

Again Namey failed to respond, as if he hadn't even heard the question. Then, bringing his thumbs up to his eyes and dabbing at them, he asked, "They can't play any of this stuff on the news, can they? Sometimes I see something where [cops] talk to people and they play it on the news."

"No," said Stuber, "we don't feed what we do to the news agencies."

Namey, now turning his head to face the detective, appeared skeptical. "Yeah. I seen it before. I don't know why they were interrogating a guy. It came on the news."

"I don't know how that happened," Stuber assured him. "This doesn't go on the news. Like I said, I'm interested in getting your side of the story. . . . So I'm going to give you the opportunity to tell us whatever you want to say . . . all right?" Before he proceeded any further,

Stuber read the standard Miranda advisory and made certain that Namey expressed understanding of it.

Although Stuber had been working on the case from the first hour of the shooting four days earlier, this was the first time he had come face-to-face with Richard Namey. The suspect had been brought directly from receiving emergency medical treatment for dog bites and other scratches, into the interview room. To Stuber, Namey appeared reticent, trying to act like a tough guy who wouldn't talk to cops.

In formal training, Stuber had been taught the Reed method of interviewing, which is a complex system focusing on building rapport with the interviewee. But with Namey, he decided to try a different approach. The detective just planned to keep him talking, recognizing that Namey would probably give a self-serving statement, leaving a lot of the truth out. Stuber wanted to spot the lies or omissions, and keep taking the suspect back over those to get the real facts. Part of the technique would be appealing to his emotions by angering him or making him feel guilty.

Interrogating street thugs was certainly nothing new to Stuber. He had questioned hundreds of them while working patrol and narcotics, and learned that "with ninety-nine percent of them, everything out of their mouths is a lie." He had become so accustomed to it that their idiotic games no longer angered him. "There was a time when I was brand-new, when people would tell obvious lies, it would really be upsetting. Why are you lying about that? As years go by, you get so calloused to the lies, you get so used to all the BS from criminals, it becomes like water off a duck's back."

"Okay," said Stuber, "why don't you just go ahead and give us your story?"

Just as expected, Namey said, "Normally, I would

never say anything. I always keep my mouth shut. Okay?" But, without pausing, he continued. "But this case, I—I got to take responsibility for my actions. Someone died. What do you want me to tell you? How everything happened?" He brought both hands up to his face, and his voice broke as if trying not to cry.

Nodding, Stuber uttered a simple, "Yeah."

"Well, I was at my girlfriend's, Sarah—she's been my girlfriend for about eight, nine months or something. I loved her with all my heart." Allowing a ten-second pause, he repeated the assertion while his voice broke into a sobbing falsetto. Using frequent hand gestures, palms up, as if pleading, he spoke falteringly. "I did everything for her. . . . For Christmas and for Valentine's Day, I spent like three hundred every time. I didn't even have enough money for rent, or nothing. I loved her. I mean—she left. And this guy—we had a problem with trust because I knew she—I felt like she was lying to me. But she said she wasn't, so we were still together for a long time. Just little dumb things. I love her still with all my heart."

Now openly sobbing, but with no tears evident, Namey's words came in a singsong pattern. "And then one day, we were at—I went to go surprise her 'cause I wanted to take her out afterward at her college. I wanted to see if she was there. So I drive around . . . because I had never been to this college. I wasn't even sure it was the right place where she was at. I didn't see her car around. I'm like, this has to be it. So I walk inside and I see her in the classroom and I'm walking away and she comes out. She's like, 'Hey.' I'm like, 'Hey, what are you doing? Where's your car?' She's all—what'd she say? 'It's in the parking lot.' I said, 'No, it's not. Don't lie to me. I looked everywhere.' And she's like getting all nervous and stuff."

Relaxing a bit, Namey spoke more clearly. "I started thinking, 'Oh, maybe she is lying.' And I said, 'Oh, someone's driving your car, huh? Just tell me.' Well, she's all . . . 'Oh, my friend Jennifer.'

"So I'm like—I got mad, but I was just gonna leave. I said, 'Whatever. I'm leaving.' I walked away. She was . . . on a break or something, and went back to her class. Then—I don't know why, the whole thing turned around because I thought she was—I just had this feeling that she came out of her class. So I turned around and walked back and saw her down at the end of the hall like on a cell phone talking to someone, sneaky." He pulled both hands up to ear level, and gestured with thumb and forefinger as if holding a phone. "I don't know if she was talking to a guy or what. You know what I mean?"

The detective nodded his understanding, but didn't interrupt. Namey was on a roll. Best to let him keep speaking.

The words tumbled from Namey. "So I said, 'Who's on the cell phone?' And she's like, 'Oh, nobody. Nobody.' So we started fighting; had a little scuffle. I grabbed her arm and she grabbed me, and I got her throat. I don't know if I was pushing her away . . . but I left. That was that. Then, after she called me the next day, I'm like, 'What happened?'"

According to Namey, she called him the next morning after the confrontation at school, admitted telling the cops that he had attacked her, and blamed her mother for wanting a restraining order. He couldn't understand the necessity for a restraining order. If only he could just talk to her, he could get her to admit that she had fought him that night. If only she had explained that to the police, he wouldn't be in so much trouble.

It came as a blow, Namey said, when Sarah announced that she had already obtained the court order. He described the incident of April 2, but left out details about forcing her car to the curb. "She handed me the restraining order. A [pickup truck] pulled up and I thought it was her brother." Namey said he had never met either of Sarah's brothers, but he had seen a picture of one who wore a goatee. "I took off. I left. And I didn't talk to her after that." In his account, he omitted the part about being chased by Matt Corbett.

Detective Stuber, later discussing the interview, said he understood exactly what Namey was doing. "He walked in, hinting that he wanted to take responsibility for his actions. But, because he loved Sarah so much, that made this a whole different set of circumstances and he wanted to talk to us, to come clean. To get it off of his chest. But, of course, he really didn't want to. He really wanted to say how it wasn't his fault and if she hadn't been the way she was, things would never have occurred the way they did."

Blubbering again, and gesturing to punctuate his words, Namey wiped his eyes as he spoke. "I was waiting for her to—she said she was going to call me. She never called. I waited—I don't know how many days, exactly. I was all miserable. I was not eating, doing nothing. And then I was going to kill myself. So I took my gun and I was going to go in her house and kill myself. At least just tell her, you know, because I love her." At this point, his voice shook, full of emotion. Stuber interpreted it as self-pity.

Perhaps recognizing the detective's doubt, Namey explained, "I don't want to kill myself. I was gonna if she didn't understand me." After a pause of nearly a full minute, he moved on to the crucial day. "I pulled up— I see the car and she's there, but I see her with some other guy in the car, right there. I go 'What the fuck is this?' I didn't even know. I just lost it. I did not know what happened. I just lost it."

A pattern was forming and Chris Stuber spotted it immediately. Namey had "lost it." Meaning, he wasn't responsible for his actions. He was out of his mind, being controlled by emotional forces. "His whole theme was that anything that happened to him was always someone else's fault. Richard never did anything that was his fault."

Mumbling and inaudible for a few moments, Namey faltered, then continued. "I can't believe she did that to me after I had loved her so much. I never cheated on her. I couldn't cheat . . . I never did anything to her. I was a good boyfriend to her. Basically, I think I was."

Scott Audiss spoke up for the first time. "Richard, I've got a question for you. . . . I know it's difficult to talk about. I know you're very emotional about it. . . . You said you went over to her house and you were going to—you planned on killing yourself, right? What day was that?"

The shooting took place on a Wednesday, but Namey mistakenly said he thought it was Thursday, at about three or four o'clock in the afternoon.

"Did you actually go to her house?"

"I just drove around once. I was gonna go to her house, but I didn't see her car. So I turned around and went back . . . that's when I seen her coming up. And I drove—that's when I seen this guy and it definitely wasn't her brother. . . ."

"Had you ever seen this guy before?"

"Never, never in my life." His memory apparently short-circuited. He had seen Matt Corbett reach through the driver's window of the blue El Camino exactly two weeks before the shooting.

"Do you know who the guy is?"

"No. Well, now I do. At the time, I put two and two together and figured it out."

Stuber wondered aloud, "What if it was just a neighbor that she was giving a ride to?"

Namey, now speaking rapidly, answered, "No. Because I put everything together . . . it all flashed in my head when I saw that GMC in front of her house when I pulled up." Sobbing and supplicating with his hands, he explained that Sarah had mentioned something about her brother wrecking his own car. "I thought that one of his friends let him borrow the GMC to drive." Namey vocalized the dawning realization. "I'm like, that wasn't her brother that time. That must have been this boyfriend. You know what I mean?"

The detectives knew exactly what Namey meant, even though he was leaving out the part about Matt confronting him earlier. Audiss asked, "Being that you already had a trust issue with her, all of a sudden you . . . realize that your worries have come true . . . and devastated you? What did you do? Take us through it, Richard. I know it's going to be tough. But you need to get this off your chest and we need to have the answers. Can you do that for us?"

After another extended pause, while clamping his head between cuffed hands, Namey mumbled a reply. "He was like . . . I don't even know. I was like dreaming. I just . . . pulled next to them and they stopped and I just jumped out of the car. . . . Like I was in a dream, I just ran over there."

Stuber asked, "Which part of the car did you run up to?"

"I can't remember. I think I ran up to—I'm trying to fuckin' remember."

The nonanswer didn't satisfy either detective. Stuber

repeated the question a little louder. "Which side of the car did you run up to, Richard?"

Staring off into the distance, Namey sat motionless and silent for several minutes, then turned toward Stuber as if snapping out of a trance.

Patiently Audiss tried another gambit. "You said it was like a dream, right? Okay, well, take yourself out of the picture and just tell us what the dream was. You've already said you need to take responsibility for this, and this is a way to do it. Share your actions with us so they are no longer a secret."

The two interrogators, instead of playing "good cop/ bad cop," worked in harmony. Stuber added to his partner's stratagem, "You're repeating it inside your head. I know you've repeated [what happened] a thousand times to yourself. . . . You need to get it off your chest. We know it's not easy to do."

Namey, turning off the tears, parried like a streetwise thug, but spoke softly. "You guys just want to bust me, that's all. I know that I'm in trouble a lot. Like I said . . . I've never said one thing to a cop before. I just keep my mouth shut and say I want to see a lawyer."

If Namey had actually asked for an attorney, rather than citing a theoretical scenario, the interview would have ended immediately. But since he hadn't actually made the request, the detectives felt free to proceed. Stuber said, "This is a little different, though, isn't it? What happened out there?"

Still mumbling in nasal tones, Namey gave an incoherent answer. "I still would never say anything if it was anything else. But I loved Sarah."

Audiss, exercising infinite patience, chose his words carefully. "Well, Richard, we don't think you are a stupid person. We can obviously hear the love you have for her. And she deserves to have the truth told. You know? I'm sure you wouldn't say anything about any other situation, other than this one. But Sarah's family has questions."

Breaking off his motionless stare into infinity, Namey jerked his head to the right and asked, "Like what?"

"Just what happened," said an incredulous Audiss.

"They know what happened." The words did not reflect sensitivity toward a heartbroken family.

"I think they want to know why it happened," interjected Stuber.

"I told you guys."

"You told us you were angry because she was with some other guy?"

His words spilling out like machine-gun fire, Namey said, "I was going to kill myself and then I saw her with another guy. She was with another guy—my friend told me he saw them at the movies. He said, 'That's her new boyfriend.' So I put two and two together . . . and I just flipped out."

Recalling that Namey had enacted a duplicate scenario a few months earlier, when he confronted Andrea Merino and Jim Fletcher in a parking lot, Stuber said, "I understand that you went through this once before, where you felt like your life was worthless. And you knew she had a restraining order against you." Namey stared in silence. Stuber asked, "What was the point of going up to Sarah's place to take your life?"

Facing Stuber, Namey replied, "Because I wanted to talk to her. . . . Hopefully, she would talk to me first. Maybe she would love me or something. I thought she loved me. I mean, I didn't know she had this boyfriend still, so I thought maybe—she was just telling me that her mom wanted her to have the restraining order. You know what I mean?"

"What route did you take when you went up there?

Did you go . . . somewhere else first? Was it a typical normal day, or what?"

Ignoring Stuber's query about the route taken, Namey volunteered that he had gone to a clinic that morning. "I always go there to get my methadone." He fell silent, as if pondering his next words, then added, "I even left suicide notes at my house." Instantly he tried to retract the key word. "I mean, not suicide notes. Notes for my mom and my sister and my daughter."

His attention piqued, Stuber asked, "What were they if they weren't suicide notes?"

"Well, they were just notes telling them that I loved them and stuff."

Suber looked at Namcy with an expression of disgust. "Well, you—you took the time to write notes telling them you loved them. Is that something you'd do normally? Do they get notes from you all the time or is that something special?"

Namey's voice took on a sharp edge and turned loud for the first time. "No! Because I was going to die. I wanted to die. It wasn't like suicide notes—I don't know. I guess it was suicide notes." He stopped, regaining control. "It wasn't like I was writing . . . saying I was going to commit suicide."

"Was that your way of saying good-bye, or what?"

Bobbing his head in a vigorous nod, Namey said, "Yeah. It was my way of saying good-bye. I wanted something for my daughter to read later—so she knows I cared about her."

Stuber wanted more specifics. "Is a gun something you normally carry with you for protection or you just took it out for the specific purpose of taking your own life? That's how you planned on killing yourself? Were you going to do it in front of Sarah?"

Namey, now defiant, answered. "I was going to put it

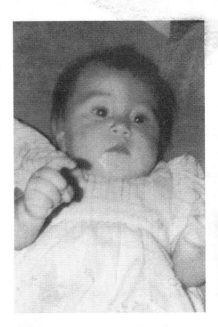

Sarah Rodriquez,
age four months.
*(Photo courtesy of
Martha Dewar)*

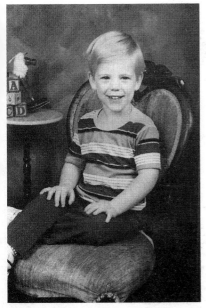

Matt Corbett, age six,
was already protective
of his twin sister, Kelly.
*(Photo courtesy of
Jill Corbett)*

Sarah Rodriquez spent hours on the phone with Matt Corbett. *(Photo courtesy of Martha Dewar)*

Matt Corbett and Sarah as high school seniors, with Sarah's sister Marilyn. *(Photo courtesy of Martha Dewar)*

Matt and Sarah after the high school prom. *(Photo courtesy of Martha Dewar)*

Sarah graduated from high school in 2000. *(Photo courtesy of Martha Dewar)*

Dennis Conway (*front row, center, wearing dark sweater*) played
on a championship hockey team in 1971.
(*Photo courtesy of Dennis Conway*)

Six of the eleven Conway kids in 1965. Dennis is fourth from the
left. (*Photo courtesy of Dennis Conway*)

Dennis Conway's father, Donald Joseph Conway.
(Photo courtesy of Dennis Conway)

Mary Conway, Dennis's mother, with his older brothers Pat and
Don. *(Photo courtesy of Dennis Conway)*

Patrick Conway, Dennis's oldest brother, seemed to have a death wish. *(Photo courtesy of Dennis Conway)*

Dennis Conway at ten already felt rebellious, but kept the "leprechaun" inside him bottled up until he left school. *(Photo courtesy of Dennis Conway)*

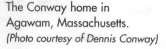

The Conway home in Agawam, Massachusetts. *(Photo courtesy of Dennis Conway)*

At his 1976 high school graduation, Dennis Conway's behavior during his senior year caused him to receive a blank diploma. *(Photo courtesy of Dennis Conway)*

Dennis with girlfriend Lisa Barrett in 1978. *(Photo courtesy of Dennis Conway)*

Richard Namey led police on a high-speed chase and foot pursuit before he was arrested for carjacking a van. *(Photo courtesy of the Placentia Police Department)*

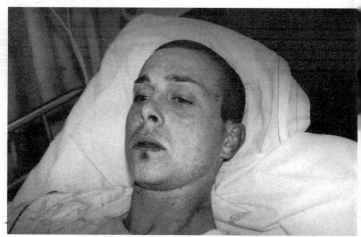

In the hospital for minor injuries sustained when captured, including a K-9 bite, Richard Namey faced a bleak future. *(Photo courtesy of the Placentia Police Department)*

Namey during transport in a police vehicle.
(Photo courtesy of the Placentia Police Department)

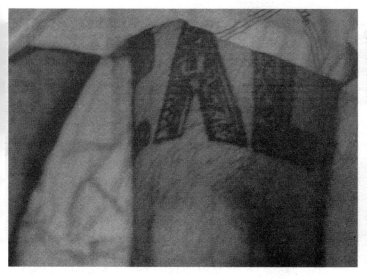

The hospital examination of Namey revealed strange tattoos on his legs. *(Photo courtesy of the Placentia Police Department)*

When police learned Namey was a murder suspect, a homicide
detective interviewed him on camera.
(Photo courtesy of the Placentia Police Department)

Sarah's mother walked to the murder scene, where she could see
her daughter's foot protruding from under a tarp.
(Photo courtesy of the Placentia Police Department)

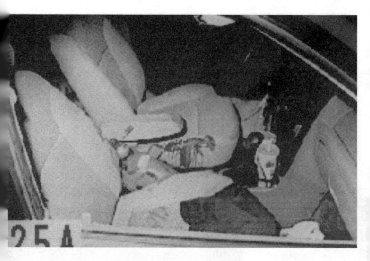

Bloodied interior of Sara's Kia Rio. She died in the driver's seat.
(Photo courtesy of the Placentia Police Department)

Strip mall where the owner of the van that Namey carjacked
searched for a parking place. *(Author photo)*

Five-shot .357 Magnum revolver used by the killer. *(Photo courtesy of the Placentia Police Department)*

At the end of the chase, Namey abandoned the carjacked van, hopped over a fence, and fled into a drainage tunnel. *(Photo courtesy of the Santa Ana Police Department)*

A box of ammunition found in the van turned out to be crucial evidence. *(Photo courtesy of the Santa Ana Police Department)*

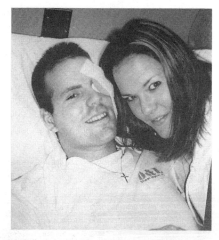

Matt's twin sister Kelly visited him in hospital. His left eye was destroyed by a shot into the back of his head, and another bullet paralyzed him. *(Photo courtesy of Jill Corbett)*

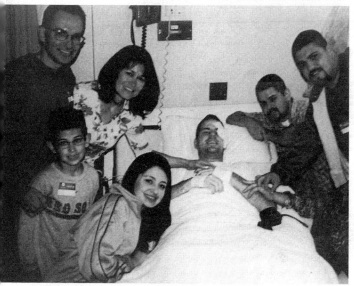

Sarah's family visits Matt in the hospital after the shooting. Left side of the bed: Bob Dewar, Martha Dewar, Michael, Marilyn. Right side of bed: George and Javier Rodriquez. *(Photo courtesy of Jill Corbett)*

Santa Ana P.D. K-9 officer Mike McCarthy and his "partner," Chris. *(Author photo)*

D.A. Investigator Ernie Gomez inside the three-quarter-mile tunnel where K-9 Chris subdued fugitive Richard Namey. *(Author photo)*

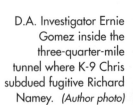

At trial, Dennis Conway used his own life lessons to prosecute Richard Namey. *(Author photo)*

Placentia P.D. Detective Chris Stuber headed up the murder investigation and conducted the videotaped interview of Richard Namey. *(Author photo)*

The Corbett family in 2005: Jill, Kelly, Tom, and Matt. *(Author photo)*

Matt still maintains close contact with Sarah's family. In the Dewar home are *(left to right)* Bob Dewar, Martha, Marilyn, George Rodriquez holding his daughter, and Matt in a wheelchair. *(Author photo)*

Sarah Rodriquez's grave. *(Photo courtesy of Martha Dewar)*

to my head and tell her, 'I'm going to kill myself,' and then if she didn't talk to me or just say something, I was going to pull the trigger."

"Why didn't you?"

The cold, direct question seemed to catch Namey off-guard. He stammered, "Because—I saw—I ran into them."

"I mean after what had happened, why didn't you take your life at that point?"

Namey could only sputter, "I was going to."

"What happened? What changed your mind?"

Perhaps grasping for something that would sound reasonable to the detectives, Namey said, "My daughter. I started sitting—I went and got a drink of water and I was sitting there for a long time. I had the gun right there. I called my mom and told her 'bye.'" He seemed on the verge of tears again.

"Where'd you go afterward?"

"Uh—I went to a—I was just driving around. I can't remember. I—all's I know I ended up somewhere where there was a gas station. And I—my mouth was really dry and I needed some water. So I drank some and sat on the curb. I can remember that part."

In Stuber's years of experience, he had heard every excuse in the book for criminal behavior, and dealt with all kinds of evasive answers. Namey, he thought, evaded the point as well as anyone. "He feigned a lot of sadness, but could change to ask self-serving questions. The facial expression would change and the tears were gone instantaneously. He was calculating and only wanted to talk about whatever would make him look good. We had a hard time drawing out of him any statements admitting responsibility."

Digging deeper, Stuber asked, "If your anger was

directed all toward Sarah for what she had done and what she put you through—"

Interrupting, Namey said, "That wasn't it."

"Well, you got angry when you saw her with another guy, that she had lied to you, that you trusted her, that she went behind your back. Am I right about those kinds of feelings?"

"Yeah."

"Why did you shoot the guy? He didn't do anything. As far as you know, he may never even have known that you existed, that she had a boyfriend she was cheating on. Why would you shoot him?"

Namey's cold reply was a perfect example of his faulty logic. "I would have rather shot him than Sarah."

Still, Stuber pressed for a meaningful answer. "But what if he didn't know—say if you were dating some girl and you had no idea she's got a boyfriend?" The detective really didn't expect Namey to acknowledge the irrationality of his actions. "We had a hard time drawing out of him any statements admitting responsibility."

Dancing away from the questions' core, Namey said, "People ain't stupid. You know? What do you mean he didn't know? He saw—that supposedly—unless that wasn't him that night. Unless it was her brother. Because I don't know that was him. Because that guy had a goatee. Maybe—that was . . ." His voice faded to an inaudible level. Namey was not going to admit making a mistake. He continued to rationalize. "I told you, I lost it. I did not know what I was doing. So I didn't—I thought since, yeah. Since, I've thought, you know what I mean, it's gone through my head a couple of times. Since I've thought."

Wondering if Namey could show any compassion for the horror he had inflicted on Matt Corbett, Stuber asked, "Do you know what happened to him?"

"My friend told me that Sarah died and the guy lived." Namey claimed that he had not read any newspapers about the murder.

"Do you know he's paralyzed?"

"No."

"Do you know you blew one of his eyes out?"

Namey muttered, "No," then turned away from Stuber and stared off to his left, still as stone.

Suber wanted him to understand the horrific impact of the crime. "His left eye is gone and he's paralyzed. He's twenty-one years old. Ricky, that guy didn't deserve that now."

Trembling and beginning to sob again, Namey's answer showed no pity for the victim. Instead, he croaked, "Stupid Sarah. She's the evil one, man. She's the one that's bad. She never should have done that."

Namey sobbed and sniffled for a full minute. Maintaining a poker expression, despite a roiling inside him, Stuber asked, "Richard, when you went up to the car, did you have any conversations with Sarah or this guy?" Namey said he couldn't remember. "Well, did you ask or give them a chance to explain what they were doing together?"

"I can't remember. I don't think so. It was very fast. At least I think it was. Like it said, it was like a dream. . . ." He was able to recall that neither victim got out of the car.

"Were they armed? Did you see a knife or a gun in their possession?" The detective, thinking ahead to possible defense tactics in a trial, wanted to dispel any notion of a self-defense strategy.

Perhaps Namey had already given that idea some consideration. Crossing his arms, with hands buried under his armpits, and facing away from Stuber, he said, "I thought I saw something. Maybe. I don't know.

Like I—I cannot remember, after all that. Everything was like blurry. Honestly, I've never—I mean, you guys have probably never done anything like that, but if it ever happened, it's like you're not all there."

Raising his eyebrows, Stuber said, "Yeah. And it's all over, right? Your whole world has changed."

Apparently complacent with his answer, Namey repeated it. "It's not like you are there. I was not there. That wasn't me."

Without hesitation, Stuber snapped back, "Well, it was you. And you were there." Softening a little, he allowed that Namey may have meant that his acts were not consistent with his normal behavior. "But what happened, happened. You can't change that."

Namey, shaking his head, stayed with his rationalization. "It wasn't me. It wasn't me. I didn't do that. Someone else went in."

As if not wishing to dignify the denials, Stuber shifted course to tell Namey that his sister wanted her Nissan, now in police custody, and asked where the keys had been left. Namey appeared petulant that the detective was ignoring his suggestion that the killing was like an out-of-body experience. Now turning to face Stuber, he replied, "Don't you guys want to search it too, and all that?"

"We're going to search it, but she wants her car back."

No longer weeping, Namey barked, "Well, I don't care. You guys can have—I mean—you guys always lie to me. I understand that's your job. Okay. Okay. But the car's over there at the market." On the subject of cars, he quickly asked, "Did you guys impound my El Camino?"

"Your mom has it."

"Where's my daughter at? With my mom?" Stuber nodded.

Leaning forward suddenly and clasping his arms against his stomach, Namey groaned and complained, "I feel really sick right now."

Ignoring it, Audiss asked Namey if he really meant his claim that he wanted to take responsibility for the crime, then brought up the suspect's drug problems. He pointed out that addicts, in order to change their lives, must first admit the addiction. Namey sat up straight again and countered, "Well, my life is fucked. As soon as I get to prison, I'll be doing all kinds of drugs. I won't be trying to redeem myself."

Again both detectives appealed to Namey's self-esteem, suggesting that he clear his conscience by admitting what he did. He would only say that it was all a big blur. Asked which victim he shot first, Namey argued that the officers already had that information.

"How could we? We weren't there."

Namey, referring to Matt Corbett, said, "He's alive. He would tell you."

It struck both cops that Namey's acceptance of personal responsibility was no more valid than a hooker's claim of chastity. Concealing disgust, Stuber said, "He might tell us if he could. Where did you shoot him? What part of his body?"

"I don't remember."

"Where do you think you shot him?"

"Well, obviously you're telling me I blew his eye out, so somewhere in the head." Namey reiterated his belief that Matt probably had already told police all the details.

The five-shot revolver Namey used had been recovered in the tunnel. Stuber asked where and when Namey had obtained it. Again demonstrating unwillingness to give up any meaningful information, he replied, "It's been a while . . . a couple of months. I never carried it with me. I had it for home protection." Stuber wished he had a dollar for every thug who had claimed his handgun was for "home protection." According to Namey, he had never previously fired the weapon.

To inquiries about his record of brushes with the law, Namey said, "I've been staying out of trouble for the past five years. I've got friends, my family. . . . I was trying to be good. I was getting pissed off at Sarah. . . . The whole time I was with her, I thought she was really a nice girl. Because it's like I had very bad girlfriends before—gangbangers, drug addicts, you know what I mean? I just thought this would make my life better. . . . This girl is good. Stupid other girls were frickin' evil." He spoke of Sarah "trying speed" for the first time, probably to please him. Namey admitted that he had been using drugs from the age of thirteen.

Redirecting the conversation back to the shooting, Stuber refused to accept Namey's memory lapses. "What were you thinking when you first saw them together?"

"It was like a million things all at once. I was just heartbroken. And I just wanted to die. I planned to kill myself real quick."

"You keep saying that . . . you wanted to die," said Stuber, reminding Namey that it was Sarah who died, not him. "You've had a ton of opportunities to take your life and you still haven't done it." Namey muttered something unintelligible. Stuber, in a more goading tone, challenged Namey "to be a man and take responsibility." It resulted only in more ambiguous contradictions.

No spent bullet casings had been found at the crime scene. Stuber asked Namey why.

Frowning, Namey said, "Well, I reloaded [the gun] because I was going to kill myself . . . and I just dumped them on the [floor] of the car. I was going to shoot myself real quick." He spoke of driving to some vague destination and deciding that he needed to call his mother to tell her good-bye. But during the conversation, he'd heard his daughter's voice in the background. "That's the only thing that kept me from killing myself."

Turning up the heat, Stuber asked if Namey regarded himself as a cold-blooded killer who would always be devious and insensitive about taking the life of someone else. "Is that you?"

Suddenly defensive, Namey responded, "No. No. If it was, I would have shot those people back in the drainage ditch. I didn't even kill the dog. It bit me. I didn't even shoot the stupid dog . . . I let it bite me. I mean I could very easily have shot it, but I didn't even want to hurt the stupid dog. I don't hurt nobody . . . for no reason at all." The interrogators thought it more likely that Namey's compassion for the K-9 was actually fear that if he opened fire, the pursuing officers might not have taken him alive.

Still pressing for Namey to admit the crimes, Audiss asked, "If somebody were to hurt your daughter . . . would it bother you to know they did it but refused to take responsibility for it? Would that piss you off? Would that make you feel bad and angry?" He suggested that Sarah's family deserved to hear that her killer acknowledged what he had done.

Namey could only speak in generalities. "Their lives are ruined. My life is ruined. Everyone's life's ruined, no matter what."

Suber had a suggestion. "What if I give you a pen and a piece of paper and you write them a letter?"

"No. No."

"No? Because you're sitting here concerned about Richard, not anybody else. Just like the day you shot those people, your concern is not about—"

"What do you want me to—"

"Be a man."

232   *Don Lasseter*

"I'll write them a letter, but I'm not going to write exactly what happened."

"You're going to lie to them?"

"No. I'm going to tell them that I'm sorry and stuff. I'm not going to write a confession. I know that's what you are trying to get me to do." Namey's attitude did nothing to change the appearance that he was playing a verbal chess game with the detectives.

Stuber voiced it. "So you don't want to confess? You told us that you wanted to take responsibility, but you don't. You are concerned about you. You're concerned about getting convicted and going to jail. You're concerned about your future, not your daughter's future. And you certainly weren't concerned about Sarah and Matt. You weren't thinking about their parents at the time."

Again Namey fell back on his amorphous rationale that he "wasn't there." It sounded like preparation for a legal defense of temporary insanity. "I may be one of those people who are messed up in the head," he muttered. Gesturing toward his throat, he asked if could have a drink of water.

If Namey was sincere about agreeing to write a letter to the victims' parents, Stuber wanted to see it. He produced a pen and paper, handed them to Namey, and said he would go get him some water. The two officers left the interview room. Namey sat motionless for several minutes, then held the pen to the paper, but didn't write anything. Instead, he muttered, "Fuckin' camera right there. I knew they were lying to me, man. Fuckin' liars. Oh, c'mon, I can't write shit with this. . . . Fuckin' with my kid, man. Where's my water at, man?" He turned toward the door and yelled, "Officer!"

When Stuber and Audiss reentered, Namey volunteered, "I didn't write nothing because you guys know you

ain't goin' to give it to [Sarah's mother] anyway. . . .
This is just like in the movies and stuff. That's what it feels
like."

Impatience finally betrayed Stuber's voice. "This isn't
the movies. This is real. This is your life." To emphasize
the reality, Stuber brought up the murder weapon
again. "Why would you put five rounds into a gun if you
were going to shoot yourself in the head? What—what
are the other four for?"

"I don't know why I did that."

"You intended to shoot some people. All you need to
kill yourself is one round."

Namey hesitated, stammered, then came up with his
brand of logic. He said that he was afraid that with only
one round, it would be like Russian roulette with the gun
clicking on empty chambers several times. "It might be
five clicks before I shoot myself in the head. You know
what I mean? So I put them all in there . . . *boom!* Round
one goes in my head."

"Well," said Stuber, not hiding the sarcasm, "that
plan didn't work very well. Because you are still sitting
here. You seem fine."

"It will work," insisted Namey. "I'll get myself somehow.
Don't worry . . . I do want to kill myself, but I don't because of my daughter. That's the only reason I don't want
to. I don't want to be here no more. I don't like this
place. It's a fuckin' bullshit world. . . . This whole world
is fucked up. It's an evil place and I hate it. I want to die.
The only thing is my daughter. I wanted to get her
somehow to Mexico . . . work my way down, find a job
or something."

Stuber shrugged and accused Namey of using his
daughter as an excuse, and lying about everything else.
He wanted the truth, and said that Namey didn't have
the courage to tell it. "You get to the hard part, where

it's time to tell the truth, and you chickenshit out."
The detective repeated his opinion that Namey simply
had succumbed to rage and killed Sarah.

"No," Namey snarled. "I felt like I was dreaming. And
I didn't know what was going on. And you—you are sitting here telling me. How would you know? You weren't
ever there."

Leveling a cool stare, Stuber suggested that Namey
take him through the events and truthfully reveal what
happened. "How about from the first minute you see
them? Remember, first of all you have a restraining
order. You're not even supposed to be near her anyway."

That was unimportant, said Namey. "I was going to kill
myself, so that wouldn't really matter, would it? . . . I told
you, from that point, I just lost it. I did not know what
was happening. . . . It was like I was dreaming. I wasn't
even—I told you, it wasn't me."

After leaning again on his mental-fog excuse, Namey
decided to support it with an odd slant. "If I was planning on killing somebody . . . I would have put hollow-
point bullets in the gun." He explained that he had
loaded the weapon with conventional bullets; so when
he shot himself, his head wouldn't have been mangled,
thus his mother could have her wish of having an open-
casket funeral for him. To the detectives, Namey's rationale was reaching the point of absurdity.

Stuber snapped, "Well, the rounds you used put a
pretty good-size hole in Sarah's head. Her parents didn't
get an open casket. . . . So don't try to make me feel sorry
for you, like you weren't going to kill somebody. You
went there for a reason. And you accomplished your
reason . . . I think you went there because you stopped
her a couple of weeks before and you didn't have a
gun with you at that time. [Matt] came out, fended
you off, and you ran away. And you felt shitty about it.

You felt like a coward, like this guy dissed you. And the next time you came back with a gun."

The assertion seemed to unnerve Namey. He denied that Matt had chased him in the earlier confrontation. "He just got out of the car."

"Yeah. And you took off."

"Because I thought it was her brother."

"So you probably felt like you looked like a chickenshit in front of her because this guy comes out and you split."

For the first time, Stuber felt like he might have found a vulnerable crack in Namey's armor. His pride and fear of being called a coward. "How come you shot the guy first, and not the girl? You went to the guy because he was a threat, so you took him out. Because you were afraid."

Perhaps Namey recognized the strategy, because he fell silent and refused to discuss that aspect of the shooting. But Stuber made another thrust. "You know what I think? I think it made you feel like a big badass when you shot the guy, and when you shot her, and that's why you didn't kill yourself because that's the way you liked it."

To the detectives, it didn't make sense that Namey would shoot the male passenger unless he knew it was Matt Corbett. "What if it was just a neighbor she gave a ride to? What if it's someone from her class? What if it's someone whose car broke down and she gave him a ride? And you jump out of your car and put two fucking bullets in his head. He didn't do a damn thing to you. And you sit here and tell me you can't remember. You're a fucking coward. You're afraid to admit it. And that's it. Simple. You need to admit to yourself that you're afraid. Because I know you are. . . . You haven't got the guts to sit here and admit what you did."

If Richard Namey was on the edge of a confession, he managed to regroup and control himself. His only response to the detective: "You're an evil person, man."

"Sure," said Stuber, "everybody's evil except you. . . . The good girls, they're the ones that are evil witches. I'm evil. Everyone's evil except Rick."

"I never said I wasn't."

"What you did was evil. It was cruel. It was inhuman. What if someone did that to your daughter? . . . It's okay for you to play God and decide who lives and dies?"

Namey's next comment made Stuber sick to his stomach. Without a change of expression, Namey muttered, "Sarah killed someone. She had an abortion. She killed a baby."

Stuber clenched his jaws. "Why do you keep turning it around to somebody else . . . somebody else's fault? I thought you said you loved Sarah."

"I do."

"You killed her. You murdered her. But you loved her? . . . You did kill her, didn't you?"

"No."

"No? Somebody else did it?"

"Maybe it was the Devil."

Stuber didn't bother to dignify the comment. He asked a few more questions. Namey finally said, "I hate myself for what I did. . . ."

"I don't think so. I think you hate it that you've been caught."

Surprisingly, Namey agreed. "Well, of course, I hate that. Of course, I hate that I got caught."

After a few more minutes, Stuber repeated his assertion that Namey had gone in search of Sarah with the intent to kill her. Namey denied it. Said Stuber, "So the whole thing was just a result of dumb luck?"

"It was dumb luck that I ran into them together."

"Was it dumb luck that you happened to have a gun with you? It was dumb luck that you happened to be in her neighborhood when you shouldn't have been there because you had a restraining order? It was dumb luck that you took your gun out of the car without even talking to anybody; you got out of the car with the gun in your hand? It was dumb luck that you walked immediately to a window and immediately shot somebody, and then went around and put a gun right to her head and pulled the trigger? That's not dumb luck. No one made you do any of those things. It was on your mind. It was your body and your brain that did it. You did it. Period. You can sit here and say the Devil made you do it, and everyone else is evil . . . that they have it coming anyway. So fuck them because she treated me bad."

Again Namey insisted that he was not in his right mind. "I told you, I lost it. I was not thinking. I was not myself."

The litany of denials, evasions, and arguing finally ended after nearly two hours in the minuscule interview room.

CHAPTER 17

A Profile in Courage

Shortly after an ambulance transported critically injured Matt Corbett to Western Medical Center in the late afternoon of April 16, it appeared that he wouldn't live through the night. Blood had gushed from his multiple wounds, leaving his life hanging by no more than a fragile spiderweb strand. A slug had lodged in his spinal cord and paralyzed him from the chest down, including his arms and legs.

Doctors informed Matt's parents that their son was in critical condition. No one could believe he was still alive after the massive assault to his body with a .357-caliber handgun.

The severity of his wounds prevented medics from accurately counting how many bullets had been pumped into his flesh and bones. Jill recalled, "Even the doctors didn't know. They said originally that Matt had five holes, gunshot holes, and so we were like, 'Oh, my God, he got shot five times.' Eventually, through deduction, we started to believe that he was shot three or four times. They were looking at entrance holes and exit holes. You really couldn't tell right away because there was so much blood. We finally found out that he was going to make it, but that he would be paralyzed."

It took more than eight hours just to stabilize Matt's vital signs, while Jill, Kelly, and Tom sat or paced all night in the waiting area. At last, just before sunrise, Matt was wheeled from surgery into the critical care unit (CCU) and his family was finally allowed to see him.

Tom Corbett recalled, "All I could do is just thank God he is alive."

One of the most difficult moments came when Matt could utter his first words and asked about Sarah. Claiming they didn't know her fate, Jill and Tom postponed telling Matt until the next day that the girl he loved had not survived.

The truth about Sarah would not register in Matt's mind. When his father told him about her, Matt refused to accept it. "I didn't believe them. No, no, it can't be." Later asked if he was unable to understand due to the pain or medication, he replied, "No. I knew I heard right, but I just didn't want to believe it. No way. I thought I'll try to get up and find out myself. I figured she was next door and I'd go see her. So I didn't know. At the time, I thought I could get up and walk. I was thirsty and wanted to get a glass of water. My dad said "I can get it for you.' But I thought, 'I'll get it' and I went to get up . . . and it all hit home. I couldn't walk. And I knew I had lost Sarah."

A common perception is that paralysis numbs the whole body. Even though the limbs are useless, at least there is no pain. In Matt's case, just the opposite was true. Flames shot from multiple nerve endings, searing every muscle. He later described it: "It was like having a million pins sticking in my body. And burning, like my hands were on fire. I don't know what it was, just all the nerves messed up due to the trauma on my spine. Just unbearable pain."

His mother said that Matt would scream at the slightest touch from anyone. And his inability to move, or make the slightest adjustments of his supine position, exacerbated the misery. Jill's voice cracked in recalling the horror. "I'll never forget it. You'd say, 'Hi, Matt, how are you doing?' And if you'd forget and touch him, he'd scream, 'Don't touch me, don't touch me!'"

At first, doctors administered drugs, including heavy doses of morphine, to reduce the discomfort. The next day, though, Matt asked them to stop all medication. He later explained, "I wanted to know what I was going through. I don't like being on all kinds of drugs." He preferred to face reality and not float in an unreal world in which his mind was numbed along with his body. "I prefer to know what I'm doing and saying."

Kelly understood. "Yeah, 'cause he was talking kind of funny. He was saying there was a bed on the ceiling. He was saying this weird stuff."

The doctors did insist on administering a drug called Neurontin, which is often used to relieve the burning nerve pain that may persist for months or even years. These are symptoms usually associated with shingles (herpes zoster), but can also result from trauma to the spinal cord. The medication allows patients to function more normally in their day-to-day lives.

Two days after his arrival, doctors performed surgery to repair the eye socket, which had been destroyed, restore the damaged nasal cavity, and remove bullet fragments from the orbital bone structure.

In the ensuing days, a gamut of emotions made Matt's nightmare even worse. At first, the idea of living without Sarah and being paralyzed made life seem untenable. "I didn't want to live. I thought about suicide all the time. I always put myself down a lot. I started not to care about a lot of things. I've always had a great family and a lot of friends, always there for me, but it just didn't matter at the time. I was just so caught up in everything I just wanted to end it. Sometimes you feel you'd just be better off to die than to live. Living without people you love. It was really hard."

The depression lasted several weeks. Much of it revolved around the loss of his beloved Sarah. To Matt, it seemed impossible that he could pull through without her. It wasn't fair that he was alive and Sarah wasn't. "She was my little angel." A feeling of guilt tore into him like another barrage of bullets. "I felt like I was partly responsible for her death because her mother felt Sarah was safe when she was with me. And so did I. It took me a long time to realize, even today, it's still hard, that I couldn't stop it from happening. I tried."

Little by little, with the help of his loving family, rays of light pierced the darkness in Matt's mind. When he was transferred from Western Medical to Long Beach Memorial Hospital, Jill Corbett's optimism for her son's life grew markedly. "That's where he was born and survived a near-death experience. When they moved him to Long Beach for therapy, it was like we were home. I knew he was going to be okay. I knew it at that time."

Matt's natural gift of courage took over and with it came increasing confidence. It helped his state of mind when therapists took him from the bed more frequently and placed him in a wheelchair. An elating, major breakthrough came when he first found that he could wiggle a couple of fingers. From that foundation, he struggled to move his hands, and in time could lift his arms. It thrilled his parents when Matt actually wrote a note to Jill, telling his mom and dad how much he appreciated their love and support.

His thoughts of Sarah also underwent a metamorphosis, changing from sorrowful guilt to recalling positive happiness they had shared. He acquired a pendant, a tiny soaring angel, to symbolize her and wore it around his neck every day.

The future had seemed dismal and impossible to face, but Matt's inner-strength took charge and he made the conversion to seeing bright possibilities. It helped, too, when cosmetic surgeons reconstructed Matt's eye socket and equipped him with a virtually perfect prosthetic eye. Learning to live with constant pain represented another challenge. Matt refused to let it hinder his progress. He dealt with it through minimal doses of medication supplemented by willpower and mind control. Things that had seemed impossible now appeared hopeful. Matt even entertained thoughts of returning to his job at the air-conditioning company. He felt certain he could be a productive employee despite being confined to a wheelchair.

When Dennis Conway inherited the duties of prosecuting Richard Namey and began preparing the case in early 2004, he spent time with the Corbett family. Jill was impressed with the personable deputy DA's understanding of problems experienced by young people. At that time, she had no knowledge of Conway's personal background and wondered how he had acquired such a perfect grasp of teenage tribulations. Matt learned that Dennis was the father of a youngster and attributed Dennis's comprehension to that. "He takes cases like this personal. I think that's why he does so well."

Dennis's discussions with Matt and his family resulted

in one of the most courageous acts yet by the paralyzed young man. Matt had learned that the bullets surgically removed from his limbs were in such poor condition that they were useless as forensic evidence. He asked Dennis about it, and made a remarkable decision. Matt volunteered to undergo additional surgery for removal of a slug still lodged in his body. He hoped it would provide the ballistics comparison that would help seal the case against Namey. Conway spoke in glowing admiration about the brave act. "Matt asked the doctor to remove the bullet from his back, and subsequently gave it to me to be used as evidence. It was high up on the spine, hit his shoulder blade, then hit his spine and lodged. He had it in there for about a year."

The surgeons also removed another bullet from Matt's right arm, just below the shoulder. Both chunks of lead were given to Conway.

A trial date was set for September 2004.

CHAPTER 18

Strange Betrayal

Dennis Conway's reputation as a prosecutor with the Orange County District Attorney's Office earned admiration from peers and from his boss. They trusted him to present the state's case in several difficult trials.

When he was assigned to handle the Richard Namey murder case, he fully expected a defense strategy claiming that Namey was in a mental fog at the time of the shooting, thus incapable of premeditation or malice. Conway discussed it: "A lot of our homicides are built up around mental defenses. I thought that's where Namey would go. When you don't have the law on your side or the facts on your side, you go and hire an expert witness to build a defense."

In all probability, Conway thought, evidence would be presented to the jury suggesting that Namey's emotional problems stemmed from a difficult childhood, or that he had experienced mental abuse. In addition "I wondered if they would also try to dirty up Sarah. She didn't know she was playing with a keg of dynamite. Also, I worried they would try to say he didn't know what he was doing because his judgment was impaired by drug usage."

In preparing for the case, Dennis hoped that Namey would take the witness stand. "A defendant who testifies sometimes crystalizes the case. I like cross-examination. Sometimes I get to take the gloves off."

A perfect example of Dennis's skills in questioning a defendant had taken place in a November 2002 trial. The high-profile case attracted national news attention, book authors, and television documentary producers.

The murders, for which a woman named Adriana Vasco faced charges, had languished as an unsolved mystery for a full year. On a chilly November night in 1999, the bullet-riddled bodies of anesthesiologist Dr. Kenneth Stahl, fifty-seven, and his optometrist wife, Dr. Carolyn Oppy-Stahl, were found slumped over in her car. The late-model Dodge Stratus, with the engine still idling and headlights illuminating the lonely shoulder of a mountain highway, sat motionless and alone. The twisting road, known as Ortega Highway, winds over craggy highlands separating Orange County and Riverside County. It is notorious not only for a long history of deadly auto accidents, but also as a dumping ground for the bodies of murder victims.

The two doctors had been shot to death on the night after Carolyn's forty-fourth birthday.

Investigators were stumped. Multiple gunshot wounds to both victims, plus the absence of a weapon, ruled out the possibility of a murder-suicide. Nor did it seem likely that a case of road rage had escalated to homicide. It couldn't have been a robbery either, since the victims' wallet and purse were untouched, and Carolyn's jewelry remained on her body. Even though the dangerous road is well traveled, no witnesses turned up.

Interviews of the victims' families and workplace acquaintances revealed no helpful clues. Detectives did learn that Kenneth Stahl had spoken of surprising his wife for her birthday by taking her to a restaurant near the well-known San Juan Capistrano Mission. The mission is only a short distance from the Ortega Highway's intersection with the I-5 Freeway. No one could understand, though, why the doctor would drive fifteen miles up a winding mountain road after the dinner celebration, since their Huntington Beach home was more than twenty miles in the opposite direction. Autopsies indicated that both victims had eaten approximately ninety minutes before they were shot to death. Whoever pulled the trigger had apparently fired through the rolled-down driver's side window. An intensive search of the surrounding area produced no shell casings or other forensic evidence. The absence of casings suggested that the gun was probably a revolver that did not eject the shells.

Had a patient of either Kenneth's or Carolyn's sought revenge for some real or imagined act? Detailed probing of their backgrounds failed to support that theory, especially with the complete absence of any malpractice suits. Both doctors were well respected in their professional fields, and had won commendations from peer groups. At funeral services, Kenneth was remembered as a quiet, private person who loved camping out, hiking in the mountains, bicycling, and cross-country skiing. A heart attack and bypass operation had curtailed his physical activities. Carolyn's family and friends described her as a sweet, angelic, friendly woman who kept her home immaculate. She had lovingly helped Kenneth recover from his heart ailments.

Eleven months passed with no new clues to help solve the double homicide. Before relegating the case to "cold case" status, a pair of new investigators decided to have a look. Their discoveries cracked the mystery wide open.

Gradually a dark side of Kenneth Stahl emerged. When the investigator learned that $30,000 had been withdrawn from Kenneth's savings account before the murders, they suspected a link.

Through intensive, probing interviews, the detectives were able to piece together a sordid story. Previously divorced, Stahl had married Carolyn in Las Vegas on New Year's Day, 1988. While their childless relationship appeared perfect to their families, he had assaulted his wife physically more than once. Six years after they were married, she came home early from a trip one day and found Kenneth with another woman. Marriage counseling seemed to help, but Kenneth continued to stray. He carried on a nine-year sexual relationship with a medical assistant named Adriana Vasco.

Vasco, thirty-three, who would call Kenneth the love of her life, shared something in common with him. Neither of them could maintain mutually exclusive sex relationships. Twice divorced and the mother of two young children, Adriana kept more than one boyfriend. Through Stahl, she met a former psychiatric patient, dated him, and moved in with him. Acquaintances hinted that the lover and Dr. Stahl sometimes participated in sexual threesomes with Adriana.

If Stahl shared Adriana carnally with the psychiatric patient, that wasn't the only close confidence between the two men. While drinking together, Kenneth revealed that he wasn't happy in his marriage, but he didn't want to go through a divorce and pay alimony the rest of his life. He asked about the possibility of finding someone to get rid of Carolyn.

With the confidant's help, Stahl visited a gang member to discuss the plan, but nothing developed from the contact.

Stahl also spoke several times with Vasco about his fantasy of having Carolyn killed.

A few months before the shooting in November, Vasco met the maintenance man at her apartment complex and began dating him. Dennis Earl Godley, thirty-one, a heavily tattooed, habitual lawbreaker, who wore a goatee and parted his black hair in the middle, seemed to satisfy Adriana's needs. She told Godley about Kenneth Stahl's desire to get rid of his wife, and suggested that the doctor might be willing to pay generously for having it carried out. "Woman," he reportedly said, "I need money. I want you to call your friend and tell him I want to meet him."

Within a few days, Kenneth and Carolyn were savagely shot to death. Godley left California and resettled in his native North Carolina.

With suspicion mounting that Adriana Vasco was deeply involved in the murders, and might even have participated in them, officials decided to arrest her in October 2000. But without enough evidence to charge Vasco with homicide, they booked her on outstanding traffic warrants, and kept her in jail forty-four days. Interrogated about the killings, she repeatedly refused to talk. Avoiding the stereotypical third degree often depicted in old movies, the investigators treated Vasco with kindness, offering her refreshments, cajoling her, and even providing her favorite music. Hints were dropped that her family might be in danger. "You are not the only suspect in this case," they mentioned.

Perhaps out of fear, or a guilty conscience, Vasco at

last told them everything she knew. The entire confession was recorded on twelve hours of tape.

Vasco's account stripped away all the cobwebs and shadows from the year-old mystery: On the night of November 20, 1999, she and Godley, dressed in black clothing, including trench coats, had left the apartment complex. With him in the passenger seat, she drove her car up the treacherous curves of Ortega Highway until they spotted Kenneth and Carolyn sitting in the Dodge Stratus.

What happened next is disputed between the killer couple. According to Vasco, Godley exited her car, approached the other vehicle, and began shooting. He was supposed to execute Carolyn only, but also killed Kenneth, maybe because Godley thought it better to eliminate the witness. Or, perhaps Godley's jealousy, inflamed by the knowledge that Adriana had been Kenneth's lover, motivated him to keep firing.

Later, Godley fled to North Carolina. Before leaving, he had casually tossed a shell casing from his revolver to a youthful neighbor. "Here," he said, "is a souvenir for you."

Using information provided by Vasco, investigators turned to Dennis Godley. They found him in a Suffolk, Virginia, jail cell, facing separate felony charges. Extradition proceedings would bring him back to California.

In late March 2001, a preliminary hearing was held in Orange County Superior Court to determine if the evidence against Adriana Vasco was sufficient to conduct a murder trial. Judge Everett Dickey listened carefully to Vasco's public defender, who stated that his client, while being interrogated by detectives, had mentioned the possible need for an attorney several times. Judge Dickey ruled that Vasco's rights had been violated.

Therefore, he said, the twelve hours of taped confessions could not be used as evidence in a trial. Without this crucial element, little chance existed of a conviction.

But Adriana had told someone else all about her involvement in the murders. Inexplicably, she had granted an interview to a newspaper reporter. The district attorney, through complex legal procedures, arranged for the reluctant reporter to testify about the story he had written. This way, the incriminating details could be placed in front of a jury even without the confessions Vasco had made to detectives.

Dennis Conway inherited the duty of prosecuting her only six weeks before the trial date.

In his recollections of preparing the state's case, Dennis said, "I was thinking about how I dealt with the problem of Donnie's mother being drunk all the time, and how at one point it even flashed through my mind to push her out of the car. Sometimes people have the governor in their heads stop working. Maybe the result of drugs, or emotions, other pressures, or a combination of these. You snap and someone is killed. Sometimes there is planning involved. On the other hand, you have sociopathic killing, with cold-blooded premeditation. It can be argued that almost all people are capable of murder—perhaps with the wrong combination of problems and drugs in the equation.

"Then there are the ones in which a loathsome coward, this doctor, comes up with a greedy manipulator who teams up with a sociopath. You have poor Caroline going through her everyday routine, unbeknownst to her, the die has been cast, this diabolic plan is taking place to take her life. Somebody has already decided that she is going to die. This coward can't just ask for a divorce? He needs Vasco to help kill his wife instead? It's like three meteors colliding. Like the Hillside Strangler

(Kenneth Bianchi) teaming with his cousin (Angelo Buono Jr.) or Charles Ng with Leonard Lake."

Musing about the peculiarities leading to deliberate homicide, Dennis asked, "How does the subject of murdering someone come up in a conversation between two people? That you like torturing a person and killing them? 'Oh goody, I want to help.' I guess it goes back to water seeking its own level. Like in *Silence of the Lambs*, they go to Hannibal Lecter and he seems to know all about these other serial killers around the country. What is it? Do they have a secret handshake?"

In the Vasco trial, her attempt to employ the battered-woman syndrome as a defense angered Dennis. "With murders, it's either 'who done it' or 'I did it, but I was justified, protecting my life.'" The latter, said Dennis, requires testimony from expert psychologist or psychiatrist witnesses. Too many of them, he thinks, are nothing but "whores."

This subject was obviously a sore point for Conway. He launched into a rant, the Irish twinkle and quick laugh noticeably absent. "You know, there's a popular myth that the prosecutors have the advantage in resources. Many counties provide an open checkbook to public defenders. And a million whores line up to feed on this cottage industry of expert testimony, with soft-science mumbo jumbo. They try to convince twelve people they are never going to see again to buy into it, maybe because one juror succumbs to touchy-feely niceness, or others are confused by it, to avoid conviction. Make no mistake about it, there are legitimate defenses. The battered-woman syndrome is one of them. *The Burning Bed* situation, absolutely. That has its solid place in the law. A woman who had been tortured and subjugated for years, guess what? She gets a mitigation pass. That's justice. But many defense teams bastardize it. Adriana did this.

"She attempted the battered-woman-syndrome defense. She had to testify to get her 'symptomology' before the jury. This is typically what I refer to as the 'boo-hoo' evidence to tell all the bad things that happened in your life. The purpose is to somehow mitigate or excuse the horrible crime you have committed. It had to come from her directly. You can't just sneak it in through your 'expert.'"

The core of Vasco's message to the jury was that she had been abused as a child, raped, and mistreated. Then later, Dennis Godley had duplicated the abuse. By threatening to kill Vasco and both of her kids, he had forced her to participate in the brutal murder of Carolyn and her husband. "I didn't know he was going to kill them," she insisted. "I didn't believe it was going to happen."

Exactly three years from the date the married couple were slain, Dennis Conway cross-examined Adriana Vasco. He made it clear that Vasco voluntarily had introduced the idea of killing Carolyn Oppy-Stahl to her boyfriend Godley, and suggested that Stahl would be glad to pay him for doing it. Questioning Vasco, Conway said, "The only link between Kenneth Stahl and Dennis Godley is you. That really looks bad, doesn't it?" She could do nothing but agree that it did, indeed, look bad.

The jury didn't accept her abuse excuse and came in with a guilty verdict of first-degree murder in the case of Carolyn Oppy-Stahl, and second-degree murder in the case of Kenneth Stahl. Judge Francisco Briseno sentenced Vasco to serve the rest of her life in prison without the possibility of parole.

When Dennis Godley was finally extradited to California, he decided to avoid a trial and pleaded guilty to both murders. In his version of the bloody events on Ortega Highway, Godley accused Adriana of shooting Carolyn to death. Chaos and confusion had followed, he said, and he had unleashed a hail of lead that took Kenneth's life. Godley, too, was sentenced to life in prison without parole.

In July 2005, the jury's verdict in the Vasco case was affirmed by a district court of appeals. Conway pointed with understandable pride to not only the affirmation, but also the publication of the decision in law journals, an honor rarely given.

The next assignment facing Dennis Conway was the prosecution of Richard Joseph Namey, charged with the first-degree murder of Sarah Rodriquez and the attempted murder of Matt Corbett. As Conway reviewed the facts of his case, he began to see eerie, foreshadowing parallels between the Namey and Vasco-Godley events:

- A male victim and a female victim were found in a car, with one door standing open, driver's window down.
- A bullet had entered behind Kenneth Stahl's ear and exited through the left eye.
- At least one bullet had either passed through or glanced off Stahl and entered Carolyn's body.
- A revolver was used in both cases, thus leaving no shell casings at the crime scene.
- In both cases, the male victim was shot first.
- In the Vasco trial, the jury foreman was from Placentia.
- Godley was a drug user with a history of abusing women. So was Namey.

The evidence in the Vasco trial had been circumstantial with a real possibility that the jury would let her off with a lesser degree of murder. Namey's chances of avoiding a first-degree murder verdict might be even better.

CHAPTER 19

Anatomy of a Trial

In preparing for a trial, the prosecutor must walk a narrow, precarious line. His job is not necessarily to win a conviction, but to see that justice is carried out. Every move, every word, by the prosecutor, will be subjected to appeals at district and federal levels, and will sometimes go all the way to the U.S. Supreme Court. And if a mistake is made that causes the jury to find a killer not guilty, constitutional guarantees against double jeopardy prevent a retrial, even if the defendant later confesses the crime.

Dennis described the tension. "When you are in trial, you sometimes have cold sweats all night. Stuff is bouncing around in your head. But you're also like a junkie; when you are away from it for a while, if you really like it, you need it. When I'm away from trial for a while, I have to tie off. I need that fix. It was that way from the beginning. When I started and they'd put the defendant on, or I'm getting ready for closing, it would dawn on me that this is such fun! To find a job that fits so many facets of my personality, and one that I really enjoy doing, I feel very fortunate. To be able to read people and communicate with people and the intellectual stimulus too, matching wits, the evidence code, and the excitement of thinking on the fly. Being on your own in there. You're all alone. It's just you on the case. Some people are petrified by standing up in front of twelve jurors and engaging them and having a judge yelling at you. I've had judges yell at me, and all the while I'm sitting there, thinking, 'You know what, you can't touch me. I've got rhino skin. I've been through so much chaos. Do you think that yelling at me is going to upset me?' And I've always kept in mind that my client, the people of this county, are the ones who are punished if I misbehave. Somebody told me my first day on the job, this is the ultimate exercise in self-restraint. It didn't ring truer to anybody than somebody like me."

Conway learned early in his trial career about the necessity of maintaining a certain demeanor in front of a jury. He realized that defense lawyers might see him as a street fighter, and he acknowledged the image, noting that he "grew up scrapping." An experienced defender once took advantage of Dennis and taught him the hard lesson. "When I was a young starting lawyer, some of the older defense lawyers, at the break, would deliberately rattle my cage. I had a lawyer do that to me, an old salty guy from LA, and the result was a hung jury. I told him, 'I'm going to try this case again.' I said to him, 'That was good. You did that and I let the leprechaun out in front of the jury.' The jury punishes us, the prosecutors, if we misbehave. He hung the jury and I told him that I knew what he did and the next time I'm going to control myself."

Educated by his broad experience of interaction with people from all social strata, from poor to prosperous,

Dennis understood human behavior. Unlike many lawyers, he was able to assess his own strengths and weaknesses. "I'll tell you something. I am humble. I'm acutely aware of my insecurities. I have them and I work on them. When I'm humble and my face turns red, that's because that's how I'm feeling. There's nothing more despicable then feigned humility. Somebody with a giant ego who has absolutely not one scintilla of humility in their body and they feign it. Guess what. Those twelve people in a jury box can smell that insincerity. They also can smell when you don't believe in your case."

Trial lawyers must possess a certain skill for theatrics, but Conway deplores exaggerated use of them. Certain attorneys, he has stated, overuse the "righteously indignant" posturing. Dennis realized that in a long trial, juries get to know the opposing lawyers. And those "who are insincere or smarmy are soon found out. In a short trial, they might get away with it. But you do a trial of a couple weeks or more and the jury gets to see what you are really like. I think that's a benefit that I have. . . . I can relate to the common guy because I am a common guy. I've worked on cars and cleaned pools and framed houses, and lived in my car and from hand to mouth for years. That teaches lessons you can't learn in school, like you can't teach height in basketball, and you can't teach speed in track. Either you've got it or you don't. And it's a benefit." Those years of adversity indoctrinated him with the skill to balance his own insecurities against a sense of solid confidence, and the ability to connect with everyday people who find themselves on a jury in a murder trial.

One of the key techniques Conway learned involved methods of getting important points across to juries. "We like to use examples in explaining to the jury, things we learn from other lawyers. But sometimes I get sick of using the same ones over and over."

Always on the lookout for something new, he observed knacks used by other lawyers. It is particularly difficult, sometimes, to make clear to juries the concept of circumstantial evidence, something every trial attorney must grapple with at times. Dennis stated that he has adopted a few ideas from observing other skilled lawyers, and invented a few of his own. A couple of his favorites involved the analogy of trash collection days, or merging into freeway traffic. The best time to introduce it, said Dennis, is during voir dire, the elimination process of selecting jurors, or veniremen, from large panels of candidates.

Dennis started by asserting that a basic truth existed among criminals—that they prefer to have no witnesses. But circumstantial evidence, he explained, can be just as important as eyewitness accounts. With this established, he pointed out that circumstantial evidence was often mentioned in movies, books, and trials depicted on television, so it's important that juries understood what it really was. Often turning to an individual candidate, he asked, "Does the term 'circumstantial evidence' have kind of a negative connotation to you?" More often than not, the person would say it did. The common perception was that this type of evidence was flimsy and questionable.

The next question Dennis presented: "Can you follow the law?" True voir dire, Dennis noted, was to see if jurors could follow the law or not. "Can you follow the law that says circumstantial evidence is entitled to the same weight as direct evidence? Does that surprise anybody?"

Again this comment was often met with confused nods or expressions of doubt. "Direct evidence," he would tell the panel, "includes eyewitnesses who come in and tell you what they saw. Then you have circumstantial evidence, which is everything else." Driving home the point, he asked, "How do you think we solve so many crimes across this country in all these years without eyewitnesses? Well, of course, it's circumstantial evidence. It might be as simple as coming home and finding that a cake has been partially eaten and seeing crumbs and frosting around little Johnnie's lips. There were no witnesses, but it's an easy conclusion to decide who ate the cake. I know it has kind of a bad reputation, but let's talk about it a little bit." To further illustrate, Dennis would use the example of trash day. He would ask a venireman (or venirewoman): "What day is trash picked up in your neighborhood?" If addressing a man, Dennis would add, with a twinkle in his eye, "Of course, you're the one who takes the trash out." This usually elicited smiles and agreement. Dennis would continue, "Let's say it's a Tuesday afternoon, and you come home from work, drive into your neighborhood, and see the tail end of a trash truck moving down the road. Your trash barrels are empty. You look up and down the street, and every lick of trash is taken. What is the conclusion you reach? Of course, you assume the trash guys took it. But did you see them actually take your barrels and empty them? Well, no. Is it a reasonable conclusion, a logical inference, that is what happened? Of course, it is, because that is probably what happened." The panelists nearly always agreed.

Having raised their curiosity, Dennis commented that defense attorneys would usually attack circumstantial evidence as unreliable. That's why, he'd tell them, it's important to understand how it worked. "You know," he reminded, "that there are people, when you put your cans and bottles and newspapers out, who come by and they grab the stuff that can be recycled. Well, it's possible that on one day, they might decide to take not only the recyclable materials, but simply take the entire contents of the trash barrel. 'You know what? Today I'm not only going to take the cans and bottles, I'm going to take every lick of trash from this guy's house and from every house.' It's possible, isn't it? But is that reasonable? No, it's not." Defense attorneys, though, preyed on far-fetched "possibilities" in their efforts to create an element of doubt in jurors' minds.

It's essential, Dennis said, that jurors keep this in mind and not let possibilities that border on the impossible distract them. He sometimes took it a step further with another example. Can jurors reasonably be able to conclude what a defendant was thinking when they committed a crime? Remarkably, this was possible. To illustrate, he said, "Okay, you're on the freeway, in the right-hand lane, and there's an on-ramp coming up, with cars on it, that will need to merge in. You see a car on the ramp and it speeds up; you see the blinker on; you see the person look in the mirror, then look to the left. And, of course, you're not going to speed up to cut that person off, are you?" Most urban jurors can identify with this, and show it with knowledgeable laughter. "What do you think that person is thinking? Are they planning to merge? Do they have to hold up a sign that says, 'I have the specific intent to merge in front of you,' for you to draw that conclusion?" By logical and reasonable inference, Dennis stated, you know what that driver was thinking and planning.

He had asked jurors if they can see how powerful circumstantial evidence can be. Through this technique, he explained, you empower the jury. You get them thinking, "Yeah, I can do this." A great deal of evidence was going to be presented, from which they must draw logical conclusions. The defense would try to neutralize it with counterevidence, and would implant the idea that direct evidence, such as eyewitness testimony, was more reliable. The prosecutor must condition the jury to understand that, while direct evidence was often valid, it also was fraught with certain frailties. He pointed out that eyewitness credibility can be weak or inaccurate. The witness might deliberately lie for some personal motive, or have incorrectly perceived what took place, or simply forgotten crucial details. It's necessary, Dennis has said, to educate the jurors in advance. They must see that the great thing about circumstantial evidence was that it's not influenced by motive, agenda, fading memory, or poor eyesight. Ideally, it's best to have both direct and circumstantial evidence in which case the latter will corroborate the former.

There's one last opportunity in trials to rebut a defender's attempt to explain away pieces of circumstantial evidence, in the closing argument. Dennis liked to use the "potato salad" analogy, which was invented twenty-five years ago by the Orange County district attorney Tony Rackaukas. "He is a down-to-earth guy and was a great prosecutor."

If the prosecutor had presented a dozen or so pieces of circumstantial evidence, said Dennis, the defense attorney would try to undermine each item separately. For example, suppose a defendant was found one block from a murder scene, in possession of the murder weapon, sitting in a car stolen from the victim. The defense attorney might present a "reasonable" explanation for each element. "Well, he borrowed the car hours earlier. The gun was already in it, without the defendant's knowledge. He just happened to be in the area because he was going to get milk for his mother."

Dennis has stated, "They will come up with twenty different explanations. Some are completely made up, require quantum leaps in logic, are unsupported by the evidence, and belie common sense. Twenty explanations, all unreasonable, for twenty pieces of circumstantial evidence. So we can use potato salad. I tell the jurors, 'Well, it's kind of like the defender going up to a buffet, and going to the potato salad bowl, and picking out a piece of potato, and taking it away from the bowl, wiping away the mayonnaise and other ingredients, and saying that it is nothing but a piece of potato, that's all it is. Then going back, pulling out a piece of celery, and saying that it's nothing but a piece of celery. They don't want you to look at the bowl with all the ingredients together that is clearly potato salad.

"The prosecution offers one reasonable explanation for the evidence taken all together. This isn't rocket science, nor is it unique or novel. Prosecutors share with one another, just as defense lawyers do, their different ways of explaining to juries various concepts they may have to deal with during a trial. The key is, each lawyer, be it DA or defender, develops their own repertoire and ways of communicating with a jury. Find out what works for you. Be comfortable and genuine. Over the years, I've heard from other lawyers what I thought were brilliant ways to explain some concept to a jury, only to realize that I couldn't use it or pull it off because it didn't work for me. You can't try to be someone you're not, especially when it is critical to win the trust of the jury. Ultimately the facts drive the case. You can't undermine the power of your evidence by being a disingenuous conduit. You cannot forget that you are dealing with humans, who fundamentally operate with emotions. If you turn them off or they distrust you, it can erode the power of your evidence and prejudice the outcome of the case."

In old movies and television shows, both prosecutors and defenders often win their cases with a stunning piece of unexpected bombshell evidence or a breathtaking surprise witness. In reality, the law generally disallows such theatrics. Prosecutors are required by "discovery" laws to inform the defense, well in advance, of anticipated evidence or witnesses. Yet, Dennis explained, last-minute evidence did sometimes come into play. He and his fellow prosecutors have a special name for it, invented by a former member of the DA team who played ice hockey. They call it a "woolick." Dennis explained that "a 'woolick' is one of those things that pops up for your use during trial that the defense didn't know about because they didn't look at the evidence or overlooked it. It's like a little land mine. The reason we call it a woolick is because of what happens in an ice hockey game. When you go to a hockey game and when a player gets checked into the boards with a really hard lick, and the boards rattle, the crowd goes, 'Wooooo!' So we call that a woolick. In trials, you don't get many woolicks."

It was one of many colloquialisms Dennis and his colleagues have coined in the Orange County DA Office. With tongues in cheek, they enjoy manufacturing different phrases, some tailored for specific judges, or circumstances in court. Dennis referred to the unpleasant event of being reprimanded by a judge as "getting your snout slapped."

From his extensive reading, an inborn natural curiosity, and his Irish sense of humor, Dennis has loved to play with words. "I guess you can tell from talking to me that I have my own jokes or Conwayisms. And I have my own misconfabulations. My favorite comedian is Norm

Crosby because I like misconfabulating words, and sometimes I do it intentionally when people think they are well read, and flaunting it. One particular judge, who's really a nice guy, seemed to enjoy correcting me. Once, I was doing a trial in his court, picking a jury. I'm not a big wordsmith, but I know for example that 'irregardless' is not a word. And some people say 'pre-emptory,' referring to challenging a jury candidate, when the word is actually 'peremptory.' In my own subtle way, I was correcting the judge who kept saying it wrong. So he picks up on this and stops the proceedings, in front of the jury, to say, 'The word is pre-emptory.' Even worse, he compounded his error by explaining where he thinks the word came from. I didn't respond, but I'm sitting there wondering when it's going to dawn on him one day, and whether he's going to be embarrassed when he discovers his ongoing solecism.

"You can prevent a few snout slappings by knowing the judges," Dennis stated. "All of them have their own peculiar vagaries or pet peeves, and it's helpful for a lawyer to become familiar with them before practicing in their courts. Experienced attorneys share this information with each other. Doing so can dramatically reduce the number of snout slappings one might incur.

"Almost universally, judges abhor speaking objections and vigorously disallow them. This occurs when the attorney continues with gratuitous verbiage after saying, 'Objection,' then adding the obligatory one- or two-word legal basis for it. 'Objection, leading.' Or, 'Objection, irrelevant.' No more explanation is necessary unless the judge asks for it. I'm with them on that. I don't like it when it's a free-for-all where you have to argue your points in front of the jury about why the issue is objectionable. And you don't want the judge being mad at you. You don't want to be yelled at in front of the jury. You want to play by the judge's rules. Do your job as an advocate. No matter whether you like that person in the black robes or not, you still have to try your case in front of him or her. That's why this job is the ultimate exercise in self-restraint. You still have to do the best you can to serve your client.

"I agree with judges who won't allow speaking objections. I like it when they control the courtroom. It is to our benefit because we have a standard where we can't misbehave. Number one, the jury punishes us for misbehaving. We're their lawyer, we wear the white hat. They expect better of us, and expect misbehaving from a defense lawyer, who has nothing to lose. He's doing anything he can to get his client off. At some level, I respect that, even though I can't personally do it. At least not to that level. A judge who runs a tight courtroom inures to our benefit, because defenders tend to be more naughty. Our guidelines are here, but there are basically no fences for some of them. That helps us and I like it."

Admitting that he had limits in this respect, Dennis occasionally risked a snout slapping by indulging in one or two speaking objections. "Sometimes the speaking objection is useful, but you must learn to save them and use them only if necessary." In one case, Dennis recalled, the defendant had stabbed his wife to death by plunging a knife into her body twenty-four times. "She had the unmitigated chutzpah, the audacity, the gall, to try and leave him after years of enduring abuse from him. So he took a knife from the apartment they had shared, drove to her workplace, got her alone, and stabbed her to death." The defense lawyer, a brilliant legal mind, had coached his client and woven his story with minute facts, seemingly scripting the direct examination. To Dennis, it was an obvious ploy. The defendant testified over three hours telling a meticulous story, led every step of the way by the defense attorney. "You are not supposed to lead the witness on direct examination. But he was so smart, after doing trials for twenty-five or thirty years, he had walked his client through this scripted, rehearsed testimony. I saved a speaking objection for that trial.

"Finally, the judge began sustaining my objections to the defender leading his witness. The defender is looking at me like I'm being naughty, as if he is just trying to present his case. It amounted to testimony from the defense attorney. At one of my objections, he protested, speaking directly to me in front of the jury, he said that he needed only a few more minutes to wrap it up. That was when I opened up. I said, 'Well, *you've* been testifying here for two-and-a-half hours, and I think it's time you wrap *your* testimony.' That's a no-no, and I knew the judge was really going to be angry with me for that. He clears the courtroom to slap both of our snouts. I was appropriately apologetic. But it had worked and I had saved my speaking objection for just that moment. I really believe the jury understood exactly what had happened, that I was sick of the lawyer testifying."

Even in describing these rare scrapes with judges or defense attorneys, Dennis emphasized his deep satisfaction with his work environment. "I have a challenging and satisfying job and work with exceptionally good people. It's a great feeling to actually look forward to going to work each day."

It is the prosecutor's duty to seek justice, not necessarily a win in court. But to accomplish this, it is necessary to understand the dynamics of a trial and to know how to communicate with the ultimate triers of fact: the twelve ordinary citizens in that jury box.

In the pending trial of Richard Namey, a piece of critically important circumstantial evidence would surface. As yet, no one had even discovered it.

CHAPTER 20

Kings and Pawns

In a murder trial, some of the most important issues are decided well before a jury is seated. In pretrial hearings, as in a master's chess game, motions are brought forth by both the prosecutor and the defense team to seek advantageous rulings about procedures to be followed and evidence to be introduced.

In the Richard Namey case, one of the first requests by the defense was to sever the charges and hold two separate trials. First, Namey would face charges of murder and attempted murder. In a second trial, the accusations of carjacking and auto theft would be presented.

The proceedings would be aired in Superior Court Judge Richard F. Toohey's courtroom. A former deputy district attorney in Orange County, from 1977 to 1989, Toohey had prosecuted homicide cases for seven years. First appointed to the bench in '89, he had been elevated to the superior court in '95. With a reputation for strict, no-nonsense procedure at the bench, Toohey's close acquaintances knew of his remarkable wit in private. His thick, salt-and-pepper hair, piercing dark eyes, and stern countenance made Toohey appear younger than his fifty-four years. Well liked by his colleagues, he enjoyed the company of retired judge Donald A. McCartin. Asked about this, McCartin quipped, "I taught him everything he knows."

On Tuesday, September 21, 2004, Toohey listened as senior deputy public defender John Zitny argued for the severance. Well dressed in a neat, dark suit, slender, with brown hair, finely chiseled features, bespectacled, standing not quite six feet tall, John Zitny spoke in a slightly high-pitched voice. With a reputation for honesty and for avoiding sleazy tactics, the defender was known by prosecutors as a "straight shooter."

Deputy DA Dennis Conway opposed the motion for separate trials. Toohey ruled against the defense. All of the charges, he ordered, would be heard by one jury.

It is important that precise and exact language be used in court proceedings. Judge Toohey corrected Conway in the next round of discussions. The defender asked that potential witnesses be ordered to leave the court-room gallery during the hearings. Conway requested an exception. He said, "The only potential witness from the people's side, depending on the motions and the outcome, is the victim's mother. These proceedings, as the court can imagine, are very important to her since her daughter was murdered. She would like to attend, and I know the court has some discretion in the matter."

In a monotone, the judge at once questioned Conway and reproached his word selection. "You're referring to the *decedent's* mother?" The distinction was subtle. Legally, until a crime could be proved, Sarah Rodriquez was a decedent, not yet a victim.

Conway didn't even blink while responding. "The decedent's mother. She is only a potential witness. She's in the courtroom now, and her testimony would be very limited and narrow."

After a brief whispered conference, Zitny proposed a compromise. If Namey's mother and father could be allowed to stay, the defense had no objection to letting Martha and Bob Dewar remain in the courtroom. Toohey granted the motion.

The next topic of discussion had been anticipated by Conway all along. He fully expected the defense to bring up the abortion in an attempt to "dirty up Sarah." To Conway, it was an underhanded idea and he did not want the jury to hear anything about the pregnancy termination, at least in the opening statements. To head it off, he struck the first blow. "There is some evidence, Your Honor, that the victim had an abortion and I would like to ask the defense if they plan to somehow introduce that. If so, we would argue as to the relevance."

Toohey turned to the defense attorney to ask if he did intend to offer the abortion as evidence. Zitny replied, "Yes, I do, Your Honor. The relevance of that is that my client—we have evidence—was the father of the child. At the time this occurred, my client was the father of another child that he loved dearly. He wanted to have children with Ms. Rodriquez. In fact, they discussed having children together, and even naming the children. The abortion was very devastating to my client, and is clearly a provocative act. This is something that . . . goes to the heart of the defense of this case. Yes, I do plan to introduce it."

To be certain he understood the facts, Toohey asked, "The defendant was the father of the aborted child; is that correct?"

Instantly Conway stated, "We don't know that, Your Honor."

Zitny brought up a letter Sarah had written, which was found on her bed, telling a friend that she had undergone an abortion, and that she thought "it was Rick's baby."

Even if Sarah believed Namey was the father, Conway argued, there was no clear proof that she was correct.

To Toohey's query about how Zitny planned to introduce the issue, the defender replied, "I have three ways. . . . We do have that letter. That is a declaration . . . even by the language of the letter. She states that she was basically embarrassed by what had happened and that she was upset that her mother had access to the letter. We also have the mother and stepfather, who do have information regarding the abortion. And, it is my understanding that the person who is the subject of the attempted murder, he also drove the decedent to get the abortion. And so, he has knowledge of it."

Toohey turned to Conway to hear his argument. Dennis made it clear that he was concerned about allowing the defense to speak of the abortion in opening statements, which might prejudice the jury against Sarah and could possibly hint that it mitigated the crime. He voiced his opinion that the murder had nothing to do with Sarah's abortion. "The defendant gave a statement to the police. He says the reason that he killed Sarah and shot Matt Corbett is because he is distraught over Sarah leaving him. . . . So, according to the defendant, he takes this gun and goes over to commit suicide in front of the victim, Sarah Rodriquez, and sees her with another guy, and just snaps, and is in a cloud." The judge frowned but didn't bother to correct Conway again about calling the decedent a victim. The prosecutor said, "His only mention of the abortion is about an hour into the interview, where he is kind of justifying what he did. He says, 'Well, she's evil too. She had an abortion.' My concern is this: the defense is clearly going to try to use this information to try to establish some sort of heat of passion to mitigate this murder."

Two important reasons supported the objections to the issues being introduced, Conway explained. One, the abortion had taken place eight or nine months before the shooting. And two, Namey had stated to the police that his reason for confronting Sarah and committing the act had nothing to do with the abortion. "I anticipate that the defense is going to try to make this the centerpiece of their case, for obvious reasons." Abortion, he added, was such a controversial social issue that jurors might turn it into a "referendum" among themselves. Furthermore, said Dennis, the parents' knowledge was only hearsay, since it came from a letter they found on Sarah's bed.

Of course, Conway acknowledged, if Namey chose to testify, he might bring up the abortion as a mitigating reason for his actions or as an element to his state of mind. In that case, the prosecutor said, he would be allowed to tackle it on cross-examination. His request, at this point, was simply to disallow the defense from bringing up the abortion in their opening statements, and trying to make it the centerpiece of their case.

Zitny replied that he certainly did plan to bring it up in his opening statement. He argued that the date of the abortion was irrelevant since "provocative acts" in legal precedent can be "long-standing."

The judge, stating that he wished to examine the letter written by Sarah, seemed impatient at both lawyers for loading their arguments with extraneous matters, failing to stay focused on what he regarded as the main point being discussed.

Frustration gnawed inside Conway. If the defense received permission to introduce the abortion in opening statements, the jury would be prejudiced from the start. Trying to sound calm, he said, "Trust me, Your Honor, I'm going to speak directly to this piece of evidence."

Toohey's next words grated even more on Conway. "Just relax. Go ahead," he chided. The "relax" comment seemed gratuitous to the prosecutor, who felt like a kid being lectured by the school principal.

His face reddening, Conway explained, "Your Honor, this is how I operate. I am just in trial mode and this is how—I'm sorry if the court takes it wrong."

In what seemed to be a patronizing tone, Toohey said that he was not taking it wrong. "I'm just telling you to relax and present your case."

"I can't relax. This is how I appear. I'm sorry." Taking a deep breath, Dennis slowed his speech. "This piece of evidence of an abortion eight months prior, without something accompanying it, is not probative at all in this case. This is my point. Who knows what it means? They could have decided to do it together. It has absolutely minimal probative value without the testimony of how it impacts the defendant eight months later to cause him to commit murder. That's my only point. Thank you."

The judge agreed to think about it and issue a ruling later. Sounding as if he believed the hearing was at an end, Toohey asked the lawyers if they had any other issues to bring up. He sighed when Conway said, "Yes, Your Honor, a few more things."

Given the go-ahead, Dennis said that "search warrants after the defendant's arrest resulted in finding photographs of the victim, Sarah Rodriquez, without her clothes on." The pictures were discovered in Namey's apartment. "I would ask the court if the defense plans on trying to introduce them into evidence."

Without hesitation, Zitny confirmed Conway's fears. "Yes, Your Honor. We do have those photographs subpoenaed." They would be offered into evidence. Toohey wanted to know their relevance. Zitny explained, "At the time my client was writing the suicide notes, there is indications that he was reminiscing about his relationship with Sarah Rodriquez by looking at those photographs. So the suicide notes found by police next to the photographs of both my client and Sarah Rodriquez, without their clothes on, show the state of mind of my client being basically heartbroken and still in love with Sarah Rodriquez, and looking at those photographs at the same time, he is contemplating suicide." The defender said he would also offer the suicide notes as evidence.

Accepting the opportunity to argue his point, Conway said, "When the court looks at these photos, it will be obvious they are of minimal probative value. . . . The suicide notes are not dated. In fact, there was a call to the police by the defendant's own mother, I believe two years earlier, reporting that the defendant is emotionally troubled and talking about suicide." Without dates on the documents, how could anyone know when they were actually written?

A prompt answer came from Zitny. "After this incident happened, my client's apartment was observed by the police, and entered after the shooting had occurred. Placed on the coffee table, or the dining-room table right in the living room, were these three letters. Which, you know, being right there at that time, even though they may not be dated, it's quite obvious that they were written just before the incident happened. There is really no reasonable—any other reasonable explanation for it."

Seizing on the opening Zitny had left, Conway attacked. "And, reminiscing, there were some love letters that were recovered, from Sarah to the defendant, and dated September and October, when the relationship was fresh—"

Toohey interrupted, wanting to know if the love letters were found at the same time and place as the suicide notes. Conway said yes, but Zitny asserted that the love letters were found in a separate room.

Now Judge Toohey had several items to weigh: the abortion letter, nude photographs, suicide notes, and love letters. He promised to give them careful consideration and announce his decisions later.

The hearing moved on to another crucial topic, the admissibility of previous criminal behavior by Richard Namey. This was one of the most controversial issues in trials. Should the jury hear that a defendant had a history of breaking the law, especially if the convictions were for similar or identical crimes? Appeals courts repeatedly overturn guilty verdicts on the basis that juries were prejudiced by hearing evidence of prior criminal conduct. Most of the general public disagrees with the courts' posture and are outraged at the idea of hiding a defendant's rap sheet from the jury. Wasn't a pattern of criminality a likely indicator that the defendant had probably transgressed again? If a dog was accused of biting someone, wouldn't it be important to know if it had a long history of biting people? Defense attorneys insist that it would be unfair to prejudice jurors against a defendant by revealing past sins. The law does conditionally allow such evidence to be presented, but under narrowly constricted rules.

In Conway's opinion, the incident in which Namey had confronted Andrea Merino and Jim Fletcher, nine months before the murder, was so similar that it should be made known to the jury. A restraining order had been in effect, the defendant had used a car to force them over, he had threatened the couple with a gun (even though it was alleged to be a toy), and he had said he wanted to kill himself. To Conway, it mirrored events that led to shooting Sarah and Matt, and the behavior demonstrated Namey's intentions. Zitny, though, had filed a written objection.

Legal issues sometimes pivot on minutia. The applicable law that might allow the evidence in this case applied to "domestic relationships." Precedents had been set defining a dating relationship as a domestic relationship. Namey had dated Sarah for months, but had he been "dating" Andrea Merino? Zitny's objection stated that the affiliation between Namey and Merino was not a dating arrangement, thus inadmissible to show similarity in the defendant's behavioral pattern.

Conway argued, "The defense, it seems, is only contesting the element of dating, and attaches a police report from an officer who memorializes that Andrea Merino didn't say 'dating relationship.' What counsel didn't attach is two other reports that were also provided in discovery, where two DA investigators, on separate occasions, spoke with Andrea when she came to court. And she clearly stated it was a dating relationship for at least two months. There were no sexual relations. But it was a dating relationship. . . . As an offer of proof, I will tell the court that she was spoken to last night, and reiterates the same thing—movies, dinners, interest in one another for a couple of months, and what she would classify as dating. Clearly, that prior incident is admissible . . . and we would be seeking to introduce it."

The defense attorney stood firm in opposition. Andrea Merino, he said, had told the officer, at the scene, that no dating relationship had existed. "Her likelihood of telling the truth to the officer is much greater than what she may have told the district attorney's investigator at some other time. . . . She blurts out the truth without an opportunity to reflect. And that truth was, 'I do not have a dating relationship with this man, Richard Namey. . . .' Taking these facts into consideration, I believe it's clear that it's not a domestic relationship." He asserted that it could not be admitted according to conditions of the applicable evidence code.

Toohey postponed his decision.

Two other disputes about admissible evidence were presented to the judge. One revolved around the incident at Sarah's night school, in which Namey had pushed and choked her. The other entailed the incident in which Namey had forced Sarah's car to the curb and was subsequently chased by Matt Corbett. Should the jury hear about these? No, said Zitny. There were no witnesses to either occurrence, only Sarah's uncorroborated word. Even her journal and the police reports reflected only what Sarah said. Without a doubt, Corbett had chased Namey, but he had not seen any confrontation between the defendant and Sarah.

Conway argued passionately, citing case law and precedents, to have both incidents placed before the jury.

As in the previous motions, Judge Toohey stated that he would give the matters due consideration and hand down his decisions before jury selection the following day.

On Wednesday morning, while waiting an hour for the jury panelists to arrive and begin the selection process, Toohey used the time to discuss the previous day's issues before delivering his rulings. He was troubled by the defense's intent to introduce the nude photos of Sarah and Namey into evidence. He said, "After we recessed, the court had a concern regarding those photographs and their sensitive nature. . . . One of the photographs depicted a male with an erect penis, and I'm at a little bit of a loss as to why you would want to introduce them." Perhaps, he suggested, they should be sealed, since the defense planned only to mention them in the context that Namey was reminiscing about them while writing his suicide letters. That way, the jury wouldn't actually see the pictures.

Zitny agreed, with the reservation that if it became necessary, he might wish to use the pictures of Sarah to support the allegation of a sexual relationship. Conway expressed concern about the defense making abstract references to the pictures in which Zitny might hint that they depicted a "happy couple."

Both lawyers listened intently as Toohey announced his decisions on the matters discussed.

Regarding the incident at night school, the judge said that even though no witnesses existed, Sarah's statements were believable, since they were made while she was still under the stress of excitement. Her reports and journal regarding Namey's abusive conduct would be admissible. The restraining order would also be seen by the jury.

The incident of April 2, 2003, in which Namey had forced Sarah's car over, threatened her, and was chased by Matt Corbett, would also be allowable. It showed a pattern of abusive conduct by Namey.

The defense would not be allowed to introduce the abortion through Sarah's unsent letter or through statements made by her parents. However, if Namey testified, and mentioned the abortion, it would be acceptable testimony, subject to cross-examination by the prosecutor.

Namey's three suicide letters were "hearsay" documents and not admissible independently. The judge left the door open for Zitny to bring them in to reveal Namey's state of mind.

So far, Conway was pleased with the rulings. Only one more measure remained. Would the judge allow the important confrontation with Andrea Merino and Jim Fletcher to show that Namey previously had behaved in almost exactly the same manner?

Judge Toohey said, "One last issue. And that's in relation to the conduct of the defendant, attributed to Andrea Merino. The court is admitting a substantial amount of evidence on the fact that the defendant had a disposition regarding domestic violence in relation to his conduct with the decedent in this matter. And the court has considered the probative value of that evidence and weighed it against any prejudice that would tend to flow from it."

Dennis held his breath. Would Toohey permit the key evidence to be used?

The judge continued, "In the court's weighing process, the court finds it goes more to character than any probative value, especially when weighed against other evidence that's presented in this case. The court precludes it."

With his face turning red, Dennis avoided any overt comments. If any pattern of conduct, in any criminal case deserved to be heard, this one should have been allowed. It was such a perfect duplication, portending a future murder. It demonstrated without any doubt that Namey knew what he was doing when he took a gun with him to chase down Sarah and Matt, then opened fire.

Speaking of it later, Dennis said, "The Andrea Merino stuff should have come in. It's statutorily admissible, right on point."

A conversation about it had taken place in the judge's

chambers. Toohey had asked Conway, "Do you really need it?"

Holding back the leprechaun, Conway had replied, "Judge, I'm looking at the evidence code. It's relevant and it's admissible, and 'do you need it?' is not a consideration for admissibility." In an abundance of caution, Toohey chose to rule it out.

Disappointed, Dennis also felt sorry for Andrea Merino. "She actually moved away to save her life. The system kind of let Andrea down. So she moved away. The police weren't helping her; the court wasn't helping; Namey was out of custody, harassing her when they left court. She packed up and moved to another county. I think that saved her life, the way this guy is." To Dennis, the setback presented nothing more than another obstacle to overcome. His life had been filled with a multitude of disappointments and emotional crises. It had taught him to see pitfalls as new challenges. He would use this setback as yet another problem to be solved, not nearly as bad as dealing with the irrational mother of his son, making his way across the country with no money in his pocket, escaping a cult kidnapping, or surviving day-to-day while sleeping in his car at night.

Now Dennis faced the challenge of convincing a jury that Richard Namey had deliberately murdered Sarah Rodriquez and knew exactly what he was doing when he tried to kill Matt Corbett. In all probablility, Namey's defenders would try to sell a story of Namey being in a mental fog when he committed the cruel acts, and thus avoid a verdict of first-degree murder. With a convincing defense, they might even get him off with a short prison sentence followed by a period of therapy. A legal ruling had already imposed a huge handicap on Conway. It might be impossible to hurdle it.

CHAPTER 21

Trial: The Curtain Rises

After Judge Richard Toohey disposed of the pretrial hearing matters, he spoke directly to the assembled twelve jurors and three alternates. "At this time, the court will have the clerk read to you the information that's filed in this matter. I would remind you, the information is not evidence in the case. It merely sets forth the charges and the allegations the jury will be asked to evaluate."

In a monotone, Toohey's clerk delivered the legal language. It stated that Richard Joseph Namey faced trial for five counts of criminal conduct and several associated allegations.

1. On or about April 16, 2003, Richard Joseph Namey did willfully, unlawfully, and with malice aforethought, murder Sarah Rodriquez, a human being.

2. Richard Joseph Namey did willfully, unlawfully, and with malice aforethought, attempt to murder Matthew Corbett, a human being.

3. On or about April 19, 2003, Richard Joseph Namey did willfully, unlawfully seize, confine, and inveigle,

entice, decoy, abduct, conceal, kidnap, and carry away Alberto Zavala with the intent to hold and detain, and who did hold and detain the said Alberto Zavala during the commission of a carjacking.

4. Richard Joseph Namey did willfully, unlawfully, and feloniously, by means of force and fear and against his will, take a motor vehicle from the person, possession, and immediate presence of the driver, Alberto Zavala, with the intent to temporarily and permanently deprive said victim of possession.

5. Richard Joseph Namey did willfully and unlawfully drive and take a 1999 GMC Safari van, not his own, without the consent of the owner.

Enhancements to several of the charges included use of a firearm and discharging a firearm. In the commission of count two, it resulted in causing great bodily injury.

The clerk also noted that Namey had entered a plea of not guilty and had denied the enhancements.

For the next two hours, Dennis Conway and John Zitny delivered opening statements to the jury to explain what the evidence, in their opinions, would show. Conway read several passages from Sarah's journal and said, "Sarah is speaking to you from the grave . . . coming into the courtroom the only way she can." Zitny said that his client's actions stemmed not from premeditation but from the heat of passion. "He shot them. I'm not saying he didn't. The only issue to decide is whether it was hot-blooded or cold-blooded."

Conway, in rebuttal, said that Sarah paid with her life for trying to get out of the relationship with Namey. He cited the aphoristic rationale, "If I can't have her, no one can."

Judge Toohey informed jurors that lawyers' words

are not evidence and should carry no weight in the eventual deliberations.

After a break, Toohey invited Conway to call his first witness. DA Investigator Ernie Gomez took the oath and settled into the padded witness chair. He had been the first police officer to chase Namey on the forty-two-mile race through Orange County, and one of the team who retrieved the fugitive from a drainage tunnel. A few months before the trial, Gomez had leaped at the opportunity to leave the police department and join the district attorney's office as an investigator.

Conway rose from his seat at the counsel table and elicited from Gomez how he'd been dispatched to search for the stolen van. Referring to an easel-size diagram of freeways and surface streets in Orange County, Conway asked the former patrol officer to take jurors through the hair-raising high-speed chase led by Namey in the red Safari. Eyes grew large in the courtroom when Gomez said the van and trailing police vehicles had exceeded 125 miles per hour several times on the forty-two-mile route. It ended in a high-school parking lot when the vehicle halted adjacent to a chain-link fence bordering a drainage ditch. Gomez had seen the driver leap from the van, elude a police dog, and vault over the fence.

Even though it was dark, the witness said, visibility was enhanced by a sheriff's helicopter overhead illuminating the area with a spotlight. He and other officers had been informed by radio that the fugitive was armed and dangerous.

"What did you do next?" asked Conway.

"Obviously, we used extreme caution. We quickly formed as a team." Bolt cutters had been used to open

a gate and allow officers to scramble down the slope to
a tunnel entry.

Introducing a stack of photographs, Conway asked
Gomez to describe what was pictured. The witness verbalized images of the red van, its interior, and numerous bullets, scattered on the floor near the driver's seat.
A red-and-white box, labeled "PMC," found in the
center-console area, was packed with .357-caliber rounds.

Regarding the pursuit on foot, Gomez said, "We went
into the tunnel with our flashlights, looking around. We
could see footprints, fresh, wet footprints going into it.
There were six officers and the dog."

"At some point, with the aid of the dog, was the suspect apprehended?"

"Yes."

"Do you see that person in court today?"

"Yes." Gomez pointed to the defendant and said,
"Mr. Namey, to my right, wearing a green, long-sleeved
sweater." Namey gave the witness a cold stare. His newly
grown dark mustache seemed to bristle.

After a short break, John Zitny rose to cross-examine
Ernie Gomez. Observers would soon see a pattern in
which he formulated many of his questions by making
a statement and attaching the inquiry "Isn't that true?"
or "Is that correct?"

The defender focused interest on the parking lot
where Namey had first climbed into the red Safari.
"Now, during the time of April 2003, isn't it true that
the market parking lot, in that vicinity, was a place for
purchasing street-level drugs?" Before Gomez could
answer, Conway objected and Toohey sustained it.

Next Zitny asked, "You told us that a firearm was recovered at the end of this pursuit, true?"

Gomez wrinkled his forehead. "I don't think I said that
today."

Haltingly the defender inquired again, "I think—didn't you say that a three fifty-seven Magnum was recovered?" Gomez reiterated that he did not remember saying anything like that. "Okay," said Zitny, glossing over his error. "Do you have knowledge—was a three fifty-seven recovered at the scene at the end of the pursuit?" Gomez answered in the affirmative. Had they known that the man they chased was possibly armed? Gomez said they had.

After a few more questions reviewing the end of the long vehicular chase and following Namey into the tunnel, Zitny wanted to know, "Were you shot at by the person leaving the van?"

"No."

"Was any other officer shot at?"

"No."

"Was the helicopter shot at?"

Another negative answer. Observers caught the drift. The defendant must not be such a bad fellow, since he didn't shoot at any armed police personnel.

"So you told us earlier that my client was apprehended by a police dog?"

Gomez suppressed a smile. "I didn't say it, but yes, he was."

"Do you have any knowledge if the police dog was shot?" No, said the witness, the dog had not been shot, nor had any shots been fired inside the tunnel.

"And so, in other words," said Zitny, "my client was bitten, taken into custody by the dog." It was almost comical, picturing a dog taking a fugitive "into custody." And Gomez had said nothing about Namey being bitten. One cynical spectator silently speculated that the defender was going to ask if the dog had read Namey his Miranda rights before making the arrest.

Zitny extended the litany, emphasizing no gunplay by

his client. "And there was absolutely no shoot-out, for
him to try to escape?" Gomez agreed that no shooting
had taken place. Zitny announced that he had no further questions.

Officer Mike McCarthy, the police dog's handler, replaced Gomez on the witness stand. Dressed in a fault-
less navy blue uniform, his black hair neatly trimmed and
combed, shoes spit-shined, he very well could have
modeled for a recruiting poster. He affirmed his employment with the Santa Ana PD Canine Unit and noted that
he'd been with the Los Angeles Police Department
over three years before moving to Orange County.
Shown a photograph of the feeder tube into which
Namey had crawled, off the main tunnel, McCarthy
verified it was the one where the suspect had been captured. A hint of delight flashed across his face when
Conway asked the name of McCarthy's canine partner.
"Chris," he enunciated.

"Now, going into that tunnel, did you have information that the person you were chasing may be armed?"

"Yes, sir. This originated in our city of Santa Ana and
the call came out as a carjacking, robbery suspect vehicle . . . equipped with a LoJack. Our helicopter picked
up the signal." The witness had joined the high-speed
car chase and at one point took the lead as "primary"
police pursuit unit. At the tunnel entrance, which he
described as "over six feet high and probably ten or
twelve feet wide," he and Chris had been part of the team
hunting for Namey on foot.

"What are your concerns as a police officer going
into a location like that after a possibly armed suspect?"

"There are several concerns. One is the lighting. It was
nighttime, we had our flashlights on. So that illumi-

nates us. The suspect was armed, and if he had wanted to engage us, [he] would know exactly where we were. The other problem that we had to think about, even if this person doesn't aim at us but just fires a round, it could ricochet—the walls are solid cement through that entire tunnel. If someone were to shoot, it wouldn't be as if the cement would absorb the bullet." Depending on the caliber and velocity, it could glance off walls several times and hit any one of the six officers.

Conway formed his questions precisely to draw from the witness exactly how dangerous the situation was. McCarthy, obviously knowledgeable, intelligent, and skilled at speaking, answered in clear language. As the canine officer, he and Chris had jumped the chain-link fence in order to lead the team into the tunnel. In a diamond-shaped formation, they advanced into the darkness, tense but determined. "Because we were tactically walking, not running, it was hard for me to judge the distance we covered, but I would say we covered approximately a mile." During the pursuit, they never caught sight of the suspect. "My canine was out in front of us, checking the area."

At the same time their flashlight beams located a feeder tube on the left wall, approximated thirty-six to forty inches in diameter, and about three feet from the floor, Chris "began to bark and alert. His ears were up and he's telling me that he has detected human scent up in that tube. . . . We then gave an announcement that we are the Santa Ana Police Department." They warned Namey that the police dog was with them and asked him to identify himself. The suspect didn't respond until McCarthy sent Chris into the tube. Because the passageway bent to the right, the dog could no longer be seen even with flashlights.

From out of the darkness, said McCarthy, he heard the fugitive say he could see the dog, at which time the officer ordered Chris back. "I wanted the suspect to keep talking so I could tell where he was. I told him that he needs to come out, with his hands in our sight." If he did, McCarthy had said, the dog would not be used. "He said he was going to come out."

A few of the jurors leaned forward in their chairs, as if watching a thriller movie. In the gallery, the usual coughing and chair squeaking was noticeably absent. Some thought McCarthy would be perfect as the narrator on a reality-TV show featuring sensational police stories. The officer said, "So we waited. . . . We still didn't know for certain if he was armed or what his intentions were. Is he going to surrender? Is this an ambush, or what? That's what we needed to prepare for."

In the unfolding account, the fugitive complied with McCarthy's request to keep talking, but to the officers, his voice seemed to be moving away from them. "I advised him that I was going to send the dog." McCarthy said he gave Chris the command and watched him disappear into the tube again.

"Did you crawl into the tunnel yourself?"

"Not at first. Not until the dog was engaged."

"How could you tell the dog was engaged?"

"By his barking, kind of growling, and I heard the suspect yelling."

"So did you enter the tube to get to the dog and the suspect?"

"Yes, sir. I had to crawl on my hands and knees approximately forty yards. There was water—it was slimy crawling up this feeder tube to get where they were."

Conway drew out the gripping, tension-filled moment, knowing full well that he had the jury hooked. "Okay, and were you still concerned about the possibility of the suspect having a weapon?"

"Yes, sir. I knew my dog was engaged with the suspect, but I did not know if the fugitive was still armed or able to fight back or shoot down the tunnel. Which, again, is cement and could cause ricochet. I was in a poor position for friendly fire, if the other officers needed to engage, and also from the suspect's fire. I was in the middle."

"Did another officer come in behind you?"

Yes, McCarthy said. At his request, another cop had followed him into the tube, on hands and knees. "I didn't want to turn on my light and let the suspect know where I was until I can make the bend where the tunnel curved. So I had no light. I had made a plan with the other officer that if shooting were to occur, I would go flat in the tube, and hopefully he could fire over my head."

Several issues had occupied McCarthy's mind during the dangerous mission. "The other problem was, because the tunnel is so tight, if I was to have my dog release on my side, there is no way for the suspect to get past us and go to the other officers. I still haven't searched him. We don't know where the weapon is at this point. I had to crawl over the dog and the suspect as they were struggling. They were still engaged—he was yelling and the dog was still in drive." With some difficulty, McCarthy had managed to scramble past them and gave the command for Chris to release. In this position, the fugitive was caught between McCarthy, with Chris at his side, and the officer who had followed them into the tube. The second cop snapped handcuffs on the suspect.

The prosecutor wanted every detail. "Then how did

you get him out this feeder tube, where you had crawled one hundred yards, when he is handcuffed?"

"The problem with the way the tunnel was, we ended up pulling the suspect through the tube back to the main tunnel. My partner is crawling backward, pulling the suspect. I was up-tunnel, helping."

"And did you recover any kind of a handgun?"

"Yes, sir. Right near where my dog was engaged with the suspect. As we handcuffed him, I was able to illuminate my flashlight and there was a weapon lying in the tunnel right next to where—within an arm's reach of where we took him into custody." McCarthy had also found a leather-bound black planning calendar.

Opening a sealed cardboard box, Conway withdrew the handgun. McCarthy described it. "It's a chrome revolver. It appears to be a five-shot with rubber or black tape grips, three fifty-seven Magnum." The chrome was splotched with rusty spots, probably from being immersed in the slime at the bottom of the drainage feeder tube. Etched on the short barrel were the words "CHARTER ARMS CORPORATION, STRATFORD, CONN."

Bringing the dramatic testimony to a close, Conway asked the witness to point out the suspect he had helped apprehend in the hellish tunnel. McCarthy pointed to the defendant, Richard Namey.

On cross-examination, Zitny recapitulated some of the facts, that McCarthy was part of the high-speed vehicle pursuit team, that other officers were involved, and that a helicopter joined in. He again brought out the absence of any shoot-out, either during the wild freeway chase or in the tunnel. "Did you ever see him brandish the firearm that you showed us today?" No, said McCarthy, he had never seen Namey point the weapon at them. "Okay. Now, you told us that, when you entered the tunnel, you used flashlights, correct?"

"Not at first. Once we were inside, there were different times that we would have to illuminate and then not illuminate for tactical reasons."

"So you're turning on and off your flashlight?"

"At different points; yes, sir."

"So, then, when you have your flashlight on, you're telling us you are an easy target, true?" Zitny apparently wanted the jury to see that his client had plenty of opportunity to open fire on these easy targets, but admirably restrained himself. Could his strategy backfire? Would it also demonstrate that Namey was in complete control of his emotions, and not in the mental fog he claimed had blurred his mind just a few days earlier? Zitny rammed home the point anyway. "And at the time you were an easy target, you didn't receive any gunfire from my client, correct?"

"No, sir." McCarthy's negative answer could be interpreted that Zitny's query was not correct, but everyone accepted that he meant there had, indeed, been no gunfire.

A few more questions by Zitny verified statements already made. The defender then focused on the canine "alerting."

"You say your dog alerted the second time—he is now inside the tunnel, true?"

"Yes."

"Was that because your dog was biting my client?"

McCarthy was having no part of it. "No," he snapped.

"The dog was barking, true?"

"Yes, sir."

"And then you heard my client's voice going farther away?"

"I instructed him to talk to us so I would know where

he was in the tunnel. And it appeared to me, based on the sound, that he was getting farther away from us, not closer."

"Now, you never had your dog jump back out of that tunnel, true?"

Not true. McCarthy had called him back once, and then, minutes later, sent the dog again.

"Okay, and then you heard the dog start to bite my client, true?"

"I heard a struggle—I would assume that my dog had engaged the suspect."

"You heard your dog bite other suspects before, correct?" The witness said he had. "And it's a rather unique sound, your dog growling. You recognize the sound of your dog's growl, true?"

"Yes."

"And your dog, you could hear him biting my client, correct?" Zitny was unrelenting in branding the image into jurors' minds.

"I could hear the fight; yes, sir."

"And was your dog injured in any way?"

"No."

Namey, who had shot two people, wouldn't stoop to injuring a dog—an impression the defense apparently thought important. Zitny painted the picture even brighter. "So [Chris] didn't have any bruises or he wasn't hit or anything of that nature, true?"

"I didn't see any injuries on him. I don't know if he was hit or kicked."

Like a bulldog himself, Zitny wouldn't let go. "Part of your duties is to check your dog after your dog seizes somebody for any type of injuries, correct?"

"Yes."

"And you did that?"

"Yes."

"And to the best of your knowledge, your dog didn't suffer any injuries, right?"

"Not that I could see."

"And now, where did your dog bite my client?" More effort to depict a snarling animal attacking a gentle human being?

"Like I said, when I crawled up, I saw the dog engaged on the leg bite. But, according to statements from the defendant and injuries, he also had bit the suspect on the forearm."

"And did you see any injuries?" No, said McCarthy, and he wasn't looking for any. Even though he had witnessed a fellow officer handcuff Namey, he hadn't personally observed any bite marks. Zitny asked, "You found the handgun close to my client's hand, true? Within reach?"

"Within arm's reach, yes."

"So the gun was there, available to shoot the dog; would you agree with that?"

"Yes."

"But the dog was never shot, true?" McCarthy said the statement was true. Apparently satisfied, Zitny changed direction and asked where the long underground tunnel led. McCarthy didn't know, having never gone any farther into it than the site of the side tube. "So you didn't follow it to the exit?"

The witness's expression told observers his opinion of the question. "No. I was pretty tired from crawling up the feeder tube."

Zitny backed away from it and asked, "Were you the person who actually recovered the gun?"

"Yes, sir."

"And you looked to see if it was loaded?" McCarthy had, and verified that the weapon was fully loaded. To the next query, he replied that he had not searched Namey. "Were you present when he was searched?"

"I don't recall. Once he was handcuffed, I was controlling my dog."

After a few more inquiries, Mike McCarthy was excused.

Dennis Conway called another police officer to the witness stand, Placentia PD detective Gene Stuckenschneider. He told of being the first officer, along with his partner, Cory Wolik, at the crime scene where Sarah Rodriquez lay dead in her red Kia, alongside Matt Corbett, who was wounded and paralyzed. The stricken youth had tried to answer questions. Stuckenschneider said, "He told me that [the shooter] was in a black vehicle and that he lived in the city of Santa Ana, and that he had been in trouble with the law before."

His face a scarlet hue, Zitny rose and objected. The judge partially agreed. "The last part is stricken. The jury is admonished to disregard it." Toohey stood on firm legal ground in his decision. Previous "trouble with the law" could not be allowed as evidence against the defendant, except within restrictions tinier than a busboy's tips. Conway knew all about that. Still, the words resonated in the courtroom, and jurors, being human, might ignore instructions to erase "trouble with the law" from their minds.

The detective concluded his short testimony by stating that he had stayed with Matt until the ambulance arrived and took him away. Zitny chose not to cross-examine Stuckenschneider, but he reserved the right to recall him if needed. The jury filed out for a long lunch break.

When Judge Toohey opened court for the afternoon session, a hearing was held outside the jury's presence. Defender Zitny asked Toohey to abort the trial. He stated, "I would be making a motion for a mistrial based on Officer Stuckenschneider's last comment." According to Zitny, the officer had tried to "sneak in" a comment about Namey's prior record of being in trouble with the law. "And now we cannot unring the bell. And I know that the court has already admonished the jury. But with that evidence being brought forward in such a manner by Officer Stuckenschneider, I'm asking for a mistrial."

Toohey turned to Conway for argument. The prosecutor said, "Your Honor, it was completely inadvertent. It was a snafu. . . . There was an objection, and an admonition. And we moved on. There was really not much made of it." Earlier, Dennis had listened carefully to Zitny's opening statements. Recalling the defender's own words, he commented, "If what counsel said bears out, it appears that the defendant is going to testify. The jury, in the long run, will hear about a prior—at least one prior contact with the law. I would submit to the court."

Toohey was obviously not very happy with the detective's utterance, but ruled against Zitny's request. "The motion for mistrial is denied. . . . the court struck the comment and ordered the jury to disregard it. The motion is denied."

The next witness Conway summoned portrayed himself as yet another victim. "Your Honor, the people call Alberto Zavala." Namey was accused of carjacking the witness's van, and Detective Gomez had suggested that Zavala might be involved in drug trafficking. What could he, or would he, tell the jury about Richard Namey?

The portly, pockmarked van owner waddled to the stand and agreed to tell the whole truth. If he was really a drug dealer, as had been implied, would he really honor the oath, or rely on street-style mendacity?

Conway produced several photographs of the red Safari van and Zavala identified it as the one he had owned for four months, and was taken from him in April 2003. Asked to identify the person who took it, Zavala pointed to Namey.

To the next question, inquiring if the witness had previously known the defendant, Zavala grunted, "No." In recalling the parking-lot incident, Zavala said that he had stopped to let pedestrians pass when Namey appeared at the passenger side of the van and asked for a dollar for bus fare. "I reached in my right pocket and I didn't have any change. So I was going to get my wallet. And that's when he approached with a gun." Zavala couldn't remember whether the weapon was a revolver or a semiautomatic. "It's a black gun. I'm not too familiar with guns. . . . He opened the door and got into the seat and pointed the gun at me."

Namey, the witness said, had given explicit directions where to drive and Zavala had followed them exactly. Why? "I was scared." They had taken a circular route, ending not far from the market, and Namey had ordered him to stop. Zavala had obeyed instantly, he said, braking in the middle of a street. "He told me to put it in park and give him my wallet." Instead of handing over his wallet, the witness had jumped out of the vehicle and sprinted away. "I went behind the van. Then I went a couple of cars behind there and [was] hiding. . . . I ran to my house." How far was that? "A good—I would say, close to two miles, maybe."

According to Zavala, he had been unaware that his van was equipped with a LoJack device. After he had made a police report, he was startled when an officer called that same night with information that his vehicle had been recovered. A patrol car had picked him up and provided transportation to Foothill High School, where the high-speed chase had ended. When they arrived, Namey was ordered to exit the rear seat of a police cruiser and stand in the beam of a spotlight. Zavala readily identified him as the person who had stolen his red Safari. After investigators searched the van "three times," they released it to Zavala and had allowed him to drive away.

Conway decided to tackle the issue of drugs being found in the van. "Did anyone ask you or confront you about transporting any narcotics or any kind of controlled substances in the van?"

"No, sir."

"If I was to tell you that there was some controlled substances in that van, and I asked if those were yours or not—".

Zavala didn't wait for the full question. "No, sir," he declared.

"They were not?"

"No."

Nodding toward the defense table, Conway thanked the witness and sat down.

John Zitny's questions on cross-examination seemed to be aimed at exposing Zavala as a drug dealer. What would that prove other than suggesting Namey had planned to buy drugs and wound up trying to take everything from Zavala? It couldn't mitigate the murder. Perhaps Zitny was simply trying to undermine the charge of carjacking.

"Now, sir," Zitny asked, "you told us that you were never confronted with the drugs in that van being yours; do you remember you just said that?"

"I didn't know nothing about that."

"Weren't you confronted by the police who asked

you if you were selling drugs?" The witness seemed to
be hedging by saying he didn't understand. Zitny asked
if two police officers had visited him at home.

Zavala's face wrinkled in apparent confusion. "That's
the next day, or two days. I can't remember." Zitny clar-
ified it. Had the police accused him of selling drugs? The
witness mumbled, "They say something like that. But I
told them it's not mine."

"Did they tell you they had some outside information
that implicated you in the selling of drugs?"

The corpulent man's memory failed again. "Not that
I recall."

The defense lawyer pulled statements from Zavala indicating that he had never seen Namey before that day,
nor had he seen him since. He then asked, "How could
you identify him so quickly? I mean, you looked over at
him, just like that. You said you recognized him?"

Without hesitation, Zavala shot back, "Sir, when they
put a gun to you, you got to recognize the pistol, the gun,
whatever it was. And I recognize him."

Seizing on the first few words, Zitny said, "Well, you
recognized the gun. But you actually recognized him because you had seen him plenty of times before; isn't that
true?" Zavala denied it, so Zitny took another tack.
"Was the parking lot crowded or was it empty?" Local residents know that the lot is seldom full.

"It was pretty crowded." Zavala's statement to police
had indicated that he drove around the strip mall
several times in search of a parking place. He admitted
to Zitny that he had been in the lot for about ten minutes, and had planned to shop in an auto parts store.

"Did you go into the auto parts?"

"It was too full. I couldn't find a parking . . . People
have cars, sir." He disavowed searching for anyone in par-

ticular, or speaking to anyone while repeatedly driving back and forth in front of the stores.

"Now, you are saying that he pulled out a gun while he was outside your car; is that correct?" Zavala said it was. "And this is in broad daylight?" Yes. With other cars passing nearby? And people walking by?

"I imagine so. Yes. It happened so fast, sir."

But Zitny let the reference to "imagine" pass. "So, in the middle of broad daylight, you are saying, my client pulled out a gun in the middle of a very busy, full parking lot, the budget market parking lot, and pointed it at you, correct?" Yes. "And did he point it at you through the window?"

His voice lower and hoarse, Zavala replied, "Yes."

"Okay. Now, does that sound believable that the gun—"

Conway objected. "Argumentative." Judge Toohey sustained it.

The defender rephrased his question, but loaded it with skepticism, emphasizing how unlikely it was that no witnesses could be found who saw these dramatic events. He added an inquiry about the lot being a site for drug sales, but Toohey sustained another objection. "Isn't it true that my client signaled you because he wanted to buy some heroin from you?" This, too, would probably have resulted in a sustained objection, but Conway let it slide. Zavala said it wasn't true.

At Zitny's request, Zavala drew a diagram to illustrate the sequence of events, and answered a series of questions covering the same ground. The witness reiterated that he had no knowledge of drugs found in the van. The defender's interrogation suggested that Zavala might have carried some of his drugs home when he ran away from the van. Why did he speak to the police outside of his home rather than inside? Was he trying to hide a drug supply from the police?

When that line of questioning produced no real evidence, but probably cemented the desired impression on jurors' minds, Zitny shifted to Zavala's source of income, and heard the witness say he worked only part-time. "But you had enough money to buy this eleven-thousand-dollar van?"

"Yes." He didn't elaborate. To inquiries about the LoJack, Zavala professed no knowledge.

Another fifteen minutes of exchanges produced nothing new, other than Zitny posing the possibility that Zavala had met with the DA and rehearsed his answers.

A brief redirect examination by Conway made it clear that he and Zavala had met for the first time just hours earlier. The witness left in a hurry, perhaps wondering if he would soon be charged with selling drugs.

To wind up the first day of testimony, Conway summoned Marc St. Lawrence, the community college security guard who had taken Sarah's report of being assaulted by Namey at her night school. The witness said that Sarah appeared "teary-eyed, shaky, kind of panicked" when he spoke to her. From her statements, and his own observation of her bruised throat, St. Lawrence had prepared a written account of the incident, and relinquished the investigation to officers from the Anaheim Police Department when they arrived on the scene.

CHAPTER 22

"I Heard Sarah Screaming"

A drenching season of record-setting rainfall for Orange County loomed in the near future on the cloudy Monday morning of September 27, 2004. Brisk breezes swept tumbling leaves along sidewalks bordering Civic Center Drive in Santa Ana as lawyers, jurors, witnesses, employees, and court watchers hurried from parking lots to the twelve-story Central Superior Court building.

In department C-36, Judge Richard Toohey greeted the well-rested jurors, hoping they had enjoyed the weekend, then said, "Mr. Conway, you may call your next witness."

A soft-spoken, attractive teenager, Megan Gilbert, strode self-consciously through the double doors leading from an outer hallway and took the oath. She answered Conway's questions about the horrifying experience of witnessing, from her parents' bathroom and bedroom, the shooting of two people in a red car, seventeen months earlier.

At one point in her testimony, Megan had a little

trouble remembering if she had heard gunshots after the shooter had circled to the driver's side of the red vehicle. Conway offered to let her refresh her memory by examining some notes she had written to herself shortly after the traumatic incident. Zitny objected, but stepped over the "objections" line that most judges dislike.

Zitny stood and said, "Your Honor, I believe this line of questioning has already been asked and answered."

Judge Toohey snapped, "I don't want any speaking objections."

Zitny tried again with a briefer version: "Asked and answered." But Toohey overruled it.

After examining her own notes, Megan said she recalled that the black-clad young man had fired two more shots after walking to the driver's side. Forensic examiners had surmised that Namey fired four shots at Matt, through the open passenger window, and only one shot at Sarah on the driver's side. The weapon held five rounds. But it was certainly possible that Namey had pulled the trigger three times in shooting Matt, and twice at Sarah, with the final bullet missing her and hitting Matt. No one, except perhaps Namey, will ever know precisely. In Megan's memory, she heard two shots in the second barrage.

While Megan could recall seeing the shooter extend one of his arms toward the victims, she couldn't remember which arm was raised. Observers were also surprised when she was unable to make the identification of Namey as the man who had blasted away at two victims.

In Megan's testimony, and in her notes written a few days later, she recalled seeing a tan-colored car drive slowly by during the confrontation on the street below her home. But in her original 911 report, she had made no mention of the passing vehicle. On cross-examination, Zitny brought up this discrepancy. His questioning seemed to suggest that she may have enhanced her story by adding the extra car after discussing the incident with friends at school. "When you wrote your notes, you had already been to school? You had been to school at that time?"

Calmly, with a tiny hint of disdain, the sixteen-year-old girl said, "No. We were on spring break."

Zitny ended his cross with just a few more questions, turning up nothing of any consequence.

Within seconds after Megan walked out, everyone in the courtroom inhaled sharply when the next witness entered. Matt Corbett, holding his head high, rolled forward in his wheelchair. People familiar with the news media accounts couldn't resist stealing a glance at his face. They knew that a bullet had torn through Matt's nasal passage and taken out his left eye. It was a relief to see that the prosthetic replacement was virtually undetectable. To his family and acquaintances, the handsome face was unchanged, still reflecting his pride and strength. News stories had told of his quadriplegic paralysis, so it pleased many to see that he had regained the use of his hands and arms.

Matt swore to tell the truth and testified from his own chair. Conway said, "Good morning, Mr. Corbett. Thanks for coming in. If you need a break for any reason, just let us know, okay?"

After seventeen months of dealing with his injuries, and now accustomed to special courtesies from some people, rude stares and comments from others, Matt answered simply, "Okay."

"Mr. Corbett, do you know Sarah Rodriquez?"

"Yes. I was dating her for four years."

"How old were you and Sarah when you first met?"

"I was sixteen. She was seventeen."

"Safe to say, over the years, you were close?"

"Yeah."

"Your families were close?"

"Very close." Matt said that he lived in Westminster, about twenty-five minutes from Sarah's house.

Conway looked toward the defendant, but spoke to Matt. "Directing your attention to the end of the table, the person in the checkered shirt, the defendant, Richard Namey, do you recognize him?"

Matt kept his voice level, avoiding manifestation of the hatred he felt. "Sure do."

"When is the first time you ever saw him?"

"April 2, 2003."

"Prior to that, when did you become aware of him?"

"It would have to be her Anaheim night school. It was a college class she was taking."

"Were you aware of Sarah getting a restraining order?"

"Yes, I was. I assisted her. I drove her."

A silent tension hung in the room and nothing could be heard other than Conway's and Matt's voices. Sometimes in trials, human drama exceeds anything ever seen in film, television, or theater. Matt's presence and his firm answers built one of those moments. The gallery seats were all filled, and every observer glued their attention to this young man.

Conway understood what Matt had gone through in losing Sarah, the woman he loved. His own agony when Lisa Barrett died in a car wreck remained with him. Yet, as prosecutor, Conway's job demanded that he ask tough questions to get the evidence and facts on record. "Did you know—or were you ever aware of her keeping a journal?"

"No, I wasn't."

Veering away from that for the moment, Conway

took Matt back to the first time he'd ever seen Namey. Matt said he'd been with Sarah at Bible study with her father and brother, not far from Sarah's home. They arrived in their own cars and left separately just before sunset, Matt in his '96 GMC Sonoma pickup, and Sarah in her red Kia Rio. He had customized the truck. Conway asked, "Was that one of your hobbies back then?"

Matt's answer showed observers how he wasn't letting his injury wreck his life. "Yeah. Still is."

"So you were following Sarah?"

"I followed her to the point where she would go to her house and I would go straight, to go on the freeway." They had been speaking to one another on cell phones, he said, even after they turned in separate directions. "All of a sudden, she hung up. I called back and she didn't answer, so I decided to make a U-turn. . . . I was kinda worried about it. I backtracked, and that's when I saw that punk over there had her cornered. " This time, the vitriol in his voice was unmasked.

Zitny stood and avoided the speaking objection by saying simply, "Motion to strike."

The judge said, "The conclusion about 'had her cornered' is stricken." He said nothing about the word "punk."

Conway constructed his questions to establish the location, two blocks from Sarah's house, and that she was in her red Kia. The prosecutor paused when Matt gripped the arms of his chair and raised his body slightly. "Are you uncomfortable?"

"No." Matt didn't bother to explain that he did this frequently to adjust his sitting position.

"You'll let us know, right?"

"Yes."

Continuing his account of the incident, Matt said he observed that the blue El Camino had blocked Sarah's car and that Namey was "yelling at her through the window. I pulled up behind Namey."

"You were in your custom truck . . . and you could hear Namey yelling?"

"Yeah." The windows were down in all three vehicles.

"What could you hear him yelling?"

"He said, 'You're only making things worse for yourself.' She was, you know, frantic."

"If you hadn't seen Namey before, how did you know that it was him yelling at Sarah?"

"Because Sarah had told me that he drove a blue El Camino, and when I pulled up, that's exactly what he was in when he had Sarah cornered."

"What did you do?"

"I ran out and I said, 'Why don't you pick on somebody your own size?' As I ran toward him, he took off and flipped me off."

"Was it light or dark when you came upon this?"

"It was dark. It wasn't pitch dark, but the sun was just setting. Lights were on, streetlights."

"Did you get a good look at his face?"

"Yeah, as he turned around. Yes, I did."

"When you got out of your truck, he was still in his vehicle and you ran toward him?" Matt nodded and said yes.

"What were you going to do if you caught him?"

"Kick the living shit out of him." Zitny leaped to his feet with a motion to strike the comment, while Matt added to it, "He knows it."

Judge Toohey spoke slowly to cool the heat of the moment. "I'm going to strike the answer. Restate the question."

Conway worded a new one instead. The jury had heard Matt's honest answer, and whether or not it would enter into their deliberations, they undoubtedly understood how he felt. "How tall are you?" Matt said he was five-ten. "Back then, what kind of physical shape were you in?"

"Pretty good. I worked five A.M. to five P.M., Monday through Friday, unloading trucks all day. I worked out with my buddy Mike and ran. So, pretty good." Matt's answer made his current physical disability even more poignant.

The witness, in response to Conway, said that Namey had sped away, with tires squealing.

"And he flipped you off. Do you mean he gave you the middle finger?"

"Correct."

"What did you do after he drove off?"

"I ran toward my truck, and Sarah said, 'No, Matt, don't chase him. He said he had a gun.'"

Zitny made a motion to strike the quote from Sarah as hearsay, and Toohey sustained it.

"Did you get in your truck and try to chase him?"

"Yes, I did. He had taken off before I did. I ran straight toward my truck. I chased him through Sarah's neighborhood. I passed Martha's house. As she was out front trying to tell me something, I just kept going. I had lost him when I got toward Jefferson Street, and as I entered Jefferson, I asked some bystanders if they had seen a blue El Camino."

"Were you able to catch him?"

"No." In Matt's answers, he told of returning to Sarah's home and learning from her what had happened prior to his arrival. "She was very scared, shaky, scared about what might happen to her and to me. She said that she had thrown a copy of the restraining order—"

Zitny avoided a speaking objection with the simple statement, "Again, hearsay objection." But this time he was overruled.

Matt continued as if he hadn't been interrupted: "—threw a copy of the restraining order in Namey's window, and he had told her, 'You're making things worse for yourself.' And she was very scared."

In a weary voice, Zitny spoke. "Motion to strike. Now we're getting into double hearsay."

Without even glancing at the defender, Toohey said to Conway, "Ask your next question."

The prosecutor inquired, "Now, after this incident, did you see Namey again?"

"Not for a while."

"Not until April sixteenth?" Conway referred to the date Namey had shot Sarah and Matt. The witness agreed. "And from April second until April sixteenth, did you take any precautions to look out for Sarah?"

"Yes, I did. . . . Before work, I would usually drive around her neighborhood, make sure I didn't see his vehicle. I was trying to keep her—trying to make her feel safe. I always tried to do my best to make sure she was safe."

Once again Zitny stood. "I'm going to object as irrelevant." Toohey sustained it.

Advancing the action to the date of the shooting, Conway asked, "What were you doing that day?"

"I worked, went home, washed my truck, went to Sarah's to grab a bite to eat. We went to McDonald's in Sarah's car because I just got her a new stereo and she loved it, put a big smile on her face, and she wanted to drive her car." Matt was the passenger as they traveled to the fast-food restaurant about ten minutes from Sarah's home and returned along Jefferson Street.

"At some point on Jefferson, before turning onto Hill Street, did you see a black car approach?"

"Yes. As we headed down Jefferson, right before we hit Hill Street to make a right, Namey was parked at the curb. As he came peeling out toward us, we made a right. He followed us, continued until he got in front of Sarah's, where we stopped." As Matt spoke, he again lifted himself from the wheelchair seat momentarily. Conway asked if he needed a break, but Matt said, "I'm fine."

"And did the black [Nissan] actually get up next to Sarah's car?"

"Yes, very close . . . on the driver's side." The Kia's windows were down, as were the Nissan's, said Matt. He had made eye contact with Namey.

Dennis wanted to know if any words were exchanged. Namey had shouted something, said Matt, but he hadn't responded. Sarah "was yelling. She was scared, saying, 'I'm going to call the police.' Namey said, 'Go ahead.'"

"Did the cars come to a stop?"

"Yes. He pulled in front of Sarah's car just like he did on April second, same thing."

"What happens then?"

"He got out of the car. It happened very quickly. He ran toward me with a gun at his side. I didn't see it right away." As the audience listened breathlessly, Matt told of Namey stopping at the passenger side and barking, "How do you like me now?"

Spectators sat stone-still, bodies tense, afraid of missing a single word. Matt said, "He pointed the gun and I went like this . . ." He held his hands up as if signaling the assailant to stop. "As I turned my head, he shot me."

Conway reconfirmed a few of the circumstances through several questions, then asked, "Where do you recall getting shot?"

Pointing to a spot just below his right ear, Matt said, "I was shot right here . . . close underneath my right temple."

"What did you feel or experience at that point?"

The answer was chilling. "I didn't feel anything really. It went right out my left eye and I couldn't see."

"Were you able to remain conscious?"

"Yes. I heard Sarah screaming."

"Did you hear or feel any more gunshots?"

"Yeah . . . like three more. I felt only one more. After he shot me again, that's when I laid down, kind of slouched over." The barrel of the weapon, he said, had been close, ". . . probably from my mouth to the microphone."

For the record, Judge Toohey said, "Indicating a distance of approximately six inches."

Asked if he had ever lost consciousness, Matt replied, "I just heard Sarah screaming, and after that, I kind of went out of it. . . . I just remember breathing real lightly and staring at the [steering] column of her car."

"As a result of getting shot—you indicated you were shot through the right side below your ear. What was the result of the damage of that gunshot?"

"It went through my nasal passage. It's kind of hard to breathe through there. And it took out my left eye." Another round had grazed the back of Matt's head, and one had ended up lodged against his spinal cord. "It paralyzed me, and I was shot once more in my left arm."

Regarding the paralysis, Conway asked, "Your prognosis at this point for life is in a wheelchair?"

Unwilling to accept such a permanent fate, Matt spoke optimistically. "I just hope for the best."

A final shot had been fired by Namey, ending Sarah's life, but Matt said he hadn't heard that one. He did recall the police arriving and asking questions, then being taken to the hospital. And he had been able to pick Namey's picture out of a group of six mug shots as the shooter.

"How certain were you of that identification?"

"I was positive."

After Conway aired facts about Matt having bullets removed from his body months later, he said, "And I imagine you have a lot of medical difficulties and day-to-day problems?"

Matt's simple answer spoke volumes. "Oh yeah. Quite a bit."

"Thank you, Mr. Corbett."

Following a morning break, Matt Corbett remained in front of the court, still under oath. For defense attorneys, cross-examining a surviving victim can be treacherous. A slight slip of the tongue might easily alienate the jury. Yet, to let the direct-examination testimony go without any effort to clarify some points could have the appearance of capitulation. John Zitny stood to ask questions of the witness.

"Good morning. You told us you went with Sarah to get that restraining order?"

"Yes." Matt had been with her during the entire process.

Skipping to another issue, Zitny said, "I'm going to go to the April second incident. You told us you had a truck; is that true?"

"Yes."

Through his questions, Zitny challenged Matt's ability to hear anything Sarah or Namey said at the time, due to the truck's "loud" muffler.

After a few more queries, the defender moved on to April 16. In reconstructing the events, he made an interesting change when referring to Namey. Instead of calling him "my client," he now preferred to use the more intimate "Rick." Many judges insist that counsel refer to witnesses and clients by their surnames. Toohey showed no preference.

When the moving cars were side by side, "you could look at Rick's face, and he was obviously extremely upset; is that correct?" Zitny asked.

"Correct."

After a few more inquiries, Zitny asked, "You've shot guns before; is that true?" The witness said he had, and that he knew the difference between a revolver and an automatic.

"And it happened so fast, you told the officers that you couldn't identify [the weapon] as an automatic or a revolver?" This seemed puzzling. Did it make any real difference whether the wounded victim could tell police what type of handgun had been used? Weren't the injuries to Matt's body evidence enough?

Matt didn't appear to be upset by it. "At that point, yeah. I was under a lot of sedation as well. My answer was kind of—I didn't see the gun right away. It was hidden on his side. It happened really fast. I couldn't really tell."

Zitny apparently didn't like Matt's response. "Motion to strike as nonresponsive."

After having the question and answer read aloud by court reporter Kimberly Owen, the judge ruled, "The answer will remain."

Zitny asked, "Now, did you actually see Rick Namey leave Hill Street? Did you see him get back in the car and leave?"

A few observers thought the question insensitive and unnecessary. Even Matt seemed perplexed. "After everything had happened? After I was shot?"

"Yes."

"No, I didn't."

"Did you see another car drive around you while Rick Namey was still there?" Witness Megan Gilbert had mentioned another car passing the crime scene.

"No, I didn't. I don't remember anything after I was shot that many times."

Jumping to another topic, Zitny asked if Matt had dated Sarah for approximately four years. Matt corrected him. "It was five years. It would have been five years this August."

"At any point during your relationship, did you break up?"

"We argued for about—a few months. We were arguing. I wouldn't call it split up. We were kinda keeping our distance." But they were still "romantically together."

"Did Sarah ever tell you that she was having a romantic relationship with Rick Namey during August of 2002?" Judge Toohey sustained Conway's objection that it would be hearsay. So Zitny rephrased it. "Did you ever have knowledge that she was having a relationship with Rick Namey, a romantic one?" Matt said he didn't, and that he couldn't remember exactly what months he and Sarah argued.

"Okay, so do you have any knowledge that Sarah Rodriquez was seeing both you and Rick Namey at the same time during 2002?"

"No. I find it very hard to believe that she would have been. I was with her a lot."

"And if you had found that out, would that have made you upset?"

"Yeah, it would have."

Zitny thanked the witness and said, "Nothing further."

Conway accepted the opportunity to conduct a few minutes of redirect. "On the sixteenth, when Sarah drove with the new stereo in her car, where was your truck?"

"Parked in front of Martha and Sarah's house."

"Have you learned since then, that Sarah had a relationship with Namey?"

For the first time, Matt's voice seemed to falter. "I never knew she had a . . . She—"

Conway interrupted. "Did you love Sarah?"

"Very much. Still do."

"Does that change what you think of her or how you feel about her?"

"Not at all. People make mistakes. We're young. There's—"

Zitny cut him off with, "No question pending."

Judge Toohey advised, "You've answered the question. Anything further, Mr. Conway?"

"No, Your Honor."

If Zitny had considered asking anything else, he thought better of it and agreed to excuse the witness.

Matt Corbett left the courtroom in his wheelchair, head held as high as when he entered.

During a sidebar, Conway brought out three photographs taken during the autopsy of Sarah Rodriquez's body. They had been carefully cropped to excise gory aspects unnecessary for the jury to see. Conway simply wanted to show the bullet wounds to her head, arm, and right side. Stippling and gunpowder "sooting" caused by the gun barrel's close proximity to her skin would be evidence of intent, premeditation, and deliberation, said the prosecutor. Zitny objected to allowing the photos on the grounds of Evidence Code 352, asserting that the "probative value is not outweighed by the prejudicial effect." Noting that the pictures had been cropped, Toohey ruled that they were admissible as evidence.

To introduce the photos, Conway brought expert Laurie Crutchfield to the stand. Well known to the law community as a forensic scientist at the Orange County

Crime Lab, Crutchfield explained that she was currently assigned to crime scene investigation, as well as firearms examination. In addition to extensive formal training and working endless crime scenes, she had honed her knowledge by attending hundreds of autopsies to observe the precise effects of death from gunshot wounds. Her ten years of experience in the job had helped send scores of killers to prison and to death row, including Adriana Vasco.

Conway quizzed Crutchfield about procedures in determining that a slug had been fired from a specific gun. Speaking with confidence commensurate with her expertise, Crutchfield led juries through the process of microscopically examining an expended bullet: class characteristics, dimension, caliber, and direction of twist. She spoke of markings called "lands and grooves," and the striations etched as the projectile travels through the weapon's barrel. "Actually," she said, "the markings on the bullet begin with the markings made on the firearm when it's manufactured. The barrel . . . goes through several processes to not only put what we refer to as grooves in the barrel, but then it has finishing processes that buff out the burrs in the barrel. Sometimes the muzzle ends are crowned, which may put additional defects on it. When the bullet is fired, these markings create scratches on the bullet surfaces . . . unique to that individual firearm."

To make certain the jury understood, Conway asked why the bullet is so marked as it travels through the barrel. "Is it made of a softer material than the bullet itself?"

The witness said it was. "It will expand to completely fit the interior of the barrel . . . thus it is etched with the weapon's characteristics."

Removing a .357-caliber revolver from a box, along

with a speedloader, Conway showed both items to Crutchfield, who verified the handgun was the one used to shoot Matt Corbett and Sarah Rodriquez. The witness explained the use of the speedloader, which had been found among Namey's possessions. "It is a device you place unfired cartridges in, and when the cylinder needs to be loaded rapidly, instead of putting each cartridge in one at a time, you just take the speed-loader, put it at the back end of the cylinder . . . and turn the knob." All five rounds are inserted with one movement.

Testing of the revolver by Crutchfield had included microscopic examination of the stippling left on a target surface.

A box of the ammunition used in the shooting, PMC brand, had been found in the red Safari van. Crutchfield informed the court that she had searched various stores for it and finally found it available in a Santa Ana shop.

"This particular ammunition, is there anything unique about its characteristics?" Conway inquired.

The witness said that it was "made to mimic what the cowboys used in the 1880s, with a heavier weight lead bullet, and was supposed to have a lighter recoil than typical three fifty-seven ammunition." In test-firing the revolver, she had used white cotton twill in the target, which allows the retention of gunpowder particle residue. These particles are called "soot" by the examiner. The distance from the muzzle to the target can be measured by the distribution and volume of soot. Crutchfield had fired shots at "near contact" range, from distances of three, six, twelve, and eighteen inches, and one "side shot without creating a hole to show the powder from the cylinder gap in the muzzle at an angle." At Conway's request, she showed the jury targets she had used and explained the various soot deposits.

After handing the witness a photograph of the bullet wound in Sarah Rodriquez's head, Conway asked, "Do you have an opinion as to how far from Sarah's head that gun was fired?"

Crutchfield said the muzzle had been from "near contact" to less than twelve inches away.

Regarding an expended bullet found inside Sarah's car, the witness had made comparison testing, by firing a similar round into a water tank and recovering it. She had found that it was "similar in bullet type and style as the PMC cowboy-action load. It had the same class rifling characteristics as those of the submitted revolver, but it lacked sufficient quality and quantity of markings for me to identify that it had been fired from that revolver." Her answer amounted to a definite maybe.

Another bullet she examined had been removed from Sarah's body at the autopsy. It, too, was "similar," but not in adequate condition to make a positive identification. Crutchfield pointed out that bullets are distorted by whatever they make contact with. These PMC cowboy rounds were made of soft lead, which is easily damaged.

Conway tried to tighten the possibility that these bullets came from Namey's revolver by asking, "So you can't exclude the fact that those two bullets may have been fired from the same gun?"

"Correct," said the witness. She also had tested two additional slugs surgically removed from Matt Corbett's body at his request. One bullet, said Crutchfield, was inconclusive because it lacked quality and quantity of markings. But the other one, she declared, "I identified as having been fired from the Charter Arms revolver."

Matt had submitted to extra surgery in hopes that he could provide useful evidence. By all appearances, it had worked.

Satisfied, Conway turned the witness over to Zitny for cross-examination. Mentioning the entry and exit wounds to Sarah's head, he framed questions about whether the weapon had been pointed at a downward angle when fired. The inquiry didn't change any of Crutchfield's opinions, and she was excused within a few minutes.

The autopsy of Sarah had been performed by Dr. David Katsuyama, who seated himself in the witness chair. Katsuyama told of examining the bullet wound to Sarah's head. It had pierced her skull on the left side, in front of the ear, and exited "toward the back of the left side." The doctor said it entered "in a slightly upward direction toward the back of the left side of the head, going into the skin, penetrating into the skull and damaging, distorting, disrupting large areas of the brain's substance, and exiting on the top upper left portion of the left side."

"And the bullet, path of travel from entrance to exit, did it appear when you conducted the autopsy to be straight?"

"Essentially, yes. The bullet had not appeared to have broken up in large pieces." To another question, he replied, "One needs to keep in mind that the head is mobile, and it could have been leaning forward; it could have been leaning to the side; it could have even been turned to its side." One could imagine Sarah's terror at having just seen Matt savagely shot, feeling a bullet rip into her side, then seeing the gun barrel aimed at her face. It was easy to understand that she might have desperately tried to twist away from it. The doctor further commented that the bullet had not entered perpendicular to her face, but had taken an angular path.

Knowing that Sarah's family sat in the audience, Conway dreaded the answers coming from Katsuyama, but had no way of avoiding the necessary questions. "Doctor, what would the effect of this gunshot would be to the victim?"

"Essentially, it would definitely stun the—at least stun the victim, very likely rendering her unconscious, very likely causing her some incapacity in her breathing ability."

"Would it be fatal, just the gunshot wound?"

"From that gunshot wound itself, she would have died at some point in time, maybe within a few minutes, depending on whether medical assistance got to her and tried to keep her alive. They might have been successful in that aspect for some period of time." He spoke also of a separate injury. "The decedent had another wound on the side of her chest, almost in the armpit area, on the outer portion of her right breast pointing in somewhat backward direction from the right to the left, very slightly downward. And during the course of the examination on her back, underneath the tip of her left shoulder blade, one could see some discoloration and slight bulging. . . . I excised, cut into that area, and recovered a gray metal bullet. . . ."

"What damage was caused by that bullet as it traveled through the decedent's body?"

"It went through her right rib cage, struck the back portion of her right lung, then struck her backbone at about midchest level and went through the lower portion of the back of the left lung and into—almost came out the back of her left chest." This was most likely the bullet fired by Namey from the passenger side, the one that grazed the back of Matt's head. Dr. Katsuyama noted that the projectile had probably resulted in severe bleeding, and perhaps some slight stunning effect. "Although I did not see any damage to her spinal cord . . . it could have rendered her more or less immobile, at least temporarily, from lower chest to waist level so she would not be able to move her legs significantly."

The actual cause of death, said Katsuyama, was blood loss. "She died as a result of bleeding to death, loss of blood from her circulatory system. Only a small amount of blood remained. . . . At that time of my examination, there was a considerable amount of blood in both sides, inside the chest, outside of the lungs, and that would have resulted in her dying, probably—becoming unconscious within a few minutes, if not shorter, and probably heart action completely seizing within, say, ten, fifteen minutes after sustaining that wound."

Conway asked who else was present at the autopsy, to which the doctor answered that Elizabeth Thompson from the crime lab was there to collect any forensic evidence, such as the bullet fragments.

Cross-examination by Zitny returned to the possible angle from which the bullet to Sarah's head had been fired. The witness indicated there were so many variables it was difficult to make a definitive statement in this regard. Zitny next inquired about Katsuyama's experience in correlating damage to a body with specific type and caliber of weapons. The witness replied, "Only to a limited extent," and spoke of the differences between injuries caused by revolvers, with softer lead bullets, versus semiautomatics, which generally use harder, jacketed bullets.

"Would you agree," asked Zitny, "that the lack of damage to [the decedent's] spinal column could have been caused by the bullet passing through another body first, slowing down, and then rattling inside the deceased in this case?" The doctor doubted that the bullet piercing Sarah's side had passed through another body first. He made no comment about it glancing from another victim.

Asked if the bullet he removed from Sarah was "distorted," Katsuyama said that it had been handed to a criminalist, and it was a ballistic expert's job to answer that question, not a pathologist's. He could only say that it was "relatively undeformed, not badly bent out of shape."

On redirect, Conway wanted to clarify the bullet-angle issue twice raised by Zitny. "Could a possible scenario for the bullet wound to the decedent's head be if she's seated in a car and the person with the gun that's doing the shooting is outside her window, window down, standing, and her head is tilted at an angle upward, looking at the person as they shoot her, is that a possible scenario of how she could be positioned when receiving that wound?"

The doctor nodded in the affirmative. "Yes, that's a possible scenario . . . as long as the trajectory, the course of the bullet into her head lines up with the barrel of the weapon, any position that those two are in configuration would be satisfactory to me."

Jurors scribbled notes in pads provided to them as Dr. Katsuyama left the courtroom.

Heavy clouds could be seen out the windows of the ninth floor that Monday afternoon as Conway announced, "The people call Elizabeth Thompson." The senior forensic scientist had worked for the Orange County Sheriff's Crime Laboratory for sixteen years. She took the stand a little after three o'clock, and told jurors she had been at the crime scene on Hill Street to search Sarah's red Kia.

Conway inquired if either of the occupants was near or around the vehicle when Thompson arrived after dark. She said, "The female victim was on the asphalt near the vehicle." Corbett had already been transported to an emergency hospital.

"Did you recover any bullets or bullet fragments inside or around the car?"

"I collected one bullet from underneath the front passenger's seat." She had also noticed uneaten burgers and untouched drinks from McDonald's in the car.

"Did you see any skid marks on the pavement?"

"Yes. There were two, parallel to each other, and they were approximately twenty-five to thirty feet [in front] of the Kia Rio." Of course, there was no way to tell exactly when they were made, even though they looked "fresh."

Responding to Conway's questions, Thompson told of attending the autopsy of Sarah Rodriquez and collecting her bloody T-shirt, with a bullet hole in the right side. She had also conducted a search of the Black Nissan Sentra Namey had driven and abandoned in the market parking lot. "I collected a short-sleeve white T-shirt from the floorboard area of the driver's seat." Large bloodstains smeared the front, body, and right sleeve. From the neck band, Thompson cut pieces of the material containing dried perspiration and skin cells, from which DNA samples could be extracted to show who had been wearing the garment.

After Namey's arrest, his clothing had been given to Thompson, including a pair of white "Fila" tennis shoes. One of them was marked with a spot of blood on the tongue.

Educated and experienced in DNA testing, Thompson had personally carried out the lab procedures. She compared the stains to samples taken from Sarah at the autopsy, from Matt Corbett, and from Richard Namey. DNA from the T-shirt neck band matched the Namey profile. Blood on the front and the sleeve of that same shirt was consistent with Matt Corbett's DNA. And a tiny spot of blood on one of the shoes statistically matched DNA samples from Sarah Rodriquez.

"How could the victims' blood been found on the shirt and shoe?" Conway asked.

"It could be some spatter," Thompson answered. Bullets slamming into the bodies of both victims could have sent "blowback" spots of blood onto the shooter's clothing.

When Zitny took the witness, he wanted more information about the skid marks in front of the Kia. Thompson repeated her earlier answer that they had been found about twenty-five to thirty feet away. Zitny asked, "So there's plenty enough room for somebody to walk in front of the Kia if there was, let's say, that imaginary car parked where those skid marks are at?"

Thompson simply answered, "Yes."

A dark smudge had been observed around the hole on the side of Sarah's T-shirt. Thompson characterized it as "bullet wipe." Zitny asked for a definition of that term.

Thompson explained. "As the bullet passes through the barrel of a gun, it picks up residues from the barrel, and it could be . . . from oil that's present, it could be dried gunpowder residue, metal shavings, so it's stuff that the bullet will collect on its way out of the gun." She acknowledged that this particular bullet wipe was larger than normal.

That seemed to satisfy the defender. He thanked

Thompson and said, "Nothing further." Conway agreed, and the witness stepped down.

After a short recess, Sarah's mother, Martha Dewar, took the long walk from double-entry doors, through the gallery, and to the witness chair. She surprised observers by saying she had never seen Namey prior to his appearance in court. Conway asked her about the incident at night school, on March 27, 2003. "Did you go up to the school in Anaheim and meet your daughter there?"

"Yes, I did." She described her daughter as scared and frightened. Martha verified that photographs of Sarah's neck and arm taken that night showed bruising, and said they were even more evident two days later.

"Did you get a call from Sarah on the morning of April first?"

"Yes. She sounded frantic, scared, very scared. She goes, 'Mom, Mom, he's here. He won't leave me alone.' And I said, 'Who?' She said, 'Richard Namey. He's here. He won't let me go to work.'"

Zitny objected, citing hearsay, but was overruled.

"Did you call the police for her?"

"I did."

"Did you go meet Sarah later at—where was she going that morning, by the way?" Martha said Sarah was on her way to work at the preschool and was about one block away when she called, saying that Namey wouldn't let her proceed. Police officers from the adjacent city, Brea, had arrived and Namey had quickly departed.

Conway inquired if Martha had seen anything of the confrontation on April 2 in which Matt had chased Namey away. She said she had heard the noise of moving cars and seen Matt's truck drive by in pursuit of the blue El Camino. Again, she said, Sarah had been extremely frightened.

On cross, Zitny wondered if Martha had called the police from her home or after she had joined her daughter. Neither, said Martha. She had called from her cell phone en route to the scene, and arrived before the police did.

"And Sarah didn't have any injuries from the April first incident, did she?"

Martha answered, "She still had the same ones from the twenty-seventh of March." To Zitny's persistence, she acknowledged there were no new injuries.

"And you told her that she should get a restraining order?"

"No."

After several more questions, Zitny asked if his client had ever been by Martha's house to visit the family. Martha crisply answered, "Thank God, no."

"All the time since August of 2002, he had never come over to your house?"

"Not to my knowledge, no."

"Did Sarah ever mention him during the time period from August to April?"

"Not in detail." But her daughter had mentioned the name.

"Now, at this same time, was Sarah still going out with Matt Corbett?"

"I can't answer that. I don't know." Martha did say that Matt sometimes came by to pick Sarah up.

"How often, let's say, in September of 2002?"

"I don't recall." She insisted that she didn't know whether the dating was regular or periodic.

"And you are very fond of Matt, right?"

"Yes, I am."

Zitny caught everyone off-guard with his next question.

"Now, you knew your daughter had an abortion in September of 2002?"

Conway jumped up. "Objection, relevance, hearsay."

"Sustained," Toohey barked.

Zitny stayed the course. "Did you have any knowledge that your daughter had an abortion in 2002?" Another objection was sustained. Zitny sat down. "I have nothing further."

Conway abstained from conducting any redirect examination, and Martha left, grateful that her testimony had lasted no longer than a few minutes.

Only two more witnesses remained for the prosecution, and they would be called on the following day.

To Conway, as he left the courtroom, something was missing. He racked his brain, trying to scan all the details. He just couldn't pin down the notion that a key element hadn't yet turned up to convince this jury.

CHAPTER 23

Of Cars, Quakes, and Killing

Spectators filing into Judge Toohey's courtroom on Tuesday morning, September 28, buzzed about the national elections, just a few weeks away, in which President George W. Bush would face Democratic challenger John Kerry. Orange County residents are predominately Republican, even though the state's electoral vote would go to the Democratic candidate.

Dennis Conway made his way through the double doors, carrying boxes and binders, his usual cheerful expression replaced by a frown. The coming election was the least of his worries. Something was still missing in his case against Namey, but he hadn't yet pinned it down.

Before Toohey took his seat, quiet conversations turned from national politics to the trial. Questions hung overhead like a threatening storm. Had the prosecutor presented enough evidence for jurors to convict

Namey of first-degree murder, or even a lesser charge, which might get him a light sentence and freedom within a few years? And when the defense took over, would Namey testify in his own behalf? Conway planned to put only two more witnesses on the stand. The crowd waited eagerly to see who they were.

A slim young man, nineteen, took the witness chair and identified himself as Jeremy Chiong. He lived on Hill Street in Placentia and had witnessed the shooting. After backing his car into the driveway of his home, Chiong had sat in the vehicle using his cell phone when the black Nissan blocked the red Kia. Chiong saw it only peripherally, since he was concentrating on his phone, until he heard a loud scream. "I put my phone down and looked straight ahead. . . . The red car was in front of the black car, and I saw the black car overtake the red one and sort of cut it off at an angle between the curb and the rest of the street."

Even though his windows were up, he realized that the girl driving the red car had screamed. "It appeared like something was really wrong. She had her hands up, and it was high, shrill. . . ."

Conway asked, "What did you see after the cars came to a stop?"

"I saw the man in the black car get out with a gun, and he held it sort of down by his left side, walked around the front of both cars to the passenger's side of the red car and started shooting."

"Did it look like the people in the red car, from the position they were in, would be able to see the gun?"

"I don't think so, because the hood of the black car would be blocking it." When the assailant opened fire on the passenger, Chiong thought he heard two shots.

"Did you see the passenger's reaction to what you describe as gunshots into the car?"

"Just strong body movements, like he was being hit by something pretty hard." The witness had been frightened, he said, causing him to dash into his garage, lock it, hurry into his living room, bolt the door, and then call the police. During this time, he heard more gunshots, but couldn't recall how many. After calling 911, he'd glanced outside again and observed that the black car was gone.

On cross-examination, Zitny asked what color shirt the man with the gun wore. Chiong thought it was black. The defender suggested that the report Chiong made to the police differed in some aspects from his testimony.

"I don't know what you are talking about," the witness protested.

"In the police report, didn't you tell the police officer that you heard two people arguing back and forth from the red car to the black car?"

"I couldn't make out words, but yeah—yes, I could hear."

"Why, today, did you say that what directed your attention was initially a scream?" Conway objected to the question as argumentative and Toohey sustained it. Zitny said, "You never told that first police officer that your attention was directed by a scream, did you?"

"I believe I did."

Zitny seemed skeptical. "The officer just didn't write it down in the report?"

"I guess not." Chiong reiterated that he had heard what sounded like an argument, or loud conversation. "With my windows rolled up, I couldn't make out any words."

Still angling to undermine the testimony, Zitny continued. "Okay, you also told that officer that it appeared to you that they were just friends talking back and forth. Is that what you told the officer on April sixteenth?"

"Yes. That's what I thought, because . . . Can I explain?"

Attorneys seldom allow a witness to explain. They can't predict what might be said. So they generally pretend not to have heard the request. Zitny said, "Well, let me just ask you this: If you told the officer that, why are you telling us today that it sounded like the woman thought that something was very wrong by her screams? It seems like they're two inconsistent stories."

Observers fully expected Conway to object. Apparently, so did the judge, who interposed with, "Excuse me. Is there an objection?"

Conway, though, saw it as a welcome opportunity for the witness to provide details. "No, Your Honor. I'll let him explain."

If Toohey was amused by the turn of events, he didn't show it. "All right, go ahead."

Chiong seemed happy for the chance to articulate what he'd been trying to say. "The reason I thought they were friends is our neighborhood is right next to a park." He referred to the giant greenbelt sports complex on the next block, along Jefferson Street. "And there's a lot of young people that live around there and I see cars sort of—friends talking to each other on that street when they drive, so when I heard a conversation, I didn't think anything of it. I thought it was just some other teenagers, some other friends talking to each other, giving directions."

Undiscouraged, Zitny stayed with it. "You told the officer initially that you heard two people arguing back and forth, true?" The witness patiently reconstructed the sequence of events of the Nissan chasing the Kia, overtaking it, and cutting it off to a halt, and hearing an exchange of unintelligible voices. Zitny asked, "How are they having a conversation if the black car was behind the red car?"

A few of the jurors' expressions seemed perplexed. Observers thought it not so difficult to understand that teenagers might shout at one another from moving cars. It wasn't really a conversation as such, but an exchange of shouted words. Why was the defender so doggedly pursuing this? Was he laying the groundwork to suggest that Namey was not in control of his mind at that moment?

Chiong answered simply, "Sort of yelling out the window."

Perhaps Zitny had achieved whatever his purpose was. He posed a few questions about Namey exiting the Nissan, seeming angry, and moving to the Kia while carrying a gun. "Okay, then the gun came out and you hear two shots?" Chiong said yes, and then added that he'd heard another shot while entering his garage. Zitny asked if Chiong had counted a total of three shots, but the witness said he'd heard at least one more while he was calling the police.

Again the defender referred to a police report indicating a discrepancy in the number of gunshots heard, but Chiong said, "I believe I told the police exactly what I told you."

In what appeared to be an attempt to confuse or rattle the young witness, Zitny said, "Now, earlier when the prosecutor asked you the same question—a similar question—you told him, just twenty minutes ago, that you didn't remember what you told the police, so how come now you can remember what you told the police?"

Absolutely calm, unrattled, Chiong replied, "From the gunshots, to my house, that was the big thing I remember."

It was a nonanswer, unspecific. But it seemed to stop

the defense attorney, who said, "Thank you. Nothing further."

Wishing to clarify the point, Conway had only a couple of questions on redirect. "Prior to you looking up and noticing these two cars, you don't know where they were or what they were doing?" Chiong agreed. The prosecutor asked if Chiong's view had been blocked by anything, and the witness said it wasn't. The remarkably calm youth was excused.

For the final case-in-chief witness, Conway called Detective Chris Stuber. As the case's lead investigator, Stuber had been sitting next to Conway at counsel table during most of the trial. He had been watching the jury carefully and later commented, "A couple of them were causing me to be concerned."

Conway's initial questions and Stuber's replies established that several bags of evidence had been properly collected and secured. They included material collected from five sources: the Nissan's interior, Namey's apartment, Sarah's Kia, her room, and items confiscated by Santa Ana PD investigators. Stuber also testified about checking Namey's blue El Camino and finding that it started four times without any difficulty. The black Nissan, said Stuber, legally belonged to Namey's mother, but unofficially was his sister's car.

Regarding evidence taken from Sarah's room, Conway asked if any photos had been found of her with the defendant, or of the defendant alone. No. Were there any letters in there from him? No. Any drug paraphernalia? No.

"How about in her purse or in the Kia Rio? Any of those items?"

"No, sir."

Conway said, "Thank you. Nothing further." The brevity of testimony from the state's final witness surprised everyone, including Stuber. He had expected the prosecutor to ask questions about the long interview with Namey shortly after the arrest, but it hadn't happened.

Defender Zitny wanted the jury to hear about some of the evidence contained in the bags mentioned during direct examination. "Did you happen to find any letters from Sarah Rodriquez to my client in my client's apartment?" Stuber couldn't remember. Zitny referred him to a police report and stated, "There were several . . . miscellaneous notes and letters. . . ." He asked, "Also, at my client's apartment, you found photographs of Sarah Rodriquez; is that true?" It was. It appeared that Zitny might be angling to have nude pictures of Sarah introduced, but he changed the subject to the El Camino.

Establishing that Stuber was familiar with auto mechanics, and had personally rebuilt engines, Zitny asked, "Now, this El Camino, you took this car and you started it four times?"

"Yes, sir." But Stuber hadn't driven it, prompting Zitney to ask if that wouldn't have been a good idea in order to evaluate any mechanical problems. The detective disagreed. Zitny thanked him and sat down. In a short redirect, Conway asked if Stuber was looking for anything in particular when he tested the El Camino. The witness said, "I was told the problem with the vehicle was the starter."

Chris Stuber had spent no more that twenty minutes on the stand.

Within moments after he stepped down, another event startled and frightened people throughout the building. At 10:15 A.M., the structure seemed to vibrate and tremble slightly. Californians had no trouble recognizing an earthquake. Those who felt the movement realized immediately that the epicenter was a long distance from Santa Ana. The notorious San

Andreas Fault had slipped near the town of Parkfield, more than two hundred miles north of the courthouse. Registering 6.0 on the Richter scale, the temblor was felt from Sacramento to Orange County, a distance of about four hundred miles. News reports later noted that a bridge near Cholame had split. The tiny community was the site of a car wreck forty-nine years earlier, almost to the day, where the movie icon James Dean had been killed on September 30, 1955. Fortunately, the earthquake resulted in no deaths or widespread damage.

Conway announced to Judge Toohey that the prosecution was resting its case. After a break, Zitny called the defense's first witness, Richard Namey's mother.

Dorothea Namey began by identifying the defendant as her son. In August 2002, he, his sister, and Richard's six-year-old daughter had lived with Dorothea in her Tustin home, she said.

Zitny asked, "Did you ever meet Sarah Rodriquez?"

Mrs. Namey answered yes, noting that Sarah had visited the Namey home several times that August. It appeared to the mother that Sarah and Rick were involved in a "romantic relationship." She had never met or heard any mention of Matt Corbett until after the shooting. In October, the witness said, she had assisted her son with moving to an apartment in Santa Ana. Her help had included selecting the place and paying for it. Sarah, she said, had continued to visit. "I saw her many times when I went to the apartment. . . ." Dorothea visited frequently to see her granddaughter. Sarah, she said, sometimes stayed there overnight.

Answering Zitny's questions, Mrs. Namey stated that the relationship between Sarah and her son continued through the fourth quarter of 2002 and into the new year. Dorothea and her fiancé had seen Sarah at the apartment in March 2003 when they had arrived to help Richard work on his El Camino. She told Zitny of paying a mechanic to make needed repairs on the vehicle.

Now it was Conway's turn to do the cross-examining. He began with an inquiry about Namey's age when he moved into this apartment. The witness answered that her son was twenty-five when he moved in. He celebrated his twenty-sixth birthday on February 21, 2003.

"He couldn't support himself?"

"No."

"You were paying for his apartment, his phone bills, all his necessities, right?"

"Yes."

The witness's direct testimony had suggested that she knew Sarah quite well and had spoken with her numerous times. Yet, police records, from an interview of Mrs. Namey by detectives shortly after the murder, did not mention such interaction between Dorothea and Sarah. Conway questioned the witness about it. She replied, "I said we didn't get into long conversations. I asked her how she was."

"Would it help you remember if you looked at a transcript of a tape-recorded interview that the police had with you right after your son killed Sarah?"

Conway's words "after your son killed Sarah" resonated through the room. The witness, showing no emotion, said yes. But after glancing at a sheaf of papers, she still maintained her belief that she had given the police information consistent with her testimony.

Conway shifted the subject to cars. He believed that Namey had used his sister's black Nissan Sentra, on the day of the murder, as part of a deliberate plan.

Both Sarah and Matt would recognize the blue El Camino. But, Conway theorized, Namey would be able to catch them by surprise if he showed up in a car they had never seen.

"In regard to the car, did you tell the police that on April sixteenth, the defendant, your son, had called you to ask if he could use his sister's car, the black Sentra?"

"Yes."

"What was the reason your son told you he needed to use your daughter's car?"

"I think because his car had no seat belts and it had not been running well."

"Did you tell the police that your son told you he had to transport a number of friends and he didn't have room in his El Camino?"

"I may have."

"And when your son came to borrow the black Sentra, he drove his El Camino to your residence, correct?"

"Yes, he did." To observers, this indicated that the El Camino was running okay, contradicting the possible excuse that it was malfunctioning. Observers now understood why it had been important for Detective Stuber to say he had started the vehicle four times and found no problems.

Having established that point, Conway made a few inquiries suggesting that Mrs. Namey had rehearsed her testimony with the defense attorney. Toohey sustained most of Zitny's objections. Returning to the vehicle issue, Conway asked, "Just to clarify on the statement your son gave you about borrowing the car, did he say he needed it to take some friends to the airport; that he claimed his friend said he had two small children and they would not fit into the El Camino?" If Conway could convince the jury that Namey had lied about his reasons for wanting to drive the Nissan, it might help prove that he was premeditating the murder.

"He may have. He exchanged cars with us on several occasions."

"I'm talking about April sixteenth, which the police were asking you about."

"I know. It was a horrendous time, and I don't remember exactly." The witness may have realized what Conway was aiming for, and wished not to say anything to incriminate her son.

Believing that he had pursued the issue as far as cross-examination rules allowed, Conway thanked her and sat down. Zitny had no redirect questions. Mrs. Namey appeared weary as she made her way out of the courtroom.

At a sidebar, Zitny said his next witness hadn't yet arrived, and asked for a brief delay. Judge Toohey addressed the jury. "Ladies and gentlemen, I just discussed timing with counsel. The witness is supposed to be here at eleven. . . . You certainly haven't earned another break. Arnold Schwarzenegger would really be on me for my use of time." Laughter rippled through the room at his reference to the state's governor, after which the judge told jurors to return at 11:15 A.M.

Unfortunately for Zitny, the doctor he had planned to question failed to show up. The defender announced that the next witness would be his own client, Richard Namey.

CHAPTER 24

On the Hot Seat

Perhaps the toughest decision in a murder trial rests on the defendant's shoulders. Is it better to follow the usual advice from the defense attorney and remain silent, or to take the witness stand in an attempt to sway the jury? The risk in choosing to testify comes in cross-examination by the prosecutor. The defense attorney can ask carefully tailored questions designed to reveal only the defendant's point of view, but the prosecutor will attack with the ferocity of a hungry crocodile. Any attempt to evade these questions, or reply defiantly, might alienate the jury. Most trial spectators hunger for testimony by the person on trial, wishing to hear just how the individual will deny, alibi, or justify the crimes.

Richard Joseph Namey chose to take the stand. He wore dark slacks, a crisply pressed white, button-down dress shirt, and looked considerably heavier than when he was arrested. His previously shaved head now sported a half-inch of lustrous black hair while a newly grown, matching black mustache gave him the look of a 1930s gangster.

His attorney, John Zitny, opened with a simple, direct question. "Mr. Namey, did you know Sarah Rodriquez?"

"Yes, I do." He put it in the present tense, as if she were still alive.

"Did you shoot Sarah Rodriquez?"

"Yes." Eyebrows shot up in the gallery.

"And also Matt Corbett?"

"Yes, I did."

Most observers and reporters had correctly speculated that the trial would not question whether or not Namey had pulled the trigger, but would pivot on the degree of responsibility. This initial gambit by Zitny confirmed it. It remained to be seen just what strategy would be employed to mitigate the acts. If the jury could be convinced that Namey was mentally out of control at the time, they might issue a verdict proclaiming him not guilty of first-degree murder.

"How did you feel about Sarah Rodriquez?" Zitny inquired.

"I loved her." Namey phrased this answer in the past tense. But when Zitny gave the impression of not hearing and asked for a repeat, the answer came out, "I love her."

"How do you feel about her still today?"

"I still love her."

"How do you feel about what you did?" Conway objected and Toohey sustained it. Chris Stuber, at the counsel table, wondered if Namey would express remorse, since he regarded Namey's conduct during the long interview as generally self-serving.

Zitny next asked Namey to look back in time to when he had first met Sarah. But the defendant couldn't remember the exact month, able only to recall that it had happened in 2002. "How did you meet her?"

"Through a friend. It was on the phone. I don't remember which friend exactly. . . . She came by my house—my mom's house." It led to a romantic "dating relationship."

"Was it a sexual relationship?"

"Yes."

Zitny again tried to pin down the approximate month they had started dating, but Namey's memory failed. He made a rough estimate. "Possibly summer, but I really don't remember."

The next few questions established that Namey's daughter, who would soon be eight, had lived with him and interacted with Sarah.

"Did you have any future plans where you included Sarah Rodriquez?"

If Zitny was fishing for possible marriage plans, Namey didn't bite. "Yeah. I liked her a lot. You know, she was my girlfriend. I didn't plan on—I planned on being with her."

The defender wanted something more specific. "Did you plan on someday being married to her?"

His client remained evasive. "Possibly."

"Did you plan on someday having children with her?"

"Yes. I wanted to have more children."

Was Zitny paving the way for introduction of the abortion? He had asked Martha Rodriquez two questions about it, but objections to both had been sustained. Still, the jury, reporters, and everyone else in the courtroom had heard and knew that Sarah had terminated a pregnancy. Zitny, though, dropped it, at least temporarily.

"You love your daughter, right?"

"Yeah. Yes, I do."

"You have a substance abuse problem; is that true?"

The defender obviously planned to reveal his client's vulnerabilities, thus denying the prosecution the opportunity to do it.

"Yes. I use heroin."

"And during that time, did you seek treatment on your own?"

"Yes, I did."

"Why did you—"

Judge Toohey interrupted. "Excuse me. Counsel, this is very vague as to time. Let's establish some time frame for your question."

No lawyer likes to be corrected in front of the jury. Zitny simply, uttered, "Okay." He reworded his question and got Namey's agreement that the addiction problem was present in August 2002. Namey had sought counseling and treatment at a Santa Ana methadone clinic. "During the summer months of 2002, were you on methadone?" Namey said yes. "And were you trying to live a life of sobriety?"

"Yes, I was . . . because I had my daughter and I was just sick of all that. I was sick of the lifestyle. I was trying to clean up because I had my daughter."

Asked when he had moved into the apartment, Namey couldn't remember, but when Zitny reminded him that Mrs. Namey had said it was in October 2002, the date sounded about right. "Yeah. I know it was before Christmas because I had Christmas there that year."

"Were you still seeing Sarah Rodriquez?" Yes. "Did she ever write you any letters?"

"Yes," Namey said, and he had saved them. Why? "I don't know. I always—I loved her. Something that you do sometimes when someone writes you a letter, you save it, maybe for further—in the future I can show her, 'Look, I saved these letters.'"

Namey answered questions revealing that he had

never been invited to Sarah's home, nor met her parents. Despite this, he had introduced Sarah to his mother and to his daughter.

Zitny made another reference to the letters Sarah had written, asking Namey to tell what one of them said, but Toohey sustained Conway's objection. Zitny repeated a request for permission to allow Namey to read the letters "based on his state of mind." Toohey turned to Conway and asked if there was any objection. The prosecutor said there was, and the judge sustained it again. Zitny handed the letters, one by one, to Namey and asked if he remembered and had saved them. Namey answered in the affirmative.

Another aspect of Namey's past came out. "Now, you've previously been convicted of a felony; is that correct?"

"Yeah. Yes." Neither lawyer nor client elaborated on the subject.

"During that time that you were with Sarah in September and October, did she ever mention to you, or [did] you have any knowledge of Matthew Corbett?" Namey said he was ignorant of Corbett's existence in Sarah's life.

If spectators were wondering how often Namey and Sarah had seen one another during their relationship, Zitny gave Namey a chance to tell them. Referring to the apartment, he asked, "Did Sarah ever come by and visit?"

"Almost every day except for Sundays, because she would go to her grandma's, and Wednesdays she would go to her brother's." Matt Corbett had spoken in his testimony of being with Sarah frequently during that same period, making him unable to understand how Sarah could have spent much time with Namey. The discrepancy would remain unexplained, and the jury would have to decide which man they believed.

"Did you feel that Sarah would make a good parent to your children?"

"Yes, because she worked at a day care. She liked kids—yeah, I thought so."

"Sometime during September and October, did Sarah become pregnant?" Zitny had kept the audience and the jury in suspense about his intention to spotlight the abortion. Now he brought it to center stage.

"Yes, she did, to my knowledge. She told me she was pregnant."

"Do you know who the father of the child was?"

"She told me it was me."

"When she told you, how did that make you feel?"

"I was happy, because like I told you before, I wanted to have some kids. I wanted my daughter to have brothers or sisters, because she was the only child." Zitny asked if they discussed naming the baby, but Toohey ruled it out.

"At some point in time, did Sarah Rodriquez have an abortion?"

"Yes, she did. She told me she—to my knowledge, she did."

"But you weren't there, right?"

"No." The negative answer meant "yes, that is right."

"And how did that make you feel?"

"I was hurt, because I don't really like abortions to begin with, and then it hurt me because I didn't quite understand . . . why. I did a little bit, because she was young, so I understand that, but she said she wanted to—you know, she liked kids and she wanted one before, so I was kind of confused a little bit." Namey believed it had happened in September or October 2002.

"You didn't break up at that time?"

"No, I was still with her."

"Was there some tension because of this?"

"A little bit, yeah."

"Did you have any arguments because of this?"

"Yes." Namey said that Sarah had continued to come by the apartment and sometimes spent the night. "She usually stayed until late, and sometimes she'd come early, like on her lunch break or whatever she said it was, in the morning. Usually almost every day, like I said, except for Wednesday nights, because she went to her brother's." The witness didn't mention that Wednesday nights were Sarah's time for Bible study, leading some to believe that the omission was intentional. If the defense's purpose, as Dennis had suggested, was to "dirty Sarah up," then it wouldn't do to speak of her interest in the Bible.

The relationship had prospered in November and December, said Namey. "It was good. I loved her." He still had no knowledge, he professed, that she was seeing Matt Corbett.

"Did you feel she loved you?"

"Yeah, I did."

When physically apart, Sarah and Namey had spoken frequently on the telephone. Zitny introduced into evidence Namey's phone bills, handed him a page, and asked him how many times he had called her during the last week of November.

"It says . . . sixty-one times."

"Take a look at the minutes. What is the longest amount of minutes you spoke to Sarah?"

"One hundred and five." Other calls had lasted from ten to fifty minutes. In the next ten days, November 30 to December 10, he had called forty-seven times, and the longest duration was also more than one hundred minutes.

"Would it be safe to say that you talked to Sarah every

day for an extended period of time, by telephone, during October and November of 2002?"

"Yes. Usually at night, because during the day she would call me—or we'd talk during her breaks and stuff." Sarah's calls to his number were usually collect, so those charges also showed up on his bill. Observers who had heard Mrs. Namey state that she had helped support him financially wondered what she thought of the staggering expenses for all those toll calls.

The pattern of telephone contact had continued through March. In the last half of February, Sarah had called him fifty-nine times, all collect, and in the first week of March, forty-four times.

"Would it be safe to say that your relationship with her was rather intense?"

"What do you mean by 'intense'?"

"I mean you couldn't go through a day without talking to her; is that true?"

"Yeah, I liked to hear from her every day." Multiple times daily.

"And she couldn't go through a day without talking to you; isn't that correct?" Namey agreed.

Zitny announced to the judge that he planned to "go into an entirely different area" and asked if they could break a little early for lunch. Toohey ordered the jury to return at 1:30 P.M.

In less dramatic trials, early afternoon can be a miserable time for jurors. Too much lunch combined with droning lawyers and a warm room can sometimes result in a losing struggle with drowsiness, but this group took their seats and listened eagerly, alert and wide awake.

Zitny opened the afternoon session by questioning

Namey about the incident on March 27, at Sarah's night school. "Did you go over to that school?"

"Yes," replied Namey, "I wanted to surprise her and take her out to eat or something." Earlier that day, he said, he had invited her over to his house.

"When you went to the school, did you look for her car in the parking lot?"

"Yes." But he hadn't seen it anywhere. Although Namey had never been there before, he knew the location because Sarah had told him it was across the street from a familiar strip mall. Unable to locate her car, Namey said, he decided to find a front desk and ask about her.

"Did you find her in a class?"

"I found her—no. She was in the hallway. I guess it was a break or something."

"Did she seem surprised to see you?"

"Not too surprised. A little bit, yeah." It was his intent, he said, to tell her why he was there.

Instead, "I asked her where her car was. She said it was in the parking lot."

"But you had already looked in the parking lot, correct?"

"Yeah, pretty much." And he confronted her about it.

"Did you feel she was telling you the truth at that time?"

"No. I had a feeling. You know . . . but I feel she was acting funny." He suspected her of lying. "I asked her, 'Well, where's your car really?' She said she had to go because the break was over. I don't know if the bell rang or whatever. It was a fifteen-minute break. I started to walk out, and I guess she started to walk back to class. And then before I got to the door, I was going to turn around and tell her—something like 'don't even come over later' . . . because I was a little bit upset already. When I walked around, it was like a T-shaped hallway, she was on the other side of the hallway, and she was on a cell phone." His story differed from Sarah's report to the police in which she had returned to class, delivered an oral presentation, then gone to a restroom and encountered Namey as she exited.

Zitny asked, "She walked around the corner so you couldn't see her?"

"I don't know if that was it, but she was around the corner. I don't know if that's where her class was or—"

The defender didn't allow him to complete the sentence. "Okay. Had she actually made it back to her class at the time you had spoken to her?"

"No, because—well, I don't know which class it was exactly, but she was outside in the hallway." Now he recalled that she "was near a restroom, maybe. I'm not sure. . . . She was on a cell phone. I heard the last words, like 'Rick is here.' That's when she saw me and looked up."

"Did she look surprised?"

"Yeah. I asked her, 'Who are you talking to?'" Namey said he couldn't remember her answer. "Maybe her girlfriend or something. I'm not sure. Or her mom—"

"Did you want to take a look at her cell phone?"

"Yeah. I asked her, because I wanted to see who she was talking to."

"Did you try to grab the cell phone out of her hand?"

"Yes. . . . And she tried to—she put it in her pocket, and I was trying to grab her arm to pull it out, and she . . . was pushing it in there as hard as she could, I guess."

"Did she try to push you away?"

"Yeah. We just kind of got in a little scuffle. We tripped over each other, I guess, and I pushed her, kind of like . . . by her neck."

"Did you try to strangle her?"

"No. I didn't try to strangle her."

"You pushed her aside by pushing her upper chest?"

"Yeah, somewhere around there." Namey also denied making any threats to Sarah.

"Did you ever say you had a gun and you were going to shoot her right then and there at the school?"

"No, sir."

The next morning, Namey asserted, they had spoken by telephone, and she had said she still loved him.

Moving on to the April 1 confrontation, Zitny asked Namey if he had driven over to Sarah's home. "Yes," he said. "Because I wanted to talk to her and see what was going on with what happened." They hadn't spoken since the school incident four nights earlier. "I was worried. I was sad. I didn't know what was going on, so I went to her house." From there, according to Namey, he drove to the preschool, where Sarah worked, and spotted her in the Kia. They both pulled over to a side street and parked. He got out of his El Camino and approached her. "She said, 'I'm going to be late to school. I have to go.' I was like, 'Okay.' She had some water in her car and I asked her if I could have a drink. She gave me some water, and she left and I went back home."

Once again, Namey's story differed considerably from Sarah's account to her mother and to the police. She had called her mother, saying that she was terrified because Namey prevented her from going to her job.

Zitny asked, "At any point, did you see her on the cell phone while you were speaking with her?"

No, Namey said. He commented that they had agreed to talk later and work out their problems. "She said she was going to call me either from her break at school or after. I don't know exactly what time." But Sarah never called.

"How did that make you feel?"

"Well, I mean, I felt terrible. How do you think?"

Zitny ignored the rhetorical question. "When she didn't call you, did you go back . . . the next day, on April second, in the evening?"

"Yes. It was in the evening, maybe seven or eight. . . . She was coming in one way in the entrance of her house." Namey probably meant the residential tract in which she lived. "I was coming in another way, and—or was I going out?" Another slight memory lapse. "I turned around, pulled up next to her, was talking to her again, and she started arguing with me, telling me, 'I have a restraining order. My mom made me get this restraining order.'"

"And she actually gave a copy of that to you; is that true?"

"Yeah. I don't remember if she threw it or I reached and she handed it to me, I can't remember, but somehow I got it."

"Did another car pull up?"

"Yes."

"Had you ever seen that individual before in that other car?"

"No." Namey described the vehicle. "It was an S10, a GMC, but an S10 pickup truck."

"Who did you think that person was . . . in that truck?"

"Initially I thought it was her brother, because she had told me that her brother drove a Honda Civic, and he got in an accident and his friend was letting him borrow an S10, so that's what I thought it was when he pulled up. And then another thing is, when the guy jumped out real quick, he had a beanie on. . . . A couple weeks before, there was a beanie in her car, and the seat was real far back, so I asked her, 'Whose beanie is this?' She said, 'That's my brother's.' So when the guy jumped out and he had the beanie on, I thought it was her brother, so that's when I took off."

It seemed to some observers that Namey was pushing awfully hard to convince jurors that he thought the man was Sarah's brother. And if that's what he thought, why did he suddenly flee?

"That was the first time you had ever seen that person?"

"Yeah. I never even met her brother, but I saw a picture of him before. That's it."

"You were still seated in your car?"

"Yeah."

"That person in the truck, did he follow you?"

"I didn't look back. I just left. I don't know." Namey made no mention of flipping off anyone, as Matt Corbett had described.

"Did you run any red lights?"

"I don't believe so. No." This, too, conflicted with Corbett's version.

Zitny skipped back to Sarah. "When was the last time Sarah told you she loved you?"

"It was the morning when she called after . . . the school incident. That was the last time."

"What did you do for that two-week time period from April second to April sixteenth?"

"I just stayed at home. That time was a bad time. . . ."

Zitny didn't seem to think the answer strong enough. "Explain to the jury what you were doing for that two-week time period."

"Well, I believe I took my daughter to my mom's house, because I wasn't feeling in the right state where I could take care of her that good; so I was just staying there sleeping and not doing much, just basically staying there."

"Were you hurt?"

"Yeah, I was hurt."

"Were you upset?"

"I was upset, depressed. I was very depressed. I wasn't eating that much."

"Did you want to talk to Sarah?"

"Yeah, I wanted to talk to her."

"Did you hope she would call you?" Namey voiced his assent, but his hopes had not been fulfilled.

"On April sixteenth, you went and borrowed your sister's car?" Zitny referred to the black Nissan Sentra.

"Yeah, I borrowed it."

"How come? How did you get that car?"

"Because my car wasn't running right. That's one thing that was bugging me. I always borrowed my sister's car a lot too and drove it around."

"Were you thinking about committing suicide?"

"Yes."

"What time did you get your sister's car?" Namey couldn't remember. "Did you get it to take to the airport?"

"No, I didn't."

Zitny handed his client an envelope and asked him to open it and describe what was inside. Namey complied and said it was a letter. "What was your intention in writing that letter?"

"Well, this particular one was—it was for my daughter, so I could . . ."

"What were you telling your daughter in that letter?"

"That I love her." Zitny asked if he was telling his daughter good-bye. "Yeah." Was it a suicide note? "I guess you can call it that. I was just—it was just a note telling her that I love her, and no matter what—I just wanted her to know I loved her if I wasn't around."

"The time you wrote that letter, were you thinking about killing yourself?"

"Yes." Namey volunteered that he had written three letters, the other two being for his mother and his sister. Zitny had him open the remaining two and asked for

explanations. The one to his sister, said Namey, was
written because "I wanted to tell her too. I never got
along with my sister that much, so I wanted to let her
know that I loved her and everything." He didn't know
at what hour of the day he wrote them, nor in which
order they were completed.

At this crucial point in his client's testimony, Zitny
needed specific answers. He asked if Namey had written
them on the morning of April 16, the day he shot Sarah
and Matt. Namey said, "Yes, it was. I believe so."

"And did you write this letter while you were contemplating killing yourself?"

"Yes. Well, I had already thought about it before. . . .
I had already made up my mind that's what I was going
to do, I guess. That's why I wrote those letters."

"Did you plan on going up and talking to Sarah that
day?"

"Yes. I was going to try to talk to her."

"Were you going to beg for her to take you back?" Yes.

"If she did not, what did you plan on doing?"

"I planned on killing myself." The defendant finally
said the words needed to show a distraught state of
mind.

Introducing another item of evidence, Zitny heard
Namey identify it as a ring for his daughter. But Zitny's
questions aimed at Namey's supposed intention to place
it on his bed pillow collapsed like a punctured balloon.
Namey couldn't remember. "How come you can't remember everything that happened that day?"

"Well, because I wasn't obviously thinking clearly at
the time." There it was. Another brick in the mitigation
fence being built. Namey wasn't thinking clearly—so how
could he have committed premeditated murder with
malice aforethought?

"Did you think that there was a good chance you would not be alive until the end of the day?"

Namey hesitated and asked, "At that time?"

"Yes," said Zitny.

"Yeah, I guess. I didn't really think about that." If the objective had been to score dramatic impact points, it missed the goal.

"You had a gun, right?"

"Yeah."

"Did you take that gun and go to Sarah's house?"

"Yes, I did."

"There were also a lot of bullets and a speedloader there. . . . How did you grab that gun? Explain that to the jury. Where was it located?"

"The gun was up above my kitchen sink. I had it in a hat turned upside down, and I had my bullets in there, and my speedloader and the gun and everything."

"Why did you have the gun?"

"I had it for home protection. I had previous problems before."

Zitny objected to his own client's statement, an action seldom seen in trials. "Nonresponsive."

Judge Toohey frowned and said, "I'm sorry?"

"Motion to strike. Nonresponsive."

Perplexed, Toohey asked for the question and answer to be read back. Court reporter Kimberly Owen complied. Without missing a beat, the judge said, "The answer will remain." Spectators scratched their heads.

Zitny asked, "Now, when did you buy this gun?"

Namey wasn't certain, but said, "It was maybe a year ago. I don't remember. Six months to a year."

Dennis Conway had been listening intently. He leaned forward and scribbled notes onto a yellow legal pad.

"When you took the gun and you put it in the car, did

you take everything separately, or did you take it as a bundle?"

"No, I took the hat. I took the whole hat." It contained the bullets, the gun, and the speedloader. Namey also stated that he couldn't remember if he had placed the items in his car or in the Nissan.

"At some point, you drove up to talk to Sarah; is that true?" Yes. Namey complained that he had been unable to sleep or eat very much in two weeks. He said he had driven to Placentia on April 16 with the intention of talking to Sarah. If she wouldn't take him back, he would kill himself in front of her.

Reconstructing that day's events, Namey said he had first driven to the preschool to see if Sarah was at work. "When she wasn't there, I drove back by her house. . . . Her car was not there. . . . I think I was going to go maybe back by the school or back home. I can't remember. I was just leaving out of the community."

"As you were leaving . . . what did you see?"

"I saw Sarah's car coming. As I was coming out, she was coming to the left of me." He had immediately recognized her car. "It turned in to go back toward her house. I turned around and sped up to pull up next to her."

"Now, when you pulled up next to her, did you look across and see her?"

"Yes . . . at first we were right next to each other." The windows were down in both cars, Namey said, and he believed that he yelled something at her.

"At that moment, what did you want to do when you saw Sarah in the car when you were adjacent to her? Did you want to talk to her?"

"At that point—well, because when I saw her, that's when I saw the—I guess Matt at the same time . . . When I was going toward them, when I passed, I saw like a glimpse of—I saw a male in the passenger seat, but it was from a little distance, and I didn't see who it was. That's when I turned around and sped up to see who it was, and that's when I pulled up next to her, and I saw him and her."

"When you saw him, what happened? Do you remember?"

"Vaguely."

"Do you remember . . . getting out of the car?"

"I remember opening the door."

"Do you remember walking over to the car?"

"Not really."

"Do you remember which side of the car, the red Kia, that you got to, the passenger's side or the driver's side?"

"No. I remember seeing myself there. I just don't remember which one I went to first."

"Do you remember who you shot?"

"No."

"Do you remember how many bullets you shot?"

"No, I don't remember how many bullets I shot."

"Can you describe to the jury what it was like at that moment?" This actually could be the most critical moment in the trial. If Namey could present a convincing account of being in a state of mind that robbed him of all self-control of his actions or emotions, he might get a lenient verdict from the jury.

He replied, "It was nothing like I ever felt before. Kind of dizzy, kind of cloudy a little bit."

"Was it like a dream?"

"Yeah, like a dream. And like I said, I just remember bits and pieces. I remember standing in front of the car. I remember seeing Matt there afterward. I think he was kind of slouched over."

"It was like a flash of an image?" It appeared as if the

defense attorney was helping his client create word pictures and provide good similes.

"I guess it was like a flash, and then—I remember standing—I remember seeing a little bit of smoke."

"And then it was over?" Met by silence, Zitny repeated his question.

"I don't remember. I remember getting back into my car, I guess, and I drove it away. I don't really remember everything too easy."

"Now, when you got back in the car, how did you feel?"

Amazingly, his memory of this part was less cloudy. "Sick. I still felt the same actually. I still kind of felt the same as I did, dizzy and all that."

"Where did you go?"

"I drove down the street. I don't remember where. I got off the freeway somewhere. I don't remember exactly where I got off, but . . . I pulled over because I was still feeling dizzy. I couldn't drive that good. I was by a gas station somewhere. I believe it was on the other side . . . by a parking lot or something."

"Were you shaky?"

"Yeah, I sat there. I just sat there and I thought about killing myself again."

"Did you start to cry at all?"

"Yeah, I was crying before, I think, when I was in the car. I was a little more shaky just thinking about— I started crying later. First I was going to—I thought about it, but I had the gun in my hand."

"Did you try to kill yourself?"

"I didn't try. I had the gun right here." Namey gestured with a hand near his throat. "I remember that. I was going to do it, but—"

"Did you point the muzzle at any part of your body to try to kill yourself?"

"I had the gun right here. I pointed it at my chin. I couldn't kill myself."

"You couldn't pull the trigger?"

"No. And I thought, I don't know why—this sounds crazy, but I was really thirsty. My mouth was really dry. I thought, okay, I need to get some water, so I walked into the—I guess it was a gas station, and then I got some water. I drank some water and I sat down outside of my car, and that's when I—there was a phone right there. I called my mom."

Zitny refocused the exchange back to his client's state of mind. "Did you lose control of yourself?"

Namey asked, "At what point?"

"Just before you saw Matt, did you intend on killing Sarah?"

"No, I didn't."

"Did you intend—"

Apparently anticipating that he was being asked if he intended to kill Matt, Namey hurried his answer. "I didn't even know him."

"You intended on talking to her and then committing suicide if she wouldn't take you back?"

"Yeah."

The defendant's state of mind when he killed Sarah and paralyzed Matt had been thoroughly explored, so Zitny turned to another subject. Perhaps wishing to preempt the prosecution, he asked Namey about the meeting with Alberto Zavala, the carjacking, and the high-speed chase.

Namey first admitted that he had started using heroin again after the shooting. "Heroin calms you down . . . so I guess I just wanted to—I was depressed. I wanted to get away from everything." He contacted Zavala. "He was my drug dealer . . . one of them, for years." Namey said he drove the Nissan to an ice-cream shop and telephoned Zavala. "He always meets me around the same area."

Zitny asked, "Is that the budget market parking lot in Santa Ana?"

Namey said it was. When he had called, Zavala had said to meet him at the market.

"Had you bought heroin from him previously between April sixteenth and April nineteenth?"

"I think so, the day before, once."

Regarding the day of the carjacking, Zitny asked, "Why did you get in his car? Did he invite you in?"

"Yeah. That's what we always do, you know."

"Did you pull a gun out on him?"

"Not at that time, I didn't." Namey denied having worn a backpack, as Zavala had said in his testimony. He had carried the gun, ammunition, and speedloader in the pocket of "a big, extra-long Levi wool jacket." Recalling the sequence, Namey said, "He basically goes to the parking lot . . . pulls up to me. I had to flag him down, and when he saw me, that's when he stopped and I got in. . . . We went around the block. Then we stopped and that's when—the normal thing we always do, I get in, we drive around, I give him the money and he gives me the dope." This time, though, "he was waiting for me to pull out the money real quick. . . . That's when I pulled my gun out, because I didn't have any money. I only had a dollar or two. I actually told him, 'I'm sorry,' because I liked the guy, believe it or not. I told him, 'Sorry, but I have to do this. Get out of the car.' I said, 'Give me your dope. Give me all the dope and give me your money and get out.' He got out. He dropped his dope, but he didn't give me the money." Zavala had jumped out and then run.

"What you heard the police officers testify to—about

you driving away and driving in a speed chase on the
freeway—was that all true?"

"Yes, it is."

After a few more questions, Zitny asked, "Do you
regret what happened?"

"Yes, I do."

After showing the jury a photo of Namey and Sarah
standing together, Zitny sank into his chair at counsel
table. "Thank you. Nothing further."

Now it was Dennis Conway's turn to cross-examine the
defendant.

CHAPTER 25

The Woolick

Dennis Conway still felt something was missing. He needed to convince the jury that Namey had driven to Placentia with the intent to kill Sarah. The fact that Namey had used his sister's Nissan, rather than his own easily recognized blue El Camino, hinted of a plan to sneak up on the unsuspecting victims. But that wasn't enough. John Zitny had done a good job of questioning the defendant and creating a compelling suggestion that when Namey saw his lover with another man, Matt, he had acted out of passion rather than premeditation.

With the trial moving rapidly to a close, the prosecutor faced the possibility of time running out before he could find the amorphous link.

As Conway stood to begin questioning Namey, he fully expected to hear many objections from Zitny. It is common for defense attorneys to object more frequently than prosecutors in order to lay foundations for future appeals. Zitny, true to form, would lodge thirty-nine objections and Judge Toohey would sustain more than half of them.

If Conway had an advantage, it was in his engaging personality. Juror's faces reflected a certain affection for him when Conway spoke. It's easy to see the Irish sense of humor lurking when the crow's feet deepen, his face beams, and his animated speech is laced with colorful expressions, all punctuated by hand gestures and energetic body language. Even when Conway is being cynical, he couches it in personal charm and an easygoing knack for capturing his audience's interest. Dennis's years of bartending and interrelating with people from all walks of life, from prosperous to poverty stricken, had infused him with a deep understanding of human nature.

Standing in front of the jury box, Conway opened his questioning of Namey by asking if the relationship with Sarah had been "pretty good" up until the end of March. Namey said he thought it was. "I really wasn't keeping track of months, like I said. My relationship was good, with me, all the way up to March—"

Zitny objected. "Motion to strike, 'all the way up to March.'"

The defender had crossed the line again. Toohey said, "I don't want any speaking objections. The answer will remain."

Conway's questions covered several subjects during the next few minutes. He established that the letters from Sarah to Namey had been written in October and November, the early half of the relationship. He elicited an admission from the defendant that Mrs. Namey had paid for his utilities, rent, and phone bills. Namey had no "steady job."

Shifting gears again, Conway asked, "You testified

that Sarah told you at some point about an abortion she had?"

"Yeah." Namey snorted, but he said he couldn't remember when she had revealed it to him. He was "pretty sure" it happened sometime before Christmas. "At first she kept it from me. . . . She said she was pregnant. We had some arguments about it, and then she said a few days later that she ended up getting her period. Later on, she ended up telling me she got an abortion."

Probing to see what else Namey would say about the subject, Conway asked, "She told you she wasn't ready to have a child with you, which is why she had an abortion, correct?" Toohey sustained an objection, and Conway reworded his question. "How did she tell you? She didn't taunt you with the abortion, she informed you she wasn't ready to have a child, and she had an abortion, correct?"

"Not right away, no." Namey commented that she was crying when she informed him about it. To another series of questions, he affirmed that their romance continued despite the abortion. When not together, the couple had maintained frequent daily contact by telephone. Conway asked if Namey had given her permission to call him collect, and the defendant said he had "no problem" with it.

"Because your mother pays the bills, right?"

"That's not why."

"But your mother does pay the bills?"

"For the most part."

Sarah had never invited Namey to her home to meet her family, have dinner with them, or attend barbecues. Conway asked if that hurt his feelings.

"Yes, it did." He didn't resent it, he said, but wondered why she acted that way. "I used to ask her, 'When am I going to be able to meet your parents?' I was a single father. I wanted to meet them."

Conway dug deeper, establishing that Sarah had never invited Namey to pick her up at school and never introduced him to coworkers or classmates as her boyfriend. "Did she ever indicate to you that she didn't want to see you as much?"

"No."

"So, up until the end of March, it's your testimony that she still wanted to see you regularly?"

"Yeah. She was coming over regularly." Namey denied that he had ever demanded of Sarah that she call him, or check in with him, or that he threatened to come and find her if she failed to call. He adamantly insisted that she had never expressed fear of him.

"The gun. When exactly did you get the gun?"

"I don't remember exactly when I got it. Within six, maybe eight months prior to me getting arrested."

"Tell us, where did you get the gun?"

"I bought it from the street." Namey added that his car had once been stolen and someone had been threatening him, so he needed a gun because "I had my daughter at home."

"So you went where to purchase this gun? Down to one of those gun stores?"

"No. I already told you it was from some people that I know."

"Did this gun come with any ammunition?"

"When I got it, it had some bullets in it, yeah. It had five bullets in it."

"Now, the suicide, April sixteenth. Are you telling this jury you thought that day may be the last day of your life; you were going to commit suicide?"

"Yes."

"When did you decide that you were going to commit suicide?"

"I think it was that day. I had been thinking about it for that week. . . . I believe it was that morning I actually made up my mind."

Conway wanted to know Namey's rationale. Was it that he hurt so much inside and didn't feel like living anymore? Namey parroted the words in his affirmative answer.

"And the reason for that is because Sarah rejected you?"

"Yeah, I guess it was. I'm hurt. . . . That wasn't the only reason. There were many reasons why."

"Is that the reason why you wanted to [kill yourself] in front of her . . . basically to show her, 'Look what you made me do'?"

"No, no. I wanted to try to talk to her at first, you know, hoping everything would be all right."

"So it was suicide with a condition?"

Namey paused, looked at the jury, and said, "That was my last resort."

Conway echoed him. "That was your last resort?"

"I figured it was probably going to happen, but I didn't want it to happen."

"Despite the fact that you have a daughter that you've told us about, over and over again, you felt at that point you didn't have any reason to live?" Conway, a single father who often said that his son was the best thing to happen in his life, couldn't tolerate the idea of a parent not wishing to live for their child.

Namey replied, "I wasn't thinking clearly then. I would never do that now, believe me. I know."

"But then you felt like you had no reason to live? I'm asking. I'm not trying to trick you."

"Sure you are," Namey shot back.

"Excuse me?" Conway felt a tiny urge to let the leprechaun out, but overcame it. "Did you think of different ways that you could end your life?"

Namey sounded sarcastic. "It wasn't too hard. I had a gun there."

"Did you think about maybe taking some pills and going to sleep and killing yourself that way?"

"I don't know if that went through my head. I don't remember."

"Did you think about maybe jumping off a cliff or a high building?"

"No." Nor had he thought about drowning himself in the ocean.

"You thought, 'I'm going to put a bullet in my head,' right?"

"I wasn't—yeah."

"And you sat down to write some letters that morning to your mother, your sister, and your daughter, because this was the day that you were going to end your life, right?"

"Yeah."

"Is this the first time, April 16, 2003, that you have thought about taking your life?"

Zitny objected, but was overruled. Namey said he had thought about it before. "Okay," said Conway, "but obviously you haven't followed through, right?"

"No." Again the negative answer meant "Yes, that is right."

A series of questions explored Namey's relationship with his sister and the letter he wrote to her. "You wanted to let her know, 'Hey, I'm going to take my life,' right?"

"It wasn't exactly what you said. I wanted to let her know that I love her."

"Well, you can let her know you love her without

writing suicide notes, right?" Even though the topic was serious, some viewers had trouble suppressing chuckles at Conway's satirical demeanor.

"Well, I wanted to let her know when I was gone. You understand?"

The prosecutor understood all too well. From the loss of his brother Patrick, Dennis knew all about a nonduplicitous intent to commit suicide. And this understanding made him even more contemptuous of someone who might use the threat in a dishonest way. He asked, "Wouldn't it be nice to call her up, go see her, and tell her this?"

An objection came from Zitny, citing irrelevance. The judge sustained it.

Conway, glancing at the letters to Namey's mother and daughter, asked if he loved them, too.

Namey's affirmative answer was almost inaudible. His chin quivered and his reddening eyes glazed with tears. Conway felt no compassion for him. "Are you crying because you feel sorry for yourself?"

Zitny launched a vociferous objection. "Argumentative." Toohey sustained it.

Conway didn't hesitate. "Why are you crying?" Another objection was sustained.

Unrelenting, Conway asked, "So your daughter, your mother, and your sister get a letter, but Sarah, who you say you loved intensely, she didn't get a letter, right?"

The defendant choked out his answer. "No, because I was going to go talk to her . . . she would know I loved her."

"And if she wouldn't talk to you and take you back, then what?"

"I was going to kill myself. That's what I planned on doing, at least."

"You're thinking as you drive over, 'Unless Sarah talks

to me . . .' This is kind of like emotional extortion, isn't it?" The objection and judge's agreement didn't even slow Conway down. "So you're thinking as you drive over there, 'I'll kill myself, and the only thing that will keep me from killing myself is if she not only talks to me, but takes me back,' right?"

"I don't remember. I just wanted things to be better, you know."

The line of questioning continued for several minutes. "At some point, did you think she was evil and she needed to be killed?" Conway had chosen not to bring in the interview with Detective Stuber, but he did remember an odd comment from Namey: "Stupid Sarah. She's the evil one, man."

The defendant recoiled. "No. No, I didn't."

"So when you went over that day and you ended up shooting Matt and shooting Sarah—now she's really not going to take you back, right?"

"What do you mean, after—"

"She can't take you back because you killed her, right?"

A glimmer of anger replaced Namey's lachrymosity. "Obviously not."

Conway agreed. "Obviously not. Now are you feeling better, and you don't want to commit suicide now?"

"I wasn't feeling better."

Turning to a different subject, Conway held the revolver up. "Is this the gun you bought on the street?"

"Yeah, it looks like it."

"How much did you pay for it?"

"I don't remember. A hundred bucks or—I don't know."

With another shift, the prosecutor asked if Sarah had used any of those long telephone conversations to suggest ending the relationship and begged Namey to leave her alone. Namey vehemently dismissed the idea.

"So you go up on March twenty-seventh and you say everything's still fine between you and Sarah, right?"

"Except little things, like I said, but the majority—"

"You were not mad at her? You didn't have any thoughts, on March twenty-seventh, of either killing her or yourself?" Namey said he hadn't. Conway spent several minutes probing the incident at Sarah's night school. When Namey hadn't been able to find her car in the lot, Sarah explained that her girlfriend was using it. A police report indicated that Namey had angrily threatened to attack the friend.

The defendant denied making the threat. Conway asked, "Did you tell her during that conversation that you had a gun in your car under the seat?"

"No. . . . The bell rang. She had to go back to class."

"Did you tell Sarah that she better not tell anyone what's going on because if she does and you go to jail, when you get out, you'll find her and you'll kill her?"

"No, I didn't." This sharply contradicted statements Sarah wrote in her journal.

"So what happened to cause you to put your hands on her?"

"Well, like I said, I turned back around and I was— she was walking toward her class, I guess, and I was walking toward the exit, I turned around to tell her, 'Don't even come to my house later on.'"

"And you're mad at her. Why? Because she lent her car to a friend?"

"Because she was acting weird. That's why."

Conway brought up the possibility that Namey's fury ignited when he spotted Sarah talking on a cell phone, and that she was perhaps telling someone about being frightened of him. Namey refuted that scenario. Judge

Toohey interrupted the exchange with an announcement of the afternoon recess.

Conway spent the twenty-minute break in a nearby room where his boxes of evidence were stored. An idea had been evolving in his mind. He knew there was one more thing he desperately needed to cement his case of premeditation. Namey's testimony about acquiring the gun, and that it was loaded with five bullets, inspired Conway's search. In the cubicle room, he pawed frantically through the items police had collected during the investigation.

As if by providence, Conway's hand touched a black leather-bound Day-Timer planning calendar. It had been retrieved from the site of Namey's struggle with the police dog in the drainage tube. Conway opened it and found dozens of paper scraps crammed between the pages and inside pockets. As he leafed through receipts from Home Depot, Jack in the Box, and other stores, along with movie ticket stubs and photographs, Conway suddenly stopped. He held a tiny document that was like the last missing piece to a giant jigsaw puzzle.

Later telling of the near miracle, Conway said, "I'm in the middle of cross and I go back to my temporary office in the courthouse. I tell my investigator, 'Let's look through some of this stuff again.' I'm looking through Namey's Day-Timer, and it's filled with literally hundreds of pieces of small paper. And I find a receipt dated March 29, 2003, which is two days after Namey assaulted Sarah at the night school. On that day, he goes over to a gun shop and buys a box of high-speed PMC ammunition. It's called 'Cowboy' ammo, and it's what he used to kill her. The box was later found in the van he carjacked. So he is obviously carrying it around with him after the murder. He must have taken the random rounds out and loaded the weapon with the 'Cowboy' ammo before he headed over there."

This was it—the missing element Conway needed. He couldn't believe that neither he nor the investigators had noticed it before, despite two evidence-viewing sessions. The defense had apparently overlooked it too, while examining boxes of material made available to them by the district attorney in compliance with discovery requirements.

Back in the courtroom, Toohey announced, "Mr. Conway, take up your cross-examination."

"Thank you, Your Honor," the prosecutor said, his face brighter and a little more bounce in his step. To build a foundation for his plan, Conway picked up where he had left off, at the night-school incident. Facing Namey, he said, "You see Sarah with a cell phone in the hallway. Are you thinking that she might be talking to another guy?"

Namey also appeared refreshed and answered in a confident tone. "I didn't know who she was talking to. It went through my head. I didn't know, though."

"So you didn't ask her who was on the phone?" The defendant replied that he thought he did. Conway stayed on track. "And Sarah's reaction to you finding her on the cell phone was to shut it and try to put it in her pocket, right?"

"Yeah."

"But you went to grab the cell phone, didn't you?"

"At first I told her—I was asking her who was on the phone." He didn't answer the question.

Conway repeated it. "Did you try to grab the cell phone when she closed it and put it in her pocket?"

"Yes." To subsequent questions, Namey said it would "bother him" to learn that she was keeping the phone, and its number, secret from him.

"You grab her arm and you don't let go?"

"No, I don't let go."

"Sarah tries to pull away from you?"

"Yeah."

"You put your hands on her throat?"

"Somewhere around there, yes." He denied choking her, though, and said he had only one hand on Sarah's neck, trying to push her away, while his other hand still gripped her arm. "I can't remember exactly."

Zeroing in, Conway asked, "Sarah's trying to get away from you, right?"

"Not really, no."

"She's staying there and letting you squeeze her throat and her arm?"

Toohey sustained Zitny's objection as argumentative.

"Did classmates come out and you ran off?"

"No."

"You didn't get the cell phone, right?"

"I didn't get the cell phone. It was escalating a little too far, so that's when, you know, I knew something bad was—I would get in trouble or something bad would happen, so I left."

"So you leave, you go home, and you're mad at Sarah?"

"I was just upset."

"At her?"

"I was mad and I was—you know, I was wondering what was going on." They had spoken the next day by telephone, Namey said, but disagreed that he had threatened her. He also denied telling her that she would be making a big mistake if she obtained a restraining order.

"Did you tell Sarah on that day, March 28, 2003, that nothing better happen to you, otherwise you were going to kill her when you got out of jail?"

"No." It was a crucial question, and several jurors made notes.

"The day she threw the restraining order in your car window, did you tell her, 'You're only making things worse for yourself'?"

"No, not that. I think I said, 'You're causing a lot of problems for me too.' I never said for herself."

Conway inquired about the period between March 28 and April 1, asking if Namey had yet thought about killing himself or if he was thinking of "taking the gun and doing something to Sarah." No, said Namey. During those days, he claimed, he thought mostly about the problems with Sarah.

"Where were you keeping your gun?"

"It was up in the same place . . . above my sink, in the cupboard."

"After the telephone conversation on March twenty-eighth, did you pull your gun out?"

"I don't recall. I can't really remember. I don't think so."

On April 1, Namey had gone to Sarah's workplace, stopped his car next to hers, and spoken to her. Questioned about it, he said he'd gone there to find out why she hadn't called him. Conway asked, "You're in the blue El Camino?"

"Yes."

"That's running fine?"

"It's not running fine, but it's running." From Conway's long experience of driving rusting rattletraps, sometimes across the country, he could have testified as an expert on the running ability of old cars.

"It's running fine enough to drive over to Sarah's place in Placentia, right?"

"It made it there. It wasn't running fine. No." Conway made the point that Namey hadn't asked to borrow his sister's car on that day.

"By the way," Conway casually added, "had you,

between March twenty-seventh and April first, pulled your gun out at all?"

"No, I don't believe so."

"When you bought the gun, did it come with a speed-loader?"

"No, it didn't." He had acquired it later. Conway asked why he needed it. Namey said, "Look . . . if something happened at my door and I needed to use the gun, I didn't want to keep it loaded"—he explained that he had kept ammunition in the speedloader—"so I could get to it quick."

"When you thought about committing suicide, you were going to use this gun, right?" Namey agreed. "When you were going to commit suicide in front of Sarah on the sixteenth, you had that gun fully loaded, right?"

"Uh-huh."

"Were you going to stick the gun in your mouth or up to the side of your head?"

"Probably to the side of my head. I don't know." Namey said he hadn't practiced it.

"Did you think that you would need more than one bullet from a three fifty-seven Magnum into your head to kill yourself?"

"I wasn't thinking that at the time, but obviously not. Obviously you don't need more than one bullet—"

"But that morning, you made sure that the gun was fully loaded with five rounds, correct?"

"I didn't make sure, no," Namey retorted, but confirmed that he had been the one who loaded the weapon.

"And you made sure there were five in there, right?" This time, the defendant muttered a reluctant yes.

"And also on the morning of April sixteenth, you took extra ammunition with you, right?" The question was one of the keystones to the structure Conway was building.

"I didn't make sure. Like I said, I grabbed everything at once. It was in a hat."

"When is the last time, prior to April sixteenth, that you pulled your gun out?" Namey didn't remember. "Was it before or after the incident at night school with Sarah?"

"It had to be before."

Conway brought up the April 2 confrontation in which Matt was involved. "You drive over to her house in the El Camino?"

"Yeah, because she didn't call me like she said she would."

"The El Camino's still running well enough to drive up to Placentia?"

"I made it there." Namey probably recognized by this time that his excuse for borrowing his sister's Nissan on the day of the shooting was growing thin.

Conway's questions re-created word pictures of Namey's El Camino stopped adjacent to Sarah's Kia, an exchange of words, Sarah throwing the restraining order through his open window, and Matt arriving on the scene. "And you didn't tell her when she gave you the restraining order, 'You've made a big mistake. You've made things worse for yourself'?"

"No. I said, 'You're making things bad for me.'"

"For you?"

"Yeah."

"Didn't you care about what she wanted?"

Namey had cornered himself and could only grunt a defeated "Yeah."

"And if she wanted you to stay away from her, weren't you willing to respect her wishes?"

"That's why I stayed away for that week or two, or whatever."

With another jab toward the El Camino's condition, Conway reviewed Matt's arrival and Namey's speeding away. "So this car's not running so well. Did you drive away pretty fast?"

"Pretty fast, yeah."

"So the car was running well enough to drive fast away from the guy in the truck, right?"

"Yeah."

"Because you were scared of this guy? He looked like he meant business, didn't he?"

"That wasn't it. I thought it was her brother."

"Did he look like he was threatening to you? Did he look like he was going to kick your butt?"

Namey said he didn't know because he had left.

"Did you think maybe Sarah didn't want to be with you because of how you treated her . . .?"

"No. I treated her great. . . . I did everything for her."

Namey had left the scene after being chased by Matt. Conway asked, "You go home that particular evening and have that restraining order with you. Are you thinking you want to hurt Sarah?"

"No." But Namey admitted that he was "a little bit mad at her."

"Are you mad at the guy who chased you?" No, said Namey.

"Did you pull out the gun that night?"

"No."

"When do you go pull out the gun that was in your apartment?"

"I don't think I pulled it out until . . . ," Namey paused. "I don't really remember the exact time."

Conway reached into a bag and withdrew the black

Day-Timer. "Do you recognize this?" Namey acknowledged that it was his.

"And you had this on you when the Santa Ana police
apprehended you, right? Do you remember that?"

"Yeah. Uh-huh. It was found near me, I think." The
Day-Timer had been in Namey's pocket when he crawled
up into the drainage-tunnel feeder tube, and was recovered at the site.

Conway announced to the judge, "Approaching the
witness with a receipt from the black Day-Timer." He
then asked the question that he'd been leading up to
for the past hour. "Is there some reason, sir, you went
and bought some special ammo on the twenty-ninth of
March, the day after Sarah indicates you threatened
her—"

Zitny objected. "Assumes facts not in evidence."

The judge said, "As phrased, sustained."

Conway reworded it. "You went and bought that ammunition, March 29, 2003, three fifty-seven ammo,
Cowboy. You made that purchase, didn't you, sir?"

"I believe so. I don't remember."

"Are you having even a vague recollection of buying
this ammo?"

"Yeah."

"The ammunition that came with the gun wasn't
enough for you to commit suicide?"

Namey countered. "The ammunition that came with
the gun was already gone by then. I had only five bullets to begin with when I bought the gun."

"I thought you said you never fired that gun before."

"I never did fire it. The bullets are probably at my
mom's house still."

"You told this jury that you didn't have anything to do
with the gun during that time period."

Namey quibbled. "I said I didn't pull the gun out. I didn't say I didn't buy bullets."

"Is there some reason that you felt, on March twenty-ninth, that you needed to get some ammunition for that gun?"

"Probably feeling suicidal at that time. I don't remember the days that went through my head."

"Was it just a coincidence that the purchase was made one day after the incident with Sarah?"

Namey answered that it was just because he was feeling depressed, but Toohey sustained Zitny's objection and ordered the response stricken from the record.

In his ensuing questions, and Namey's answers, Conway reminded the jury that Namey had lied to his mother about the reason he needed to borrow the Nissan. Namey argued that Sarah had seen the Nissan before, so she wouldn't be surprised at him using it. Conway pointed out that Matt had never seen it. The prosecutor next rehashed the quarrels and confrontations between Sarah and Namey in which she might have "pushed his buttons." Conway asked, "She didn't deserve to be killed for pushing your buttons, did she?"

"No."

"And you didn't kill her because eight months earlier she'd had an abortion that she told you about, right?"

"I don't know why that happened." Conway repeated the question. Namey replied, "It might have been part of it. I don't know."

Taking issue with Namey's "I don't know" response, Conway asked, "You're the one that took the gun and put it a couple inches from her head, right?"

"I don't know."

"Right?"

"I don't know."

"That was you, right?"

"Yeah, it was me."

"And you pulled the trigger, right?"

"Apparently so, yes." Namey's shoulders appeared to slump, and he sounded weary.

"So is the reason you shot her and Matt because you're really, really mad?"

"I can't give you any reason. Sorry, sir." Conway wanted to know if this was something else Namey couldn't remember. Namey said, "No, I might have been mad. It would have been one of my feelings. There were a lot of feelings I had." He agreed that anger was probably part of it.

Once again taking Namey through the sequence of events on April 16, Conway established that the defendant had seen the S10 pickup parked in front of Sarah's house, a vehicle that belonged to the man who had angrily chased Namey away in a previous confrontation. Namey agreed that he had been looking for Sarah, and had brought with him a loaded handgun, a box of ammunition, and a speedloader.

At that point, Judge Toohey ended the session until the following morning.

Dennis Conway, later recalling his cross-examination of Namey, said, "The judge had been disallowing certain evidence I wanted to introduce, but now I have a *woolick.* That's a colloquialism we invented at the office, meaning a surprise blow. I walked Namey right into it. I asked about the gun and he said he hadn't thought about it after hiding it in the cupboard of his kitchen. Okay, then, 'How come the day after the confrontation with Sarah at the school, and less than two weeks before she was killed, you find it necessary to go out and buy some high-speed Cowboy ammunition?'

"That's what we call a woolick. And there was no defense response. They might have protested that the receipt hadn't been among the discovery material. But no. Because it was in there. The defense lawyer had looked through all the documents and evidence. He just didn't find it."

Conway's woolick had struck a hard blow to the defense's midsection. But was it a knockout punch? Twelve people would be faced with making that decision.

On Wednesday, September 29, the remainder of the drama in Judge Toohey's courtroom played out. But the zenith, like the climax of an action movie, had already been reached. Defender Zitny carried out the necessary redirect questioning of Namey, then rested his case. Prosecutor Conway called only one brief witness in the rebuttal phase, a police officer.

Toohey informed the jury that, on the following morning, they would hear summation arguments by both lawyers.

Inveterate trial watchers usually regard this final act of a trial, the arguments, as the best. Each side presents an opinion of what the evidence had shown. More important, they would have the opportunity to put the evidence and the testimony into a logical context, like a film editor assembling all the separately photographed footage of a movie into a palatable sequence. And, like with motion pictures, what the prosecutor and defense attorney say in those final hours can be powerful and convincing, or it can result in box office failure.

CHAPTER 26

"He Saved One for Sarah"

Dennis Conway stood and addressed the jury on Thursday.

"Good morning, ladies and gentlemen. Thank you for your time and your patience over the last two weeks."

Before presenting his view of the evidence, Conway spent a few minutes walking the jury through the possible verdicts from which they could choose:

1) On the charge of murdering Sarah Rodriquez, they could find Namey guilty, or not guilty of murder in the first degree, second degree, or of voluntary manslaughter. If guilty, they would need to decide if the special finding, use of a firearm, was true or not true.

2) On charges of shooting Matt Corbett, the choice was guilty or not guilty of either attempted murder or attempted voluntary manslaughter. In the case of a guilty verdict, they would once again need to decide on the firearm issue.

3) Additional charges of causing great bodily injury would also require true or not true verdicts.

4) It would be necessary to decide if the crimes were carried out with premeditation and deliberation.

5) Finally the jurors would determine if Namey was guilty or not guilty of kidnapping for carjacking, with the use of a handgun.

Forms were provided for all options.

Perhaps the weakest segment of the state's case was in asking the jury to find Namey guilty of kidnapping Alberto Zavala. If they believed that he willingly drove from the parking lot to transact a drug deal with Namey, there was no abduction. Conway spent several minutes on the issue, saying, "Okay. Maybe he's a dope dealer. Well, he can be a victim as well. . . . He seemed credible and quite up-front."

Moving on to the more serious charge of homicide, Conway carefully defined various options facing the jury. Warning them not to get caught up in a confusing "quagmire" of legal language, he spoke of first-degree murder, second-degree murder, and voluntary manslaughter.

The heart of Conway's case was convincing twelve people that Namey had acted with premeditation and malice aforethought. "What does that mean? Well, what it means in a nutshell is . . . intent to kill. That's it." The perpetrator, he said, must give at least some thought to the act before executing it. When a person points a gun at someone and pulls the trigger a number of times, Conway asserted, it most likely means that the shooter meant to kill.

Pacing back and forth, keeping eye contact with jurors, Conway emphasized that the slaying of Sarah was deliberate, premeditated murder and the shooting of Matt was undoubtedly attempted murder. Neither act, he insisted, had anything to do with "sudden heat of passion."

Objections are not often raised during the final

argument phase, since the lawyer's words are not part of the evidence, but Zitny objected on the basis that Conway was misstating the law.

Judge Toohey spoke to the jury. "Ladies and gentlemen, at the conclusion of the arguments, I'm going to give you a full statement of the law. And the statements by either counsel regarding the law are not what you should go by. But, rather, what the court gives you after the arguments. With that, Mr. Conway, you may proceed."

Conway offered his thanks and continued. "You have figured out by now that the defense is going to try to go with the heat of passion." It would be a mistake, he said, to let Namey off with a voluntary manslaughter verdict. Nor was it second-degree murder.

A major question always came up when premeditation was discussed. In legal terms, how long in advance must the killer think about doing the crime for it to be considered premeditated? Conway anticipated this curiosity in jurors' minds and emphatically declared, "The law does not undertake to measure in units of time the length of the period during which the thought must be pondered. . . ." It may take place in a split second, several minutes, or a few hours. "The true test is not the duration of time. . . . A cold, calculated judgment and decision may be arrived at in a short period of time."

Defense tactics were built on obtaining a verdict of voluntary manslaughter. Conway stated that voluntary manslaughter certainly had a valid place in the law, when circumstances warranted it. Offering an example, he said, "A man in a long marriage, no marital problems, comes home in the middle of the day and finds his wife in bed with someone else. He is so moved by emotion at that moment, he grabs a lamp and smashes the guy over the head and kills him." In this situation, said

Conway, a jury could find that the crime was manslaughter. But the verdict would be different, he pointed out, if the cuckolded husband had walked out of the bedroom, gone into the garage, rummaged around for a bat, then returned to beat the man to death. This would involve deliberation, therefore it would be murder. "So, there are circumstances where a manslaughter is definitely warranted. Voluntary manslaughter is a good thing in the law. It just doesn't apply here."

Chiding the defense, Conway urged the jury not to place importance on Namey's testimony in which he acknowledged shooting Sarah and Matt. His admissions on the stand did not mitigate the crimes, nor prove they had been committed under the heat of passion. The defendant really had no other choice, said Conway, because overwhelming evidence proved Namey's guilt. Witnesses had seen the shooting. "We have Matt's identification. We have the car that was used in the crime . . . with a shirt in there with the DNA from Matt."

Jurors might not realize, Conway explained, that even though the defendant admitted pulling the trigger, the prosecution was still required to prove the identification of the perpetrator. And there was plenty of proof. "We have the flight. We have the shoe during the flight. Flight is consciousness of guilt, especially the efforts that this person took to get away. . . . We have some DNA on his shoe. And we have the weapon that was found in his possession, with ballistics." The testimony, according to Conway, was nothing but a ploy to give Namey some credence, which might carry over to his rationalization of being in a mental fog while committing the crime.

The claim that Namey had acted under the heat of passion had not been supported by any expert testimony, Conway said. So there was no basis for a defense of mental incapacity.

Did Namey intend to kill Sarah? Yes, said Conway, in reference to Sarah's journal. "We have him telling Sarah, two weeks earlier, that he will kill her. Remember?"

Forging ahead, Conway asked jurors not to get caught up in "the dynamics of the relationship." The abortion, hundreds of phone calls, arguments—none of these offered any excuse for the cold-blooded shooting of two people, Conway said. "There is no justification for taking her life. . . . Fortunately, she wrote a journal. So you can hear from her . . . about her efforts to try to end the relationship with him, and his response to that."

Is it necessary for the prosecution to prove there was a motive? "As odd as it sounds," said Conway, "it is not legally required for a prosecutor to produce a motive. But, when you have it, it's a very strong, compelling piece of evidence." Namey's motive to kill Sarah was quite clear. "She rejected him. She broke up with him. She called the police on him. That's the reason he does it. She dares to leave him."

Did he have motive for shooting Matt? Most likely, said Conway, it was revenge for chasing Namey off and making him look like a coward in front of Sarah.

In Namey's version of events, he had driven several times to Placentia, hoping to see Sarah and talk to her about the relationship. Conway suggested that Namey, in reality, was stalking her and lying in wait, planning his actions. "On March twenty-seventh, Namey goes to her school. His intentions toward her are escalating. Violence, threats. But this guy is really *lucky* when it comes to timing." Conway's articulation of the word "lucky" signaled his scorn. "Because he walks into the school, and she just *happened* to be going on a break. Just like April first. I guess . . . she just *happens* to be there as he is driving in the neighborhood. I guess, on April second, he just *happens* to be in the neighborhood when Sarah is passing in her car. Just like April sixteenth, I guess he just *happens* to be there when Sarah and Matt are on their way to Bible study. He is waiting around, waiting for opportunities to confront her. . . . What is the logical inference to draw from that, where it keeps happening? What are the chances that every time [he goes] over to see Sarah, she just happens to be driving where he can see her? Now, you know he is waiting over there for her, to confront her, to cut her off. . . . This is a person who is angry and obsessed. And he can't let her go."

Reaching the crucial point in which he had scored a woolick, Conway said, "You know, I guess I'm not the most skillful cross-examiner. But it sure became clear when I kept asking him when he last tested the gun. When did he think about suicide? When did he pull the gun out?" In Namey's answer, he said it had been months. "He goes and buys ammo on March twenty-ninth, the day after he has threatened her life . . . just a coincidence? Oh, this is all for suicide. Yeah, we understand, that suicide you keep *not* committing.

"Oh, don't forget the speedloader. That's fully loaded too. And the El Camino that's been running well enough to get him around to chase Sarah and make it up to her neighborhood at the time that Matt confronts him. He's been chased off by the guy. You don't think he really knows who Matt is?"

Replaying the full sequence of events like a videotape of the crimes, Conway suggested that Namey maximized the element of surprise when he hid the weapon at his left side as he rushed toward the Kia. He shot Matt first, not only as an act of revenge, but to eliminate the threat of being physically stopped. "There was no standing in front of the car, saying, 'I'm going to take my life. Please come back to me.' No. There is just getting out and going directly to the guy that disrespected him before, the guy who is with Sarah, and the guy that poses the big threat or obstacle to him. Take out Matt. And then he can either take out Sarah or do whatever he wants to do with Sarah without Matt in the picture."

Scoffing at the idea that Namey had intended to commit suicide, Conway said the pattern of behavior was clearly aimed at committing murder. "He points the gun at him and shoots immediately. And he shoots him in the head. Can you draw an inference from that? He wanted him dead. Do you think he didn't appreciate the outcome, after the first bullet he put in Matt's head that blew out his eye, when he pumped a couple more in him, a second, and the third. Do you think he's formed the intent by then? He formed it long before then. He is just executing it.

"What else does he do? Matt is not the only object of his temper and his anger, not the only target. No. Sarah, she is the main target. She's the one who did it. She's the one that rejected him. She is the one he is there for. She is the whole reason he's there."

Conway emphasized that Namey had saved at least one bullet for Sarah. "Three were fired at Matt, maybe four, but three for sure. Maybe one went through and hit Sarah in the side. She has that injury consistent with reaching over, no doubt screaming, and catching one that might have grazed the back of his head. It punctures both her lungs, and makes a nick in the spine. But one thing we do know he did, he saved one. He saved at least one for Sarah. And then he walked around the car and he put that gun about three inches from her head and he executed her. And that, we do know. Does that sound like someone who doesn't know what they are doing? Does it sound like someone who doesn't want to kill?

"He wants to make sure he completes what he went there to do. There is still no suicide. I was going to go into that other stuff. But, you know, I don't mean to be cavalier. I don't mean to be arrogant, at all presumptuous. But sometimes cases have just such an overwhelming amount of powerful evidence that it's just real clear what is going on. And I just need to learn to trust in the jury system. And I have. And I do."

Winding up his plea, Conway asked jurors to ignore emotional issues aimed at denigrating Sarah. "I'm not going to stand up here and address and dignify all that nonsense about she's not very nice. She is evil. She had an abortion. . . . I think the evidence cries out to you for justice at this point. And I believe you know what it is.

"Thank you."

Toohey called for a fifteen-minute break after which John Zitny would deliver his arguments. Reporters and spectators watched the jury file out, trying to read any expressions of belief, or disbelief, in regard to the impassioned words of Conway. But no such message was perceivable.

CHAPTER 27

In the Heat of Passion

Judge Toohey turned to the defense table and said, "Mr. Zitny, you may make your final argument."

Zitny, wearing a conservative blue suit, stood to tell his version of what the trial evidence had shown. "Okay. Thank you. Good morning. Hot-blooded or cold-blooded? That's what I told you when we first started. Is it calculated or is there emotion?"

The defender read aloud from one of Namey's suicide notes:

> *Dear mom, I know you are going to be sad and mad*
> *when you get this letter. I know you will be okay because*
> *you are a survivor. And anyways, I have been nothing*
> *but trouble for you, I know. This is very hard for me.*
> *Because I do love [my daughter] with all of my heart.*
> *And she is the only thing that has kept me alive this long.*
> *And I am all messed up in the head. I know [she] will*
> *be better off with you. I don't want her to go with her*
> *mom. But if she does, she will probably be better off there*

than with me. Please don't be sad. Maybe I will finally be at peace.

Zitny lowered his eyes and said, "This excerpt of a letter . . . was found in his apartment after the shooting."

If I have control of anything in the afterlife, I will try to make things good for you guys. Heart. Love, your brother, Rick

The defender spoke quietly, asserting that emotion must be considered when weighing human behavior. Even in the prosecutor's example of a man discovering his wife cheating, he said, emotions were present leading to the person acting in the heat of passion.

Sarah, Zitny remarked, had built a house of cards. "On one side of the house, the cards were made up of Matt, a very good person. He was the one the family loved. He was the boyfriend that was open. He was the one that the mom and dad knew about, the one that they had the cell phone number. The other half was Rick Namey. They did not know about each other. Rick Namey was a secret lover. And she kept building up this house, those cards, wall by wall. And it gets weaker and weaker. Until, eventually, that house of cards has to fall over. Matt was chosen. In the end of March, it was Matt."

This history of duplicity by Sarah had upset Namey, said Zitny. His client had only wanted answers as to why she did these things. Speaking for Namey, he said, "'You called me basically nonstop for months on end, four, five times a day. . . . We had an intense sexual, romantic relationship. And now I'm cut off. . . . I'm not the one that is invited to meet the family or to spend a vacation with them. I just want some answers. I want to know what is going on.'"

Sarah, Zitny suggested, needed to justify the deceit
to her parents and to Matt, so she prepared the journal for that purpose. "It's in anticipation of possibly
going to court later on. It's not a slice of life. It's not a
diary. She was . . . working on that document, knowing
her parents were going to see it, knowing that Matt was
going to see it. And so, she had to exaggerate that
journal in order to justify her relationship with Rick
Namey."

The defender invoked the word "justice," saying that
was all he asked for. "Justice is making sure the facts fit
the crime and that a person is convicted only of the
crime for which they are guilty." Namey, he declared, was
not guilty of murder.

Reiterating that the judge would read jury instructions
to them, and they would have a reference copy in the
jury room, Zitny asked them to read it carefully. He spent
several minutes urging each juror to maintain their independence and not bow to group pressure. "You have
a duty and an obligation to stand up to the other eleven,
which is very difficult sometimes."

The focal point of Zitny's defense centered on
whether the crime was "cold-blooded or hot-blooded."
He declared that Namey had not acted in a cold-blooded
manner, with premeditation or malice. Circumstantial
evidence, he said, had proved that.

Repeatedly referring to the jury instructions, Zitny
wanted the jurors to understand how to interpret the evidence. "If there are two choices," he explained, "you
must adopt the one in favor of the defendant."

As an example, Zitny described a woman accidentally
taking a bottle of shampoo out of a drug store, distracted
by conversing with a friend, then returning it upon discovery of her error. "So there are really two interpretations of
that. The prosecution will always say, 'Well, she's stealing

something.' But you can interpret . . . that she had no intent to steal by the fact that she sheepishly walked back inside. And she was distracted by talking to her buddy. There are two reasonable interpretations of that scenario. The law says you must adopt the one that says that she was not stealing."

Constitutional law, said Zitny, is based on the presumption of innocence. We all learn it in eighth-grade civics, but people tend to judge otherwise. "Driving down the freeway, you look off to the side of the road. You see a police officer. He is talking. He has got his ticket book out, speaking to a driver. How many people here say to themselves, 'I wonder what that guy did'? Or how many people say to themselves, 'I am going to presume that person is innocent, because they haven't had a trial yet'? I can guarantee what you're going to think. You're going to think, 'I wonder what that person did.' Because you presume them guilty. And that's what happens here." He suggested that during deliberations, the jury should ask themselves, "Am I really presuming this person is innocent? Am I really presuming that it's a manslaughter and not a murder?"

Everyone knew the standard of "reasonable doubt." And in this case, Zitny said, there was plenty of room for it to be applied. "You listen to the evidence . . . and if you have a reasonable doubt, you must come back [with] not guilty of murder."

Zitny disputed Conway's definition of premeditation, in which he said it could happen in a brief instant. "The law says that you don't take into consideration the amount of time. And I assume it can happen quickly. But we talked about using your common sense. Remember that? The bottom line is . . . that it's possible it could happen in a short period of time. But common sense tells us that it's not probable."

Pushing for a verdict of no more than voluntary manslaughter, Zitny again urged jurors to carefully read the instructions. "The relevant point is this: the question to be answered is whether or not, at the time of the killing, reasoning ability of the accused was obscured or disturbed by passion to such an extent as would cause the ordinarily reasonable person . . . to react rashly, without deliberation and reflection, and from passion rather than judgment." If Namey had acted rashly, without deliberation and reflection, "from passion rather than judgment, then the case is a manslaughter."

Even in Matt Corbett's testimony, Zitny reminded jurors, he had said he would be "upset" if he had known that Sarah was seeing Namey. People do act from anger and passion, said Zitny, even to the extent of cursing or "keying" the paint on a car. Offering a personal example, the defender said that he had once grown impatient with his own young daughter and yelled at her to "knock it off." Embarrassed, he admitted, "I was not acting rationally, was not acting from judgment. I was acting from passion.

"We understand that somebody is frail when they are in an emotional state. When somebody is in an emotional state, their crime is called manslaughter. It's not called murder." Reading from the instructions again, he said, "'To establish that a killing is murder and not manslaughter, the burden is on the people to prove beyond a reasonable doubt each of the elements of murder, and that the act which caused the death was not done in the heat of passion or upon sudden quarrel.'

"Okay. What does that tell us? He has got to prove that it was not manslaughter. Right now, you must presume it was a manslaughter, to the same degree we talked about regarding presumption of innocence." If there was any reasonable doubt, "you must give the benefit of the doubt to Rick Namey. . . . That is the law. You must presume it's manslaughter.

"I'm trying to give you as much information as I can, so you can make an intelligent decision. I am not going to try to limit you. I want you to have everything, so you can work with it." He implored the jury to look at all the evidence very carefully, to examine the telephone bill records, to weigh and consider all the circumstances.

Referring to the incident at night school, Zitny said, "They had a scuffle then. And that's when they distanced themselves. He tried to call her back. She would have nothing to do with him. Now she's with Matt. My client is hurt. For people who have been in love, you realize the pain, and sleepless nights, the aches . . . the dry eyes, day in, day out, an hour here, an hour there of sleeping. Finally suicide. 'I cannot take it anymore. I just cannot take it anymore. The woman that I want to have kids with . . .' The surprise to him was that she had a boyfriend. *Snap.* Not that he didn't have any intent. He hopped out of the car, and he flashed that gun, and just started firing away.

"And the issue is this: was it hot-blooded or was it cold-blooded? I am not standing here asking you for sympathy. I am not asking you for mercy. But I am asking for a little human understanding."

Zitny had spoken for an hour. Without uttering the usual gratitude to jurors for their patience, for listening, and for their diligent service, the defender sat down. His face appeared confident that he had implanted the necessary seeds of doubt with at least a few of the twelve triers of fact.

Now Dennis Conway would have one more chance to convince the jury. Because the burden of proof is with the state, the prosecutor is given a final opportunity to rebut defense arguments. After a short recess, Judge Toohey said, "Mr. Conway, you may proceed."

A renewed vigor radiated from Conway. "Thank you, Your Honor. I will be brief. Defense talked for an hour. And one thing I really didn't hear being talked about was the facts and the circumstantial evidence."

For the most part, Conway characterized what the defense attorney had said as "ridiculous," and expected the jury to come to the same conclusions in their deliberations.

"What he didn't talk about was the facts and the circumstantial evidence. I'm not going through all the evidence again. But I think you have seen and know what all the evidence is. The thing about circumstantial evidence— and this is important. It's important to take it together. Some pieces of evidence naturally have more weight than others.

"Taking one piece of evidence out of context doesn't necessarily tell you what is going on. It's not, keep in mind, a search for doubt. . . . It's a search for truth.

"You look at all the evidence, and you take it all together, and you draw a logical inference, that the defendant was angry. Sarah left him. He wants Sarah dead. And, surely, by the time he's shot Matt three or four times, he could appreciate what he is doing. By the time he walks around and shoots Sarah, he is absolutely knowing what the gun is going to do when he points it at her head."

Conway expressed disgust that the defender had suggested Sarah's journal was written to impress her parents and Matt. There was no evidence they had ever even seen it.

Was it important to weigh Namey's purported intent

to commit suicide? There was no real intention of suicide, Conway asserted. Calling the defense strategy an attempt to build a "quasi heat-of-passion" excuse, Conway asked how a lawyer could look at twelve citizens and "even start with a straight face" in using the circumstances to justify Namey's conduct. All of the events preceding April 16, he said, would not lead a reasonable person to shooting innocent victims. "Even if you add it all up . . . he gets to kill her for that? No. He doesn't get to set his own standard, any more than he gets to set his own body temperature.

"But let's keep indulging for a minute. It's no surprise to anybody in this courtroom that somebody is not going to admit having the intent to kill. Okay. But let's take him at his word. 'I just snapped.'" Just snapping, Conway scoffed, was certainly not enough reason to let Namey off with manslaughter.

Calling the defendant's actions "goal-oriented conduct," Conway declared the defense case insufficient to warrant a verdict of manslaughter. "It's so cold, and it's so deliberate, and it shows intent on accomplishing the goal of taking Sarah's life."

Citing all of the evidence, item by item, Conway used the "potato salad" analogy. Each ingredient, by itself, is only a piece of potato, or celery, or onion. But combined, they complement one another and become a complete culinary preparation. "Circumstantial evidence is like that. All of the elements combined give the true picture, the reasonable inference of what happened. Don't let anybody go to one or two of the pieces and pull them out, away from the bowl. You take that evidence and put it with everything else, and it tells you a story. The story that he had this plan to go over there and commit a murder, and he did."

Zeroing in on Zitny's presentation, Conway said, "I
can't really blame the defense lawyer for ignoring the
facts and staying away from them. Because when the
facts are so compelling and overwhelming, the defense attorney talks about everything else. You tell
cute little anecdotal stories, or talk about the law, or
suggest that Sarah is a tramp and try to get you not to
like her. . . .

"The desire, the intent, the premeditation, and deliberation can be formed in a split second. And I just—you
know, I could go on and on. I think lawyers have a bit
of an ego to do this kind of work. And, you know,
lawyers, especially trial lawyers, probably have bigger egos
than anyone else. So we stand up here and we talk. You
know, we think we are really overwhelming you with our
brilliant argument and questioning.

"But you know what? You folks on the jury have got
four to five hundred collective years of common sense
and life experience.

"As lawyers, we have got to get over ourselves. The evidence speaks for itself. And the system works. And,
hopefully, it's not that easy just to come in and distract
or fool or emotionally choke one or two jurors, so the
wheel of justice is clogged, slowed down.

"And I'm through. I will let the evidence and final
words of what Sarah had to say talk to you. And I just
trust that you are going to do the right thing. Thank
you."

In the gallery, Sarah's mother wept softly.

After lunch, Judge Toohey read the official jury instructions aloud, then sent the twelve members into
the deliberation room.

It is impossible to predict how long a jury will be out

in a murder case. The lawyers retreat to their offices waiting for a telephone call from the court clerk. Victims' families often drift up and down, pacing the halls, or sit quietly chatting in small groups. It is a long and difficult wait.

CHAPTER 28

"The Pain That We Have All Felt"

Dennis Conway's phone rang at nine-thirty on the morning of Tuesday, October 5. Judge Toohey's clerk said, "The jury has a verdict."

Conway rushed three blocks from his office to the central courthouse and took the crowded elevator up to the tenth floor. In the courtroom, he nodded encouragingly to Martha Dewar, who, with her husband, Bob, and the rest of her family, occupied a full row. Matt Corbett, in his wheelchair, sat at the row's end, next to Martha, and near his own parents.

On the opposite side of the aisle, the defendant's mother, her daughter, and her fiancé waited expectantly. A door in the front left corner opened and two uniformed officers escorted Namey from a holding cell to a chair at counsel table. He took a quick glance at the audience as he sat down.

As soon as the bailiff called the court to order, Judge

Toohey entered from his chambers, took his elevated seat, and turned toward the jury box. He spoke directly to a middle-aged man seated in the back corner. Toohey addressed him by the number assigned during voir dire. "Juror one-thirteen, I was informed by the bailiff that you are the foreperson of the jury; is that correct?"

"Yes, sir," came the reply.

Toohey asked, "I have also been informed that the jury has reached verdicts in this matter; is that correct?"

The foreperson said it was correct, that all the verdicts were unanimous, and that they had addressed all the charges and counts. At the judge's request, the juror handed a stack of forms to the bailiff, who, in turn, gave them to the court clerk. Toohey asked her to read the verdicts aloud. She spoke in a bell-clear voice. "We, the jury, in the above entitled action, find the defendant, Richard Joseph Namey, guilty of the crime of felony to wit: violation of section 187(a) of the penal code of the state of California, murder, as charged in count one of the information and set the degree thereof as murder in the first degree."

"Guilty of murder in the first degree!" The words resonated throughout the room like a charge of electricity. Sarah's and Matt's families felt an oppressive weight lift from their shoulders. A feeling of buoyant redemption washed over them. Matt raised his arms in a gesture of triumph, then leaned over to hug Martha Dewar.

For Namey's family, the verdict seemed to turn everything dark, like thick black clouds blotting out the sunshine.

Continuing to read, the clerk announced that Namey was also guilty of attempted murder and inflicting great bodily harm, conducted willfully, deliberately, and with premeditation. More guilty verdicts came for charges of carjacking, unlawful taking of a vehicle, and felonious use of a firearm.

The jury had found him not guilty of kidnapping for carjacking. They had apparently put little credence in the testimony of Alberto Zavala, perhaps because evidence suggested that he was a drug dealer.

Judge Toohey polled the jury and each member answered that the verdicts had all been unanimous. After thanking them for their service, the judge declared that they were now free to discuss the case with anyone, or if they preferred, to discuss it with no one. The twelve people were now free to leave.

Before court was adjourned, the attorneys agreed to a sentence hearing on Friday, November 19.

Reporters rushed into the hallway to conduct interviews. Amanda Beck, of the *Orange County Register*, and Claire Luna, of the *Los Angeles Times*, spoke to Matt, who said, "Knowing that this jerk got what he deserved, Sarah can rest peacefully now. I'm just glad that she's got her closure."

Martha Dewar wiped tears from her eyes as she sobbed. "Your children are your everything. I'll never recover from this loss." She looked through the plate glass windows at blue sky and spoke toward heaven. "Sarah, you got your wish."

While waiting for the November 19 sentence hearing, Matt Corbett put his wishes in writing, along with a chilling description of how Namey's crimes had affected the lives of Matt and his family.

In his letter to Judge Toohey, dated October 23, 2004, Matt began by describing the sequence of events prior to the lethal confrontation, then said:

When Richard Namey got out of his car, he came around to my side and shot me 3 or 4 times. Due to this shooting, I . . . lost my left eye. After shooting me, he went around to Sarah's side and shot and killed her. After he shot me, I was instantly paralyzed. I tried to help Sarah, but I couldn't move. I could only watch. This haunts me every day because I was trying to protect her and I couldn't.

I lost the most important piece of my life that day. I loved Sarah very much. She was my best friend as well as my lover. . . . Besides emotionally trying to recover from Sarah's death, I was left a quadriplegic. I am in a wheelchair now and may be for the rest of my life. Although my spinal cord was only damaged, not severed, the doctors cannot be sure if I will ever walk again. I can no longer work at the job I was hired for and am reliant on the State of California just to pay my bills that my insurance doesn't cover. This has been very hard on my family and friends. It is difficult to go out with my friends. At one point they were picking me up to put me in their vehicle so I could go out with them. This was a big strain on my friends. . . . While I am lucky that most of my friends continued to come by and support me, there are still others that I do not see any more as they cannot handle my injuries.

The strain on my family has been huge. My father, Tom, had to take a leave of absence from his employment that he had held only five months. So we have been relying on my Mom's income for all the bills, including a lot of items not covered by insurance or Victim's Services. It has been a financial struggle constantly. My parents had to take a second loan on their house and a loan from my Mom's retirement account in order for us to survive. This makes me feel really bad but also much loved. I had always helped out if needed and also paid my own way. My Mom has taken many weeks off as well. At this time, her employer has been very helpful and supportive. She *doesn't know how much more time she can take off to help me and still be able to do her job.*

Besides the financial hardship this has created, my family has had to deal with all the doctor appointments, scheduling as well as transportation, Social Security, Victims' Services, insurance, hospitals, etc. It is very draining on both of them. And along with all of this, they assist me in hygiene, which consists of bowel movements, catheterization, and showers. This can take up to 3 or 4 hours a day. . . . After the shooting in 2003, my Dad took me to therapy three times a week for several months, which would take a couple of hours each time. After my release from the hospital on May 22, 2003, I have been back in the hospital 8 times with infections to the bladder, kidney, and blood. I am usually in the hospital for a week at a time and have been sent home with IVs four of those times. My Mom and Dad have learned to change the IV bags, use syringes to clean the lines, and change dressings. This is very stressful as they are constantly worried they may do something wrong and hurt me.

I will be going in for an operation on November 24, 2004 which hopefully will help to prevent the infections in the future. This will be a major surgery in which they will take part of my colon and add it to my bladder to enlarge it. The doctors believe that my injury and sitting in a wheelchair all day has led to shrinkage of the bladder. I will be bedridden for six weeks or so. This means shower and bowel care will have to be done in bed by my parents. This will be very hard on them. It seems like every time I get to the point where I am getting more independent, I get sick and have to start all over again. This has completely changed my life and my family's lives. Because they are helping me, my parents rely on my twin sister, Kelly, a lot more than should happen.

I am only 22 and was 20 when I was shot. I was

working 50 to 60 hours a week and had been thinking about attending college with Sarah and moving out of my parents' house. Now I don't know when that will happen. I know that I am very fortunate to be alive and try to think of the positives, but there is so much to do every day. There are no days off for anyone in my family.

To me, my life is nothing without Sarah. She is the only thing I really cared about. I live one day at a time, because I know now that time is precious and nobody is promised tomorrow. I live life now as if every day is my last. As hard as it is, I still have to go to work and live my life and go on without my Sarah. My work, Norman S. Wright / Airelink Mechanical, is holding my position for me until I've recovered enough to come back to work. I really don't know what I'm going to do without Sarah. She was the woman I loved, the one I wanted to marry, and the one I wanted to bear my children. I know that I will never fully recover from such a loss. Part of me died when Sarah left our lives.

Judge Toohey, I want to let you know that Sarah was a good girl. Everybody makes mistakes, but she didn't have to pay the ultimate sacrifice. Sarah worked with children along with her mother, Martha. She was a great teacher and all the kids loved Sarah. I personally think the kids liked her so much because Sarah was a big kid herself. I could go on and on about Sarah, but I'll get to the point here. I think that Richard Joseph Namey should be sentenced to life in prison without the possibility of parole. I don't want another family to feel the pain that we have all felt.

Please take the sentence I have requested into consideration, and if there is ever a possibility that he does come up for parole, please let us know. We would like to know so we can attend the parole hearing. Thank you so much. Signed, Matt Corbett.

In the weeks before November 19, Dennis Conway heard some disturbing news. Through a jailhouse informant, he heard allegations that Richard Namey had tried to put out a contract on Conway's life. Reportedly, Namey had offered his blue El Camino pickup in exchange for killing the prosecutor. Fortunately, there were no takers. Still, it caused Conway to keep his eyes open, "not to mention taking offense that my life was worth no more than what an old El Camino would fetch."

On the chilly morning six days before Thanksgiving, people filing through the metal detectors at the central courthouse's entry were still chattering about the recent elections, in which President George W. Bush had been reelected.

In Judge Toohey's tenth-floor courtroom, the conversations faded to dead quiet when Martha Dewar took the stand to deliver a victim impact statement. Donning her glasses, Martha told the court her name and read from a prepared letter:

My daughter Sarah Rodriquez was murdered April 16, 2003, by Richard Namey. Writing this letter is so painful. I sit and think, how can my beautiful daughter be gone? I want her to come through the front door, like she did every day, hearing her voice saying, "Mom, I'm home. I love you, mom," Her hugs, her kisses. She always gave me one before she left. Her smile, her carefree smile, always so happy, so trustworthy. I miss her so very much. My sweet Sarah, I love you. April 16, 2003, is a day I will never forget. My son and I just got home from work. It was around 5:10 p.m. Most days, we would come in the house, drop our belongings, and then go outside and play.

That day, for some reason, we got home, and we didn't

go out right away. Maybe twenty minutes later, we started to head out, when my husband got home and he told me the bad news. I yelled, "No, no." I wanted to run. I wanted to go running to her. But with my husband was a detective, who, when he walked in with my husband, told me I couldn't go out there. All I kept saying was, "Why, why? What do you mean I can't go out there? My daughter, she needs me. What is wrong with her? Is she hurt badly?" Finally, the detective agreed to walk me over. It was just around the block from my house. She was that close from being home, her and Matt. When we turned the corner of my street, my daughter's red Kia was there in the middle of the street. As we got closer, and then I saw a yellow tarp over her body. I said, "Please, please, no. Tell me it's not my daughter, please. That can't be her. I need to go over and help her up."

Of course, they held me back from getting near my Sarah. All I could do was sit there and cry, knowing that there was nothing I could do to help my daughter. And then to find out that Matt was [also shot], everything just went dark. Who, who would do something so evil?

It didn't take me long to realize, behind this horrible crime was Richard Namey. Everything Richard Namey did speaks for itself. Need I say more? Sarah is my middle child, born January 19, 1982. As a baby, Sarah was always happy. She always had a smile on her face. Sarah was always kind and easy to get along with. In her early childhood and up to her middle school, we did a lot of family activities. Everyone who knew Sarah grew to love her. She was always willing to lend a helping hand. She would always go out of her way to help family and friends. Sarah was very close to her grandparents. She was the only one who was allowed to take their pictures. Matt is confined to a wheelchair and is blind in one eye, because Richard Namey cowardly, ruthlessly shot him and murdered Sarah. . . . *I am thankful for my family, who has been through it all. Their lives have changed, as mine has changed, forever.*

The tremendous impact of what Richard Namey has done to my family and myself is unforgivable. He belongs locked up forever. He cannot do this to anybody, to any other person. Richard Namey is a very evil, manipulative, and a control freak, and does not belong in our society. He needs to pay for what he did to Sarah and Matt. He has taken my Sarah away. I will never see her married or see her children. One thing I do know, I am very thankful and grateful to have a loving and very supportive family and friends, something that Richard Namey never had, and never will.

Sarah was about to start college and pursue her dream at the computer graphics department. But all that came to an end when Richard Namey became greedy, evil, and, with no respect for life, murdered my daughter. My tiny Sarah, who was standing four-eleven tall, weighing 95 pounds. Now my trips to visit my daughter are to the cemetery. At least I have a place to go up and talk to her. I feel her presence. I know she comes around in the form of a butterfly or a song or when I see a red Kia, her favorite food, or when I hear a funny story about her. Oh, yes, and my dreams, that's when I can see and talk to her.

Thank you to the justice system . . . which I trust to put Richard Namey away for life. This is where he belongs, making sure he will never get out. May he endure pain and suffering for the rest of his life and rot in jail. Thank you.

Martha dabbed at her eyes as she sat down, to be replaced by a man few people recognized. Dennis Conway introduced him. "Your Honor, Fernando Rodriquez is Sarah's natural father. He'd like to address the court briefly before Matt Corbett does."

The man who had once cut all the hair from his infant's head so it would grow back thicker stood and told the court of his relationship to Sarah. "I would like to say that killing my daughter changed my life very much, dramatically. And she was my only daughter. Now I don't have her by my side. And she used to brighten up my life, and used to be around me. She used to be my little girl. And now she is no more. And now I see sorrow in a lot of people. Everywhere I go, I see sorrow. And sometimes I think that, for some miracle, maybe that person that I am looking at is Sarah. Maybe God will have mercy on me and brought her back. And I see Sarah in a lot of girls that look like her. It's very painful. I don't think I'll ever get over it. That's all I have to say."

Matt Corbett, wearing a T-shirt imprinted with a portrait of Sarah over the words "Always In My Heart," rolled his wheelchair up to the railing separating the gallery from the court. He cleared his throat and spoke briefly, reiterating some of the issues he had described in his letter to the judge. "Your Honor, April 16, 2003, was the worst day of my life. Ever since then, I have lost everything I really cared about—Sarah Rodriquez. And I not only have to deal with the fact that I lost her, the only one I could really talk to when I am having a problem, but I lost my legs. The fact is, I may never walk again. So I still keep positive, thinking that I will. It's been very hard for me since that day, trying to be positive, think positive. I go through lots of problems every day that people wouldn't really—you can't really imagine unless you are there. I feel a loss of affection. And I'm in and out of the hospital constantly. The bills are just so hard to pay for. I'm, you know, about to go through surgery here, the day before Thanksgiving, to help enlarge my bladder and fix my kidney. I just can't believe this is all happening. Sometimes I feel like it's not real. You know, I am blind in one eye. I now have to drive a handicapped vehicle, equipped, so I can start going back to work. Hopefully, I will be able to go back to work after my surgery, if everything goes well. I miss Sarah a lot. I would give anything just to have her here. I want to say that I miss her a lot and I love her." More than a few spectators, along with several jurors who had returned, blinked away tears.

With all the preliminaries now complete, the time had come for Richard Namey to hear his future forecasted.

Toohey had something to say before handing down the sentence. Referring to a twenty-five-page document, he said, "The court has reviewed this Probation Department report. . . . I was struck in reading the sentencing [recommendation], Mr. Namey. When they asked about your financial status, [you] said, 'Before my arrest, my mom helped me when I did not have money. Now I have no house, car, or money. I have nothing.' And it just struck me how centered you were on yourself as you discussed the case with the Probation Department. Because your violent conduct has created unspeakable loss to these families. There was a comment about you not being loved. But I would note that your mom, her fiancé, have been here throughout the proceedings of this case. And I'm certainly not in a position to judge them. But, if anything, they loved you too greatly, gave you too much. In relation to this matter, the court, first off, denies probation. The defendant is statutorily ineligible for probation."

Looking up at the convicted killer, Toohey said, "As to the crime alleged in count four, the jury found the defendant guilty of carjacking in relation to the date of

April 19, 2003." Observing that Namey's violent conduct indicated a danger to society, Toohey spoke of the previous behavior. "He had prior convictions of increasing seriousness, was on probation for false imprisonment of a young woman, who also had a restraining order against Mr. Namey. In fact, he also was on probation for violent conduct against his own sister, striking her with an object such that she had a two-inch laceration on her eye that required medical attention at St. Joseph's Hospital. Also, I would note his prior performance on probation is clearly unsatisfactory.

"For all these reasons, the court sentences the defendant to the aggravated term, in relation to count four, of nine years. And consecutive to that, the defendant is sentenced to the term of ten years, the jury having found it true that a firearm was used in relation to that crime . . . for a total term of nineteen years in state prison in relation to count four.

"As to count two, the jury having convicted the defendant of attempted murder and having found the allegation of premeditation and deliberation true, the defendant is sentenced to . . . a consecutive term of twenty-five years to life, as to count two.

"As to count one, the jury having convicted the defendant of murder in the first degree, the defendant is sentenced to . . . fifty years to life."

By the time all the legal language was sorted out, and all the numbers totaled, Namey faced a term of ninety-five years to life in California's state prison system. According to current guidelines for parole, he would not be eligible until after the year 2084.

Among Sarah's writings in her journal and notes, just days before the murder, she had declared, "I swear to God that I hate Richard Namey. I hope he goes to prison for life. He is just so very mean to me." Sarah's wish had been granted.

When Toohey finished speaking, and chatter in the gallery rose, Matt shot a fist into the air and celebrated with a round of high fives, slapping palms with two dozen family members and friends.

Richard Namey showed no emotion, other than a few frown lines. The same two uniformed officers who had escorted him into the room helped him rise, checked his handcuffs, and led him out.

Dennis Conway and the district attorney's staff had chosen not to seek the death penalty for Namey, realizing that special circumstances required in capital punishment cases would have been difficult to prove. With more than 650 convicted killers crowding the state's death row, it probably makes little difference. In all probability, he will spend the rest of his years in the living hell of concrete and steel—a cauldron of incessant violence, hostility, noise, and fear. Never again will he play the game of love, according to his own convoluted rules of possession, control, and vengeance.

AUTHOR'S NOTES
AND ACKNOWLEDGMENTS

In researching extensive documents and conducting interviews for this story, I was privileged to meet several unforgettable people.

Matt Corbett made me rethink a few opinions I had formed about today's youth. His strength and courage in the face of horrific circumstances is remarkable. I first encountered Matt when I was welcomed into the home of Martha and Bob Dewar. They had generously agreed to indulge my need to learn all about Sarah's life and death. As I've said before, dragging victims' families through a repetition of the heartbreak, reopening their wounds, is the most difficult part of writing true crime books. When I arrived, there was Matt in their living room, smiling, shaking my hand, and joining in the family discussion about a young couple's life, love, and tragic fate. Martha, Bob, Sarah's sister, Marilyn, and her brother George enthusiastically recalled the good times with Sarah, and shared the heartbreak of losing her.

A few days later, Matt's family hosted me in their home. Some people have a special knack for welcoming a stranger with sincere warmth and humor, and the Corbett family—Jill, Tom, Kelly, and Matt—could give lessons on how to do this successfully. I was treated like a longtime friend.

There were a few topics I was reluctant to bring up with Matt in the family environments, things I wanted to discuss with him, one-on-one. So we later met at a fast-food restaurant. He drove his green van, equipped with hand controls. While waiting for him to arrive, I wondered if he would need assistance to leave the driver's seat and get into his wheelchair. My mistake. With all the confidence and agility imaginable, Matt pressed buttons and pulled levers that opened the side doors and unfolded a ramp. He twisted around, moved athletically into his chair, and rolled down onto the pavement. I stood there, struck with admiration. We entered the restaurant, had lunch, and talked about Matt's confrontations with Namey, the abortion, the experience of being shot multiple times, and his undiminished love for Sarah. She had made "mistakes," he said, but that was only human. A lovely photograph of Sarah adorned the dashboard of his van.

In February 2005, Matt had returned to his job and began working full-time assisting customers at the counter, handling will-call transactions, answering telephones, and processing supply orders. The admirable firm had held his job open throughout the entire ordeal, and kept his insurance active. Coincidentally, the company owner lives within a stone's throw of the drainage tunnel where Namey was caught.

Matt holds out hope that one day, perhaps with the aid of medical breakthroughs from stem cell research, he will regain the use of his legs. I certainly hope and pray that it happens. But if it doesn't, this young man will find a way to succeed in whatever goals he sets. I am literally in awe of him.

This book was largely inspired when I chatted with

Dennis Conway while researching another story. The account of his life is one of the most colorful I've ever heard. I've never before had so much fun during a series of interviews. Dennis plans one day to write his memoirs, and when he does, I'm going to be first in line to buy a copy. In late 2005, his excellent performance with the district attorney's office was recognized with a promotion to a supervisory position. Dennis's son, Donnie, started college in September 2005.

Readers sometimes ask authors if they interview the convicted person in true crime books. My answer is yes, but it is not always possible. In this case, I wrote to Richard Namey at his prison address and invited him to tell his side of the story. After several weeks, he responded with a short note saying that he would like to, but that any statements he might make could potentially compromise his pending appeals. I replied, telling him that I understood, and stating that I would rely on police reports, his interview with Detective Stuber, and on trial transcripts. Even if he had chosen to speak to me, it is doubtful that he could have given any more information than these resources provided.

I am indebted to Dr. Christina Johns and to Los Angeles marriage counselor Cosette Case for their expert opinions on Sarah's relationship with Namey.

My sincere gratitude is also extended to K-9 officer Mike McCarthy and his dog, Chris; DA Investigator Ernie Gomez; Detective Chris Stuber; senior public defender John Zitny; Larry Welborn, of the *Orange County Register*; Minerva Hildalgo, victim contact coordinator with the Orange County DA; and the ever-reliable Geoff Christison, keeper of the superior court archives.

Happily, I have known Kensington Publishing's Michaela Hamilton for several years, and tip my hat again to her for making this book possible. Her associates,

Jeremie Ruby-Strauss and Miles Lott, helped guide the project through the complex publication maze.

Let me also note that this story, to the best of my knowledge, is entirely factual. There are no fictionalized passages or made-up dialogue, as some other "true crime" books contain. The information came from court records, transcripts, and interviews. To protect the privacy of certain individuals, I have changed their names in the text.

—Don Lasseter, 2006

MORE MUST-READ TRUE CRIME
FROM PINNACLE